30 Hour IBM
by
Clive Prigmore

NATIONAL EXTENSION COLLEGE
COURSE NUMBER M027

ISBN 1 85356 008 1

© NATIONAL EXTENSION COLLEGE TRUST LIMITED 1988

No part of this publication may be reproduced, stored in a retrieval system, or transmitted in any form or by any means, electronic, mechanical, photocopying, recording or otherwise, without the prior permission of the publisher.

This book is sold subject to the condition that it shall not by way of trade or otherwise, be lent, re-sold, hired out, or otherwise circulated without the publisher's prior consent in any form of binding or cover other than that in which it is published and without a similar condition being imposed on the subsequent purchaser.

Designer: Peter Hall
Cover design: Hobson Street Studio
Printed by NEC Print

First printing 1988

Acknowledgements
The National Extension College wishes to thank Benedict Freeman for his work in converting this text to IBM format and Geoff Wiles for his encouragement and meticulous checking of proofs.

Contents

How to use this course		v
UNIT 1	Simple statements and commands	1
UNIT 2	Making decisions	29
UNIT 3	Strings	63
UNIT 4	Lists	89
UNIT 5	An end to strings and PRINT	115
UNIT 6	Mainly about dice and games	141
UNIT 7	Handling numbers	169
UNIT 8	An introduction to data processing	195
UNIT 9	File handling	219

How to use this course

Aims of the course
Quite simply, to help you learn to use a microcomputer with confidence. To do that you need to master three things: (a) the BASIC language; (b) planning good program structures; and (c) using the keyboard. This course teaches you the first two. Your computer will teach you the third!

30 Hour IBM doesn't teach you all there is to know about BASIC but it does cover all the essentials. Once you've completed the course, you will be ready to use a textbook on BASIC or for a second-stage BASIC course.

Do I need a microcomputer?
You can do the course whether or not you have a microcomputer. All you have to do is to choose one of the following ways of working through the course:

Self-instructional use: With a microcomputer: do all the Exercises and Self-Assessment Questions (SAQs) and key in all the programs marked [K]. Without a microcomputer: do all the Exercises and SAQs but omit the items marked [K].

FlexiStudy use: With your own microcomputer: do all the Exercises and SAQs at home and key in at home all the programs marked [K]. Test your assignment answers on your own microcomputer. Then take/send your problems to your local FlexiStudy centre. Without your own microcomputer: do all the Exercises and SAQs but ignore the items marked [K]. Then do the assignment questions and take these to your local FlexiStudy centre to run on the microcomputers there.

NEC correspondence student: With your own microcomputer: do all the Exercises and SAQs at home and key in all the items marked [K]. Test your assignments on your own microcomputer before sending them to your NEC correspondence tutor. If the assignment programs don't run properly, tell your tutor what response you are getting from your microcomputer. Without your own microcomputer: do all the Exercises and SAQs at home but ignore the items marked [K]. Do the assignment questions and post these to your NEC tutor.

Which microcomputer should I use?
This course has been designed to relate to IBM BASICA (and GWBASIC for IBM compatibles). If you have another type of computer, check with NEC to see if there is a version of the course for your machine. If not, you should still find that most of the programs will work on your computer, with minor adaptions.

Which BASIC does the course use?
There are many versions (dialects) of BASIC, each created by a computer manufacturer modifying the original BASIC. As far as possible, we have kept to the common core of microsoft BASIC, e.g. BASICA for IBMs or GWBASIC for compatibles.

Structure of the course
The course is in 9 Units (see Contents). Each Unit includes:

Examples: These are problems which we solve for you in the text.

Self-Assessment Questions (SAQs): We ask you to stop and quickly check that you have understood a new idea that we have introduced. Answers to these always appear at the end of the Unit in which the SAQ occurs.

Exercises: These are longer problems for you to try. Answers appear at the end of the Unit in which the Exercise occurs.

K which stands for key. This is where we think you could find it helpful to key a program into your own microcomputer.

Assignment: These are questions for you to answer and send to your tutor for marking and comment. There are no answers to these in the course.

Note: When entering programs, care must be taken to distinguish between the letter 'l' and the number '1', and between the letter 'O' and the number '0'. If a program does not run properly, then you should check that it has been entered correctly, taking extra care to check that the characters 'l', '1', 'O' and '0' have not been mixed up.

UNIT 1
Simple statements and commands

1.1	What does a computer do?	2
1.2	What is a computer?	2
1.3	What is BASIC?	4
1.4	A simple problem	4
1.5	Statement numbers	6
1.6	Executions and commands	8
1.7	Execution and data	10
1.8	INPUT, PRINT and LET	11
1.9	Store locations	12
1.10	Copying and overwriting	14
1.11	Arithmetic operators	16
1.12	Numerical constants	19
1.13	The remark statement: REM	20
1.14	More complicated arithmetic	20
1.15	Literal printing	21
	Assignment 1	23
	Objectives of Unit 1	24
	Answers to SAQs and Exercises	24

1.1 What does a computer do?

In broad terms, a computer is a machine which helps us to solve certain kinds of problems. These usually involve symbols or *characters* which are familiar to us through everyday use, e.g. letters of the alphabet (capital and lower case), numbers, punctuation marks and some special *characters* such as +, #, *. The computer allows us to put in one set of symbols or characters and get out a different but related set. If this seems vague and general, let's consider some specific examples.

CHARACTERS IN	CHARACTERS OUT
Numbers representing the size of a window.	Cost of double glazing.
List of books borrowed from a library.	List of those books overdue.
A person's name.	The person's telephone number.
Standard notation for a move in a game of chess.	Picture of the chess board with the move accomplished.
Number representing height and acceleration.	Picture of lunar lander.
Pre-determined codes.	Musical sounds.

(Figure 1   Some uses of a computer)

This course is not about how the computer does these things but about how you can get it to do them by giving it the right instructions. We shall not therefore be going into any detail about the insides of a computer but you will find it helpful to know which are the major parts of a computer. This is quickly dealt with in the next section.

1.2 What is a computer?

A simple model of a computer is shown in Figure 2.

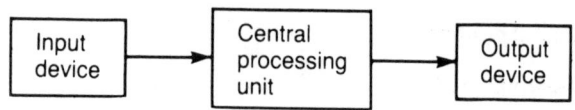

(Figure 2   A simple model of a computer)

You can see that there are three main parts to a computer:

1. The *input device* which allows you to enter either instructions or data (information) into the computer. On a microcomputer the input device is a keyboard which looks like a typewriter.

2. The *central processing unit* (CPU) which, among other things, carries out the instructions you have put in. This processing results in a modification of your data giving you the 'answer' or output that you require.
3. An *output device* which enables you to receive the result of the processing. The output device might be a monitor (screen) displaying the output or a printer which actually prints the output onto paper.

All this may sound very mundane. Indeed it would be were it not for the three key characteristics of a computer: (a) its capacity to store very large quantities of data which (b) it is able to process very rapidly, and (c) its capacity to store a program which controls its own operation. This last characteristic is by far the most important one and is the one we are going to cover in this course.

Backing store
We shall just mention one other technical detail before looking at programming. If you are using this course you are likely to own or use a microcomputer with a small internal storage capacity. It uses that storage to keep its main running instructions plus the details of the problem it is currently solving. The latter details are erased when you switch the machine off, so if you want to keep your program or data you have to keep them in a *backing store:* a separate storage system that you can link to the computer as needed. This will be a built-in hard disk and disk drive on large machines or just a disk drive on smaller machines.

So, to summarise, the main elements of a computer system are illustrated in Figure 3.

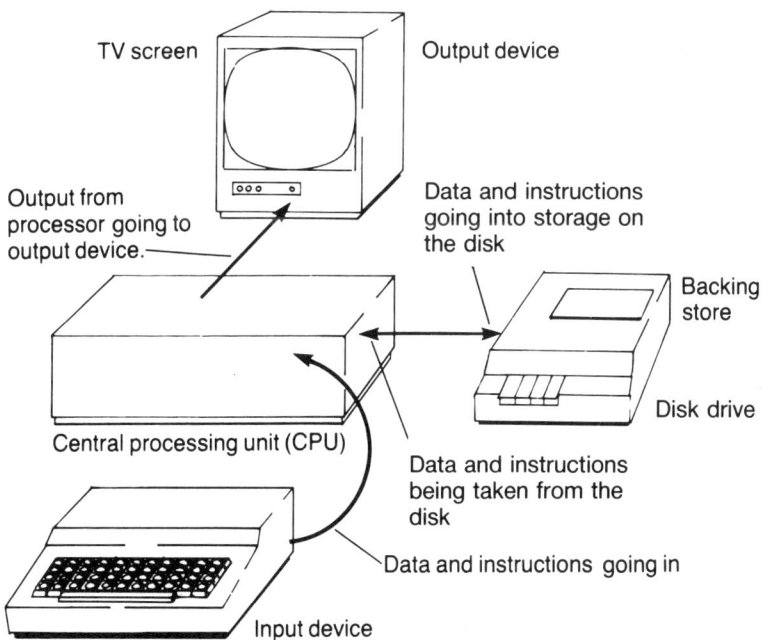

(Figure 3   A typical computer system)

1.3 What is BASIC?

BASIC is a *high-level programming language*: one which allows you to key in easily learned commands and code words. These are then interpreted by an *interpreter* program built in to the machine and converted into machine code (a *low-level programming language* which corresponds directly with the patterns of electrical signals in the computer). Once you have learnt BASIC you will be able to use it to program any computer that contains a BASIC *interpreter*. BASIC stands for Beginners' All-purpose Symbolic Instruction Code.

You may find it useful to note the sequence of events that is taking place when you program a computer.

1. You have a problem.
2. You break down the problem into steps which can be put into BASIC.
3. You write a program in BASIC.
4. You sit at a keyboard and enter your program into the computer.
5. The computer interprets your BASIC instructions into its own code and processes them.
6. The computer prints out the results in the form you specified in the program.

And that is all you need to know about what a computer is. From now on we will assume that all you want to do is to give the computer problems and to get back results, so now let's move on to a simple problem which we might want to give to a computer.

1.4 A simple problem

The main activity of programming is breaking down the solution to a problem into simple steps which can be represented by BASIC programming statements.

Imagine that you are playing the part of a computer with a young child. The child might give you two numbers and ask you to give their sum. After a short time the child will naturally try you out with large numbers which you cannot add in your head, so you will have to have a paper and pencil at hand. The following could be a typical dialogue.

CHILD: 'Start'
YOU: 'Give me the first number'
CHILD: '12157'
(You write this number on a piece of paper)
YOU: 'Give me the second number'
CHILD: '7896'
(You write the second number on the piece of paper)
(You perform the addition sum)
YOU: '20053'

We could describe the computer's part in this process more formally in the following way:

1. Input the first number
2. Input the second number
3. Add the two numbers
4. Output the result

(Figure 4   Computer processes in adding two numbers)

By this simple analogy we have arrived at a strategy for solving this problem. Broadly speaking, phases 1 and 2 would be concerned with entering numbers into the computer, phase 3 would involve a process in the central processing unit, while phase 4 would involve the output device.

Now, although we have not yet taught you any BASIC programming, we are going to show you what the problem-solving sequence would look like when written in BASIC.

Example 1
Write a BASIC program to enter two numbers into the computer and to output their sum.

Solution
We have already worked out an intuitive procedure to solve this problem in Figure 4. A program in BASIC would have the following form:

```
10 INPUT FIRST
20 INPUT SECOND
30 LET SUM=FIRST+SECOND*
40 PRINT SUM
50 END†
```
Program 1

We do not wish to concentrate on the details of the program at this stage, but hope that you can see, without stretching the imagination too far, how the strategy from Figure 4 has been changed into a program. A program then is a *'sequence of instructions composed for solving a given problem by computer'*.

SAQ 1
We now come to the first point in the course at which we want you to check your progress through trying this Self-Assessment Question (SAQ). The SAQs are designed to help you find out whether or not you have understood the immediately preceding sections of the course. In each case, the answer to a SAQ appears at the end of the Unit in which the SAQ occurs. If you get all the answers right, just move onto the next section. If you get any wrong, check back to see where you have gone wrong.

---

* The command LET is optional and can be left out, i.e.

```
30 SUM=FIRST+SECOND
```

† END is not needed on all computers, e.g. it may be omitted from programs where the exit from the program is in the last line of the program.

Select those phrases from List B below which complete correctly the phrases given in List A.

A
1. The CPU . . .
2. The main characteristics of a computer system are . . .
3. A machine code is . . .
4. A machine code is an example of a . . . language.
5. BASIC is an example of a . . . language.
6. A BASIC interpreter . . .
7. A computer program is . . .

B
(a) low-level
(b) high-level
(c) . . . holds data and instructions, controls its own processing, and controls the operation of input and output devices.
(d) . . . a series of instructions or procedural steps for the solution of a specific problem.
(e) . . . that it is capable of storing large quantities of data, is able to process this data very rapidly, and lastly that it is able to store a program which controls its own operation.
(f) . . . translates code written in BASIC into machine code.
(g) . . . a code which corresponds directly with the electrical patterns within a computer.

1.5 Statement numbers

Let's have a closer look at Program 1 again:

```
10 INPUT FIRST
20 INPUT SECOND
30 LET SUM=FIRST+SECOND
40 PRINT SUM
50 END
```

Program 1 (from p.5)

We have said that a program is a *sequence of instructions.* In the program above each line is an instruction. Thus:

```
10 INPUT FIRST
```

is the first instruction of the program, and

```
50 END
```

is the last. Instructions in a programming language are sometimes called *statements.* We will use the words 'instruction' and 'statement' synonymously.

Entering statements

Until later in the course, we shall restrict ourselves to one instruction per line.

When sitting at the keyboard of a microcomputer, the actual process of entering a statement is completed only after the *RETURN* key has been pressed. So what happens is this:

You type 10 INPUT FIRST then press RETURN. Then you type 20 INPUT SECOND and press RETURN etc. . . .

You will see on the screen:

```
10 INPUT FIRST
20 INPUT SECOND
```

You will have noticed that *each line begins with a number*. These must be whole numbers in the range of 0–65529, and they determine the order in which the instructions are processed (executed), i.e. they define the 'sequence' of the instructions. The execution of the instructions starts with the line of the lowest number, and continues in the sense of increasing numbers until instructed otherwise, or until the end of the program is reached. (More about 'until instructed otherwise' and 'ending', later.)

Why then, you may ask, was the program not written as follows?

```
1 INPUT FIRST
2 INPUT SECOND
3 LET SUM=FIRST+SECOND
4 PRINT SUM
5 END
```

Program 2

Why not indeed! The program would have done the job perfectly well! However, as you will soon find out when writing programs, you need a certain amount of flexibility. In particular you need the opportunity to slip into the program a statement which you have overlooked, or one which allow you to make an important modification. Numbering our lines 10, 20, 30 and 40 leaves 9 empty lines between statements which may be used to correct or modify the program. When running, the processing proceeds to the *next highest* line number of the program, so the gap of 9 unused line numbers does not slow down the program execution in any way.

SAQ 2

Look at the line numbers in the following programs and decide which programs would produce a correct sum of FIRST and SECOND.

(a)
```
 11 INPUT FIRST
 59 INPUT SECOND
 93 LET SUM=FIRST+SECOND
401 PRINT SUM
500 END
```

(b)
```
23 INPUT FIRST
32 INPUT SECOND
49 LET SUM=FIRST+SECOND
40 PRINT SUM
50 END
```

(c)   10 INPUT FIRST
       20 INPUT SECOND
       15 LET SUM=FIRST+SECOND
       40 PRINT SUM
       50 END

(d)   100 INPUT FIRST
       200 INPUT SECOND
       110 LET SUM=FIRST+SECOND
       190 PRINT SUM
       220 END

(e)   100 INPUT FIRST
        50 INPUT SECOND
       407 LET SUM=FIRST+SECOND
       902 PRINT SUM
      1000 END

Programs 3–7

1.6 Executions and commands

The command RUN

Execution? No, it's not the end but the beginning! Let's go on and run our first program before we get tired of it!

```
10 INPUT FIRST
20 INPUT SECOND
30 LET SUM=FIRST+SECOND
40 PRINT SUM
50 END
```

Program 1   (from p.5)

And what happens? Nothing. This is because the computer is waiting for us to give instructions to the program as a whole. *If you want to execute this program, you must give it the command RUN.* This you put on a new line as follows:

```
10 INPUT FIRST
20 INPUT SECOND
30 LET SUM=FIRST+SECOND
40 PRINT SUM
50 END
RUN
```

Program 1   (from p.5)

(Don't worry about RUN not having a line number – we'll explain that shortly.)

Then press *RETURN*. You will then see *?* on the screen which is the computer's way of asking for data. Give it your first number; then press *RETURN*; another *?* appears because the computer needs your second number. Give it the second number and press *RETURN*. The answer should now appear. Here is our version of this run:

```
10 INPUT FIRST
20 INPUT SECOND
30 LET SUM=FIRST+SECOND
40 PRINT SUM
50 END
RUN
```

```
? 12157
? 7896
20053

OK
```

(Figure 5   A complete run of a program)

What we are doing therefore is to distinguish between the *entry* of a program and its *execution*. Let's go back to the dialogue between you and the child playing computers. A very explicit infant may have said 'I am going to give you two numbers. I want you to write them down, add them together, and then tell me their sum'. At this point you know exactly what to do, but you haven't yet done anything. You've got the instructions though, you've been programmed. The dialogue may proceed thus:

CHILD: 'Start'
YOU: 'Give me the first number'
CHILD: '12157'
YOU: 'Give me the second number'
CHILD: '7896'
YOU: '20053'

Now these instructions have been carried out (run). *A program then is just a set of instructions for the computer. When the program is run or executed these instructions are carried out.*

Other commands: LIST, SAVE, LOAD

RUN is not the only command which you can give to a program as a whole. You can also use LIST, SAVE and LOAD as follows:

LIST*
For example, you may spend quite a lot of time typing a program into your machine and during that process make several corrections. You may then wish to see a fair copy of the program as a whole on the screen. If you type the word *LIST*, a complete copy of the program in line number order will appear on the screen.

SAVE*
Having developed a program to a satisfactory stage you may wish to take a copy of it on to disk; the word *SAVE* will do this for you. (Your computer will, of course, have to be connected to a back-up store such as a disk drive.)

LOAD*
Later you may wish to use one of your stored programs; the command *LOAD* will enter the program from your back-up store back into your computer.

Words like LIST, RUN, SAVE and LOAD, which allow us to handle the program as a single entity, are called *commands* and are provided by the BASIC interpreter. *A command occupies a line on its own and generally does not have a line number*, e.g. the word RUN after line 50 causes the program to start to execute, and is

---

* See Unit 9 for details on how to use LIST, LOAD and SAVE.

equivalent to the child's command 'start' in the dialogue above. Commands will be discussed in greater detail in a later Unit, but the four that we have already looked at will allow us to get by for a start.

Computer response
After a command has been successfully carried out the interpreter informs you of this fact by writing a message on the screen, e.g.

OK

Keywords
These are the BASIC words which go in the program to specify what action is to occur, e.g. INPUT, PRINT, LET.

1.7 Execution and data

You will have realised that we have written a program which will add any two numbers in a quite general way, for it is immaterial to the program what numbers we enter when we receive prompts, ?, on the screen. As the computer executes the program it must be able to request that we input actual numbers for its particular task, i.e. it must have the facility to demand specific data to do the job in hand. You need to be able to distinguish clearly between the program, as a set of more or less general instructions, and the *data* which are the actual numbers which must be input when the program is executing, in order to solve a particular problem. You can, of course, run your program repeatedly with many pairs of numbers, as you will see later.

Another way of looking at these instructions is to visualise the situation as an umpire gathers the runners at the start of a race in order to give them certain instructions: 'Go down the right-hand side of the field to the furthest corner, over the stile and turn left down the lane . . .' The umpire's instructions are analogous to a program. If the runners understand what he is saying then they know what to do; but they are still at the starting line. They haven't actually started. This is analogous to the program having been entered into the machine. Then the umpire says 'Go!' and the race starts. This is analogous to the computer starting to execute the program.

Let's extend the analogy and consider the cross-country race as a novelty race. Imagine that the umpire did not give enough instructions for the runners to complete the course but said something like 'When you get to the bottom of the lane you will find further instructions pinned to the oak tree . . .' These instructions should be sufficient to guide the runners over the next part of the course, i.e. on to the next clue, and so on until the end of the race. These clues are analogous to giving the program more data during the course of its execution. This analogy may help you to see the important distinction between entering a program into the machine, executing the program, and then inputting data during the course of its execution.

SAQ 3
Below is a print out from a computer. It contains *keywords, commands, responses from the system* and *items of data*. It also contains sections that are concerned

with *entry, execution* and *listing*. Identify as many of these items as possible as follows:

Mark keywords with   K
Mark commands with   C
Mark system responses with R
Mark data items with   D
Bracket lines concerned with entry
Bracket lines concerned with execution
Bracket lines concerned with listing

```
10 INPUT FIRST
20 INPUT SECOND
30 LET SUM=FIRST+SECOND
40 PRINT SUM
50 END
RUN
? -37
? -46
-83

OK
LIST

10 INPUT FIRST
20 INPUT SECOND
30 LET SUM=FIRST+SECOND
40 PRINT SUM
50 END

OK
RUN
? 12.83
? 48.95
61.78
OK
```

Program 1   (from p.5)

1.8 INPUT, PRINT and LET

You have seen that a program is a sequence of statements, and we have given you an intuitive idea of how each statement works. You may also have noticed that each of the three types of statement used so far (INPUT, LET and PRINT) corresponds to one of the three main devices which comprise the computer system (input, central processor and output devices). We will now look at each statement in more detail.

INPUT
The word *INPUT* is a signal to the computer that during execution, an item of data must be entered at the input device. We saw this happen when we ran our first program: after the ? we entered 12157, pressed RETURN to complete the input procedure and then found ourselves confronted by another ? requesting the input of the next number. What, then, happened to 12157, the first item of data? The answer is that it has been stored for later use in the program's execution in a *storage location* labelled FIRST. The word FIRST has two main functions in the program, (a) when written and later referred to by the programmer it reminds him that at this point in the program the first item of data should be input, and (b) when

written in the statement 10 INPUT FIRST the word FIRST is the name or label of a location in the computer's memory. So 10 INPUT FIRST means *enter a number at the input device and store it in the location labelled* FIRST.

PRINT
The statement 40 PRINT SUM has almost the reverse effect to statements 10 and 20, in that it allows us to output information from the machine. It is a signal to the machine to take a copy of the contents of the store location labelled SUM and pass it to the output device which for most users of this course will be a screen or monitor.

LET
30 LET SUM=FIRST+SECOND is an example of an *assignment statement*. It is in this type of statement that the processing takes place. As you can see, it is a mixture of store names (SUM, FIRST, SECOND) and arithmetic operators (= and +). If you read it forwards, it says

> Let the store location SUM be made equal to the contents of the location FIRST added to the contents of the location named SECOND.

However, like many mathematical expressions, it is often clearer when read from right to left of the '=' as follows:

> Add the contents of the location FIRST to the contents of the location SECOND and store the result in the location labelled SUM.

Generally the assignment statement has the form:

> LET store location name = expression.

This means find the value of the expression of the right-hand side of the '=' and store this value in the store location named on the left-hand side of the '='.

The tricky point about LET ...=.... is that it is easily confused with ...=... in mathematical equations. An example will demonstrate the difference. Suppose you have stored a number in location L and you want to make the number in that store 5 greater than it now is. You write:

    LET L=L+5

Now obviously this doesn't mean:

    L=L+5

since there is no value for L which could make this true. L is not in this case a mathematical constant, but a label for something whose value can be altered. Thus

LET L=L+5

effectively means LET new L = old L+5.

1.9 Store locations

As we have already said, one of the main characteristics of a computer system is its capacity for storing large quantities of data. We must now consider how the

BASIC language allows us to allocate store location names. If you look at our first program and recall that a computer is capable of doing only one thing at a time, it is fairly obvious that when we reach line 20 and wish to input our second number, the number that we entered in line 10 must have been stored somewhere! In this case the first number was stored in the location labelled FIRST. We can think of the storage locations as being like a set of pigeon-holes where we distinguish clearly between the label or address or name on each pigeon-hole and the contents of the hole.

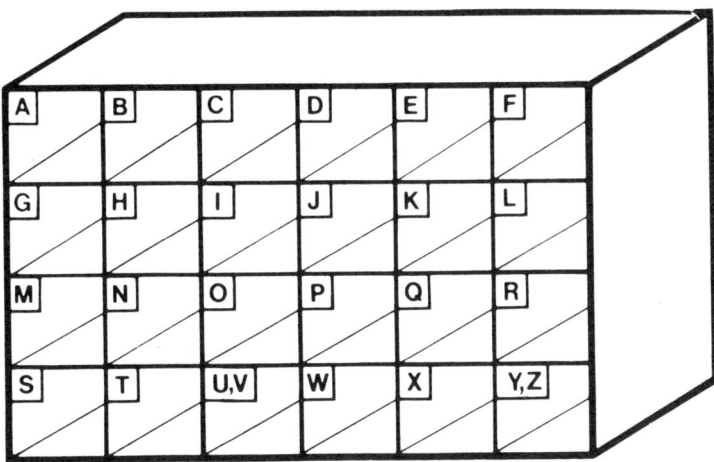

(Figure 6   A model of the store locations in a very small computer)

You will see that in our model of possible store locations we have used the labels A, B, C . . . On the other hand, in the program we have been studying we have used words of up to six characters to label our stores, e.g. FIRST, SECOND. (IBM BASICA allows variable names of up to 40 characters in length.)

Choosing store location names

Clearly it makes life a lot easier for programmers if they choose store location names which remind them of what they are storing. That is why we chose FIRST, SECOND and SUM. We could have used A, B and S so that our program would have been:

```
10 INPUT A
20 INPUT B
30 LET S=A+B
40 PRINT S
50 END
```
Program 8

[K] Program 8.

When you see the symbol [K] it means we suggest you try this program on your own microcomputer, if you have one. To do this, key in the lines, press RETURN and then type RUN. Your computer will ask you for a number. Give it one and press RETURN. It then asks you for the second number. Give it the second number, press RETURN and the sum will appear on your screen. If we had done this, then after inputting 12157 and 7896, the store locations would be:

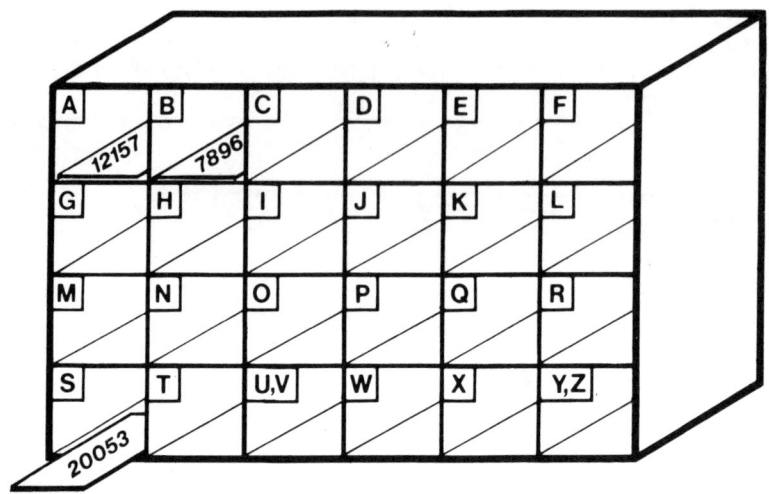

(Figure 7   State of the store locations after Program 8)

Store location names
From now on, we shall use location names which are meaningful, e.g. FIRST, PERCENTAGE. In BASICA and GWBASIC location names can be typed in both upper and lower case. However, when you list your program both commands and location names will be in upper case. So to the computer first and FIRST are the same.

A store location or variable name must not be a reserved word. A list of reserved words can be found in Appendix B. Reserved words include all BASIC, BASICA and GWBASIC commands, statements, function names and operator names.

DATE is a reserved word. If you wish to use the word DATE embedded in a variable name use ADATE or THEDATE. Never begin a variable name with a reserved word, i.e. DATE1. For example, BASIC will interpret the statement LETTER$="A" as LET TER$="A", LET being a reserved word.

1.10   Copying and overwriting

BASIC statements can have two different effects on the contents of a store location. Or rather a statement can either have no effect on the contents of the location or it can change the contents. This is illustrated below.

Effect of copying
Suppose we have the number 53 stored in location A. What happens after LET B=A and after PRINT A? In each case A still stores the number 53 after the statement has been executed:

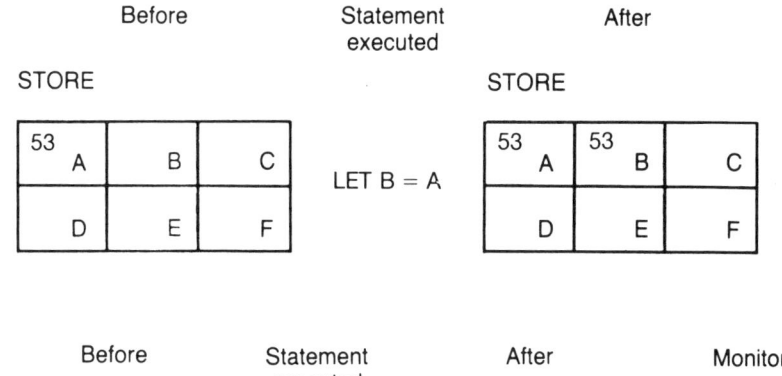

In each case the copying statements leave the original store location unchanged. It's just like getting a statement of your bank account: the piece of paper copies your account but your account still has your money in it!

Effect of overwriting
Suppose now that we still have the number 53 stored in location A but this time execute the statement LET A=A+7. The result is:

Before	Statement executed	After
STORE: 53 in A; B, C, D, E, F empty	LET A=A+7	STORE: 60 in A; B, C, D, E, F empty

The statement LET A = A+7 overwrites the contents of A. That is, the original contents disappear and are replaced by the new contents, which is in this case 60. Of course we could have made the new contents of A to be 60 in many ways, e.g. by, say: LET A = 60.

1.11 Arithmetic operators

When you do arithmetic you use four main operators: +, −, × and ÷. BASIC has the same operators, although two are printed differently:

Everyday symbol	Meaning	BASIC symbol
+	add	+
−	subtract	−
×	multiply	*
÷	divide	/

SAQ 4
Write the following expressions using BASIC symbols for the arithmetic operators. (Where the expressions use brackets, leave the brackets in your answers.)

(a) 3+7 (e) 30÷(3+2)
(b) 3×7 (f) 24−(4×3)
(c) 8÷4 (g) 5×6×7
(d) 5×(2+8) (h) 81−(27×2)

SAQ 5
If A has the value of 2, B has the value of 5 and C has the value of 10, calculate the values of the following:

(a) A+B+C   17
(b) A*B   10
(c) A*B*C   100
(d) C/A   5
(e) C/(B−A)   10/3 = 3 1/3
(f) A*A   4
(g) (B*C)/(B−A)   50/3 = 16 2/3
(h) (C−B)*(C+B)   5 × 15 = 75

The arithmetic is actually done (executed) in BASIC through assignment statements (LET statements) which tell the computer's arithmetic unit (part of the central processor) what to do. We can illustrate this with the following computer model.

Effect of LET A = B−C

STORE AT START

A	15 B	10 C
D	E	F

LET A = B−C

Remember to read this from the right to the left of the "=" sign. It says *take the number in location B, subtract from it the number in location C and put the result in location A.* So the result is:

Result of LET A = B−C

Notice that the contents of B and C are unchanged.

STORE AT FINISH

5 A	15 B	10 C
D	E	F

Effect of LET A = B★C

STORE AT START

A	15 B	10 C
D	E	F

STORE AT FINISH

150 A	15 B	10 C
D	E	F

SAQ 6
Fill in the values in the store locations A, B and C after each line has been executed in these programs.

1. Program

    10 LET A = 12
    20 LET B = 5
    30 LET C = A★(A+B)
    40 LET A = A+10

    Store location values

A	B	C
12		
12	5	
12	5	204
22	5	204

2. Program

    10 LET A = 20
    20 LET B = A★3
    30 LET C = A/4
    40 LET A = B+C

    Store location values

A	B	C
20		
20	60	
20	60	5
65	60	5

What you have just done isn't (we hope) difficult and it doesn't get any more difficult when we move on to more complicated store location names. We have to make the names more complicated because A, B, C . . . only give us 26 stores and, as we said on page 14, we are going to use meaningful location names.

e.g. LET ATIME = FINISH−START

LET ATIME = FINISH−START is no different from LET A = B−C. ATIME, FINISH and START are simply store location names. START is one name, just as XYZ 823A is one car number.

We are now ready to use the arithmetic capacity of a computer.

Example 2
Write a BASIC program to enter two numbers into the computer and then output their sum, difference, product and quotient.

Solution
This may look complicated but we've really solved this already. We had a program (Program 1) to output the sum of two numbers, so to output their difference, product and quotient, we need only change the arithmetic operator in line 30 which reads:

```
30 LET SUM=FIRST+SECOND
```

Original program
```
10 INPUT FIRST
20 INPUT SECOND
30 LET SUM=FIRST+SECOND
40 PRINT SUM
50 END
```

Now what we need is three extra versions of the original program, each with a different line 30:

```
10 INPUT FIRST
20 INPUT SECOND
30 LET SUM=FIRST+SECOND
40 PRINT SUM

10 INPUT FIRST
20 INPUT SECOND
30 LET DIFFERENCE=FIRST-SECOND
40 PRINT DIFFERENCE

10 INPUT FIRST
20 INPUT SECOND
30 LET PRODUCT=FIRST*SECOND
40 PRINT PRODUCT

10 INPUT FIRST
20 INPUT SECOND
30 LET QUOTIENT=FIRST/SECOND
40 PRINT QUOTIENT
```

Do we need to write four programs? Fortunately no, because when we copy the numbers from locations FIRST and SECOND, we don't destroy these contents, so we can use them four times over in one program:

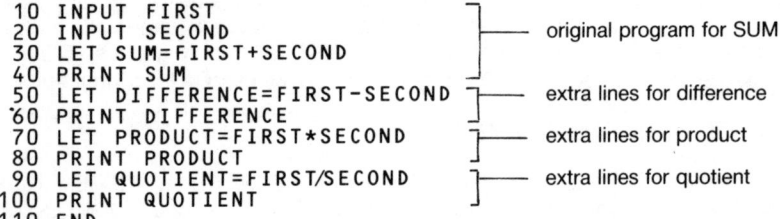

Program 9   Sum, difference, product and quotient of two numbers

[K] Key Program 9 into your microcomputer. Then key RUN and input two numbers. A typical print out should look like this:

```
RUN
? 57.82
? 19.11
76.93
38.71
1104.94
3.02564

OK
```

1.12 Numerical constants

Earlier in this Unit we saw that our first BASIC program was capable of manipulating whole, decimal and negative numbers. At this stage we won't go into detail on how numbers are represented in BASIC, but just show you that we can use numbers directly in assignment statements.

The statement LET P=427*R means create the number 427, multiply it by the number found in store location R and then store the result in location P. (Don't be put off by thinking that computers handle only binary numbers. The computer's interpreter enables us to input ordinary decimal numbers.)

Similarly, the statement LET Y4=3.142+Z8 creates the number 3.142 and adds it to the contents of location Z8, and then stores the sum in location Y4.

And the statement LET A=−48.93/B creates the number −48.93 and divides it by the number found in location B and then stores the result of this calculation in location A.

Exercise preamble

Progress in metrication has been slow and life still abounds with irritating conversions which occasionally tease us, e.g. pounds weight to kilogrammes, yards to metres, pints to litres, a knitting pattern with balls of wool in ounces which must be bought in grammes, etc. . . . If we go on holiday abroad we mentally convert kilometres into miles, and pounds sterling into other currency. Most of us still think of body and weather temperatures in terms of degrees Fahrenheit rather than degrees Centigrade or Celsius. We can imagine the home microcomputer of the future having a general conversion program in it which will do all these diverse conversions for us. The next two exercises are on writing programs to do with conversions. You need only the ideas introduced in the earlier programs in this Unit.

Exercise 1

Write programs in BASIC to carry out each of the following conversions:

(a) Input a number representing a length in inches, and output this length in centimetres, given that one inch is equivalent to 2.54 centimetres.
(b) Input a number representing a weight in ounces, and output that weight in grammes, given that one ounce is equivalent to 28.375 grammes.

(Answers to Exercises appear at the end of each Unit with the SAQ answers.)

Exercise 2
Any conversion *involves 'conversion factor x number to be converted'*. So it is possible to write a *general conversion program* where you input two numbers each time you use it: the conversion factor and the number to be converted. Write a general conversion program which will do this.

1.13 The remark statement: REM

The statement REM is the remark statement. It allows us to give a title to a program or make some other meaningful remark about the program. For example, within the body of a program it helps us to identify what the program or section of the program does. The *REM statement is not executed by the computer* and is there purely for the benefit of either the programmer or user, i.e. when the computer sees REM at the beginning of a line it ignores everything on that line. The next program is concerned with calculating percentages and so as a title to the program our first statement will be 10 REM**PERCENTAGE CALCULATION**. (The two stars have no function other than to emphasise the title.)

Example 3
Write a BASIC program to input two numbers and output the second as a percentage of the first. *Reminder:* Percentage=(second÷first)×100.

Solution
```
10 REM**PERCENTAGE CALCULATION**        ──────── (program title using
20 INPUT FIRST                                    REM statement)
30 INPUT SECOND
40 LET PERCENTAGE=(SECOND/FIRST)*100
50 PRINT PERCENTAGE
60 END
```
Program 10   Percentage calculation

Typical runs

```
RUN
? 57
? 74
129.825

OK

RUN
? 74
? 57
77.027

OK
```

[K] Program 10.

1.14 More complicated arithmetic

We have reached the stage when we can use the computer like a simple four-function calculating machine, but we will soon wish to do slightly more complicated arithmetic. Generally BASIC allows us to set out equations in a familiar way. We can use brackets, i.e. ( ), to group together certain values, and when BASIC evaluates an expression, it deals with the values *inside* the brackets first. Next come values involving multiplication or division and finally, addition and subtraction.

This *order of preference* for performing arithmetic operations is discussed more fully in a later Unit, but you will soon see that this order just formalises the way we naturally go about arithmetic calculations.

Let's show you what we mean.

Example 4
Write the following expressions in BASIC:
1. AB+C   2. A(B+C)   3. $\dfrac{A}{B+C}$

Solutions

1. A*B+C
    The order of precedence rules tell us that A*B will be evaluated first and the C added. If you were worried about this you could write (A*B)+C but the brackets aren't essential here.
2. A*(B+C)
    Notice that, just as a bracket is needed in A(B+C) so it is needed in A*(B+C).
3. A/(B+C)

Now try some for yourself.

SAQ 7
Write the following as BASIC expressions:
1. ABC   2. $\dfrac{AB}{C}$ 3. $\dfrac{A+B}{C}$

Exercise 3
Now that you have written the expressions in SAQ 7 as BASIC expressions, write a program that will allow you to input three numbers (A, B and C) and print out the values of the expressions in SAQ 7.

1.15 Literal printing

You have seen already that we can print out the values from store locations. You will find as the course progresses that the PRINT function is very versatile. One use of this statement is to print messages on the screen which will be helpful to you when the program is running. These messages are usually referred to as *prompts*. We have seen already that when an input statement is encountered during the execution of a program, a ? appears on the screen to remind us that an input is required. In even slightly complicated programs, a series of question marks on the screen is confusing since you may not know which input value the question mark is prompting. Prompts generated by PRINT statements are very useful in these circumstances.

It is very easy to get a computer to print a reminder or message on the screen. All you need is a line such as:

```
20 PRINT "MESSAGE"
```

This simply prints

```
MESSAGE
```

on your screen.

In other words, whatever appears between quotes thus " " after the word PRINT will be printed out *exactly as it stands*. Notice that, as in the case of the REM statement, the computer doesn't execute the words in the quotes. Thus

```
20 PRINT "A+B"
```

results in

```
A+B
```

on your screen and the computer does *not* add the value in location A to the value in location B.

The following example demonstrates the use of PRINT " " to remind the programmer and user of what the program is doing.

Example 5
Write a BASIC program to convert a temperature value given in degrees C into degrees F. *Remember:*

$$°F = \frac{9 \times °C}{5} + 32.$$

Solution

```
10 REM**CENTIGRAGE TO FAHRENHEIT**
20 PRINT "ENTER NEXT TEMP IN DEGREES C"  ← print message precedes
30 INPUT CENTIGRADE                         input statement so that
40 LET FAHRENHEIT=(9/5)*CENTIGRADE+32       the message is printed
50 PRINT "THE TEMP IN F IS"                 before ? appears
60 PRINT FAHRENHEIT
70 END
```

Program 11   Temperature conversion

Typical run

```
RUN
ENTER NEXT TEMP IN DEGREES C
? 16
THE TEMP IN DEGREES F IS
60.8

OK
```

K Program 11.

Assignment 1

NEC students: your solution to this assignment should be sent to your NEC tutor for marking. If you own your own microcomputer, write your own assignment in the BASIC for that computer and tell your tutor what make of microcomputer it is and which type of BASIC you are using.

FlexiStudy students: complete the assignments according to the instructions given to you by your FlexiStudy centre.

Remember to make good use of remark and literal print statements when writing your programs.

1. If you deposit £D in an account paying P% rate of interest for one year, then the yield at the end of the first year is given by the equation

    $$Y = (D+Y) \times \frac{P}{100}$$

    (a) Write a BASIC program to input values for D and P and to output the yield, Y.

    (b) If the original deposit together with the accrued interest is left in the account for a further year at the same rate of interest then the compound interest after the second year will be given by the equation

    $$C = (D+Y) \times P \div 100$$

    Extend your program for (a) to calculate and output this compound interest.

2. Consider the problem of estimating the cost of installing replacement aluminium double-glazed windows. The windows comprise 3 parts:

(a) a hardwood surround, (b) aluminium frame and (c) glass. If the height of the window is H metres and the width is W metres, then the total lengths of both hardwood and aluminium required are given approximately by the expression (2H+2W) metres; and the area of glass required by the expression (H×W) square metres.

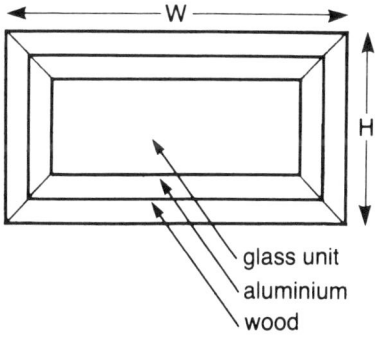

(Figure 8)

Write three separate BASIC programs which, on being given values for height and width in metres, will output the cost of

(a) the hardwood surround if the wood costs £3 per metre;
(b) the aluminium surround if the aluminium costs £4 per metre;
(c) the glass unit if the glass unit costs £40 per square metre.

Now link these three into one program to estimate the total cost of installation, if the labour cost is £50 per window.

Objectives of Unit 1

Now that you have completed this Unit, check that you are able to:

Write simple programs using:

Line numbers ☐
INPUT ☐
LET ☐
PRINT ☐
Copying from one location to another ☐
Overwriting ☐
$+, -, *, /$ ☐
( ) ☐
Numerical constants ☐
REM ☐
PRINT " " ☐

Know when to use:
RETURN ☐
RUN ☐

Know how to respond to:
OK ☐

Answers to SAQs and Exercises

SAQ 1
A   B
1   (c)
2   (e)
3   (g)
4   (a)
5   (b)
6   (f)
7   (d)

SAQ 2
(a) and (e) would run as Program 1.
(b) is asked to print SUM before SUM has been calculated.
(c) and (d) are asked to calculate SUM before SECOND has been inputted.

SAQ 3

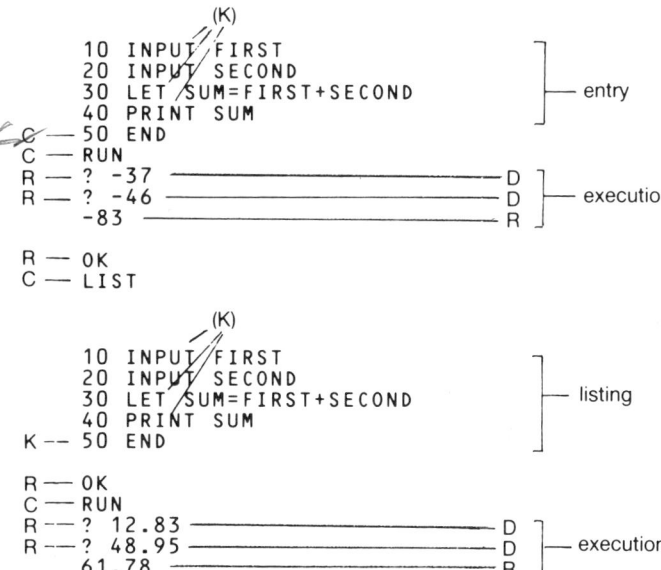

(Have you noticed that this program has coped with negative and decimal fractional numbers?)

SAQ 4

(a) 3+7
(b) 3*7
(c) 8/4
(d) 5*(2+8)
(e) 30/(3+2)
(f) 24-(4*3)
(g) 5*6*7
(h) 81-(27*2)

SAQ 5

(a) 17 (b) 10 (c) 100 (d) 5
(e) 10/3 or 3⅓ or 3.33... (f) 4
(g) 50/3 or 16⅔ or 16.66... (h) 75

SAQ 6

1.

12		
12	5	
12	5	204
22	5	204

2.

20			
20	60		
20	60	5	
65	60	5	

Exercise 1
(a)   Program 12

```
10 INPUT INCHES
20 LET CENTIMETRES=2.54*INCHES
30 PRINT CENTIMETRES
40 END
```

Typical runs

```
RUN
? 12
30.48
```
} first use

```
OK
RUN
? 36
91.44
```
} second use

```
OK
```

K Program 12.

(b)   Program 13
```
10 INPUT OUNCES
20 LET GRAMMES=OUNCES*28.375
30 PRINT GRAMMES
40 END
```

Typical runs

```
RUN
? 10
283.75
```
} first use

```
OK
RUN
? 50
1418.75
```
} second use

```
OK
RUN
? 16
454
```
} third use

```
OK
```

K Program 13.

Exercise 2
Program 14

```
10 INPUT BEFORE
20 INPUT FACTOR
30 LET AFTER=BEFORE*FACTOR
40 PRINT AFTER
50 END
```

Typical runs

```
RUN
? 16
? 28.375
454
```
} use for ounces to grammes

```
OK
RUN
? 36
? 2.54
91.44
```
} use for inches to cms

```
OK
```

K Program 14.

SAQ 7
1.   A*B*C
2.   A*B/C   [(A*B)/C is also correct]
3.   (A+B)/C

Exercise 3
Program 15

```
10  INPUT A
20  INPUT B
30  INPUT C
40  LET R=A*B*C     } calculates first expression and prints it out
50  PRINT R
60  LET R=(A*B)/C   } calculates second expression and prints it out
70  PRINT R
80  LET R=(A+B)/C   } calculates third expression and prints it out
90  PRINT R
100 END
```

Typical runs

```
RUN                 RUN
? 13                ? 13
? -27               ? 13
? 55.2              ? 13
-19375.2            2197
-6.358696           13
-.2536232           2

OK                  OK
```

K Program 15.

UNIT 2
Making decisions

2.1	Introduction	30
2.2	PRINT . . . ,	30
2.3	IF . . . THEN . . .	32
2.4	Inequalities	34
2.5	Repetitions and WHILE . . . WEND . . .	38
2.6	A note on GOTO	44
2.7	Flowcharts	45
2.8	Counting	49
2.9	Comparisons	53
	Assignment 2	54
	Objectives of Unit 2	54
	Answers to SAQs and Exercises	54

2.1 Introduction

The programs which we considered in Unit 1 were quite straightforward. They started their processing at the statement with the lowest number and continued in line number order until execution finished at the line with the highest line number. One thing that computers are very good at is lots of repetitive calculations; another is their ability to make decisions. Both of these features involve changing the sequence in which a program is executed. This Unit will introduce you to some of the statements which enable you to write programs of this type. But first we are going to introduce you to a new type of PRINT statement.

2.2 PRINT . . . ,

In Unit 1 we wrote a program (Example 3) to output one number as a percentage of another. On the screen, the calculation and result appeared in the format:

```
RUN
? 57
? 74
129.825
```

Obviously it would be better if the answer included the word *Percentage* so that it was clearer what was happening. This can easily be done by changing line 50 from 50 PRINT PERCENTAGE to

```
50 PRINT "PERCENTAGE", PERCENTAGE
```

The effect of this line is:

Version of line 50	Result on screen
50 PRINT PERCENTAGE	129.825
50 PRINT "PERCENTAGE", PERCENTAGE	PERCENTAGE 129.825

The statement PRINT "PERCENTAGE", PERCENTAGE has four items in it.

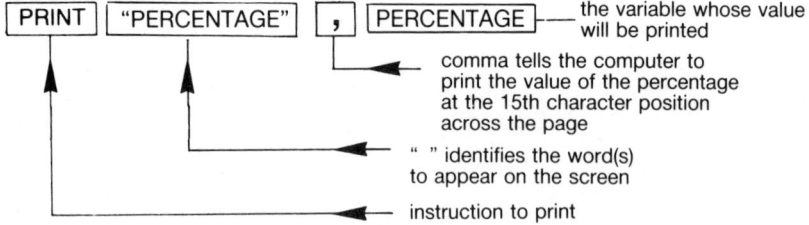

We can use PRINT . . . , to improve the percentage program from Unit 1. At the same time we can improve the appearance of the program by making use of the literal print statement PRINT " " which we introduced in Section 1.15.

Original program

```
10 REM**PERCENTAGE CALCULATION**
20 INPUT FIRST
30 INPUT SECOND
40 LET PERCENTAGE=(SECOND/FIRST)*100
50 PRINT PERCENTAGE
60 END
```

New program

```
10 REM**PERCENTAGE CALCULATION**
20 PRINT "INPUT THE FIRST NUMBER"
30 INPUT FIRST
40 PRINT "INPUT THE SECOND NUMBER"
50 INPUT SECOND
60 LET PERCENTAGE=(SECOND/FIRST)*100
70 PRINT "PERCENTAGE", PERCENTAGE
```

Program 1 Improved percentage program

Original program: typical run

```
RUN
? 80
? 37
46.25
```

New program: typical run

```
RUN
INPUT THE FIRST NUMBER ──────── effect of line 20
? 80
INPUT THE SECOND NUMBER ──────── effect of line 40
? 37
PERCENTAGE      46.25 ──────── effect of line 70
                 │
                 └────────── 16th position
                 └────────── 15th position reserved for
                             '−' sign with numbers
```

Notice how the use of literal print at lines 20 and 40, together with PRINT " ", makes the program much more friendly and understandable when in use.

[K] Program 1.

Commas in PRINT statements

You can use more commas in print statements to space out your results on the screen. BASIC usually has 5 print zones across the screen.

72 characters

Zone 1	Zone 2	Zone 3	Zone 4	Zone 5
0 to 14	15 to 29	30 to 44	45 to 59	60 to 71

Each successive comma in the print line moves the item after it one zone to the right. Thus

`PRINT "ZONE 1", "ZONE 2", "ZONE 3"`

results in:

`ZONE 1    ZONE 2    ZONE 3`

and

`PRINT "PERCENTAGE", PERCENTAGE`

gave:

`PERCENTAGE    46.25`

whereas

`PRINT "PERCENTAGE" PERCENTAGE`

would give

`PERCENTAGE 46.25`

SAQ 1
What would appear on the screen as a result of these print lines?
(Assume A=48, B=8, C=6 in these questions.)

(a) `PRINT "AREA" A`
(b) `PRINT "LENGTH" B, "WIDTH" C, "AREA" A`
(c) `PRINT "LENGTH", "WIDTH", "AREA"`
     `PRINT B, C, A`

Write PRINT lines in BASIC which would print on the screen the following words in the zones shown:

	Zone 1	Zone 2	Zone 3	Zone 4
(d)	LENGTH	8	WIDTH	6
(e)	LENGTH	8		
	WIDTH	6		
	AREA	48		
(f)	LENGTH	WIDTH		AREA

2.3 IF ... THEN ...

We are now going to look at one of the most important features of computers: their ability to make decisions. So far, in all previous programs, the computer has gone through the program in order of line number and every command has been done by the computer. What if we want the computer to do something depending on a store location, e.g. get the user to input his/her age and then print a relevant message, for example, "same age as me" or "very young".

Fortunately there is a BASIC command which will allow us to do this:

IF *condition* THEN *BASIC statement*

The condition

When the computer comes across the statement IF it looks to see if the *condition* is TRUE. The *condition* normally consists of two parts on either side of "=". E.g.

```
FIRST=SECOND
```

If the values in the store locations FIRST and SECOND are the same, then we say that the expression "FIRST=SECOND" is TRUE. If the values in the locations FIRST and SECOND are different, then the expression "FIRST=SECOND" is FALSE.

Often you need to perform calculations on each side before you can decide whether the *condition* is TRUE or FALSE, e.g.

```
(FIRST+SECOND)=(THIRD+FOURTH)
```

The above expression can be TRUE for many values of the store locations.

SAQ 2

Which ones of the following expressions are TRUE?

1. 5=9
2. N1=N2 (where N1 and N2 have the values 6 and 9)
3. B1=Z3 (where B1 and Z3 have the values 4 and 4)
4. 7=7
5. (4+5)=(3+6)

Now, returning to the original program, you can immediately see how we are going to program it. The first bit, getting the user to input his/her age is relatively easy.

```
10 PRINT "ENTER YOUR AGE"
20 INPUT AGE
```

Then come the IF . . . THEN . . . lines:

```
30 IF AGE=35 THEN PRINT "SAME AS ME"
```

and

```
40 IF AGE=1 THEN PRINT "VERY YOUNG"
```

and to round off

```
50 END
```

Program 2

```
10 PRINT "ENTER YOUR AGE"
20 INPUT AGE
30 IF AGE=35 THEN PRINT "SAME AS ME"
40 IF AGE=1 THEN PRINT "VERY YOUNG"
50 END
```

[K] Program 2.

The bit after the THEN can be any ordinary BASIC statement, and not just PRINT. E.g.

```
IF...THEN PRINT "HELLO"

IF...THEN INPUT AGE

IF...THEN END

IF...THEN LET I=I+2
```

and many more, as you will see later on.

When making IF . . . THEN . . . lines, first work out the condition (when the command should be done) and then work out the command as if it were on its own, before putting in the IF . . . THEN . . . statement.

For example, suppose you need to print "hello" when the store location FIRST has a value of 6.

The condition will be when "FIRST=6"
and the command to be carried out will be PRINT "HELLO"
and putting it all together:

```
IF FIRST=6 THEN PRINT "HELLO"
```

SAQ 3
Write IF . . . THEN . . . lines for the following situations.

(a) Write an IF . . . THEN . . . line which will increment the store location SECOND by 5 if the value of the store location FIRST is 10.

(b) Write an IF . . . THEN . . . line which will INPUT a number into the store location TELNO if the value of the location NUMBER is equal to the value in the store location AGE.

Type in and try them on your computer in programs.

2.4 Inequalities

In Program 2 we could only decide if the value in AGE was 'young' by using =. But we may want to print the message "very young" for all ages below 5, which would mean using four IF lines:

```
IF AGE=1 THEN PRINT "VERY YOUNG"
IF AGE=2 THEN PRINT "VERY YOUNG"
IF AGE=3 THEN PRINT "VERY YOUNG"
IF AGE=4 THEN PRINT "VERY YOUNG"
```

The "=" sign represents a relationship between the store location AGE and the numbers 1, 2, 3 or 4. But this is a very clumsy method and would be quite impossible to use if we wanted to print a message for any value of AGE under 1000! This section will show you how to do all these comparisons in one IF . . . THEN . . . line.

BASIC also allows expressions to include relationships:

Relationship	Example	Meaning
>	A>B	the value in store location A is greater than the value in B
<	X<Y	the value in store location X is less than the value in Y

True or false?
Consider the expression A<B. If A=2 and B=5 then A<B is true, because 2 is less than 5. Consider the same expression with values A=2 and B=1. Now A<B is false, because 2 is not less than 1. Similarly if A=2 and B=2 then A<B is false, for 2 is not less than 2. In writing programs we often find it useful to be able to know whether a statement involving = or < or > will be true or false. This is called the logical state of the assertion, e.g.

Assertion	Logical state
3>2	True
7<7	False

You will probably find this easy enough for positive whole numbers but may be less sure of what happens in other cases. If in doubt, remember the number line:

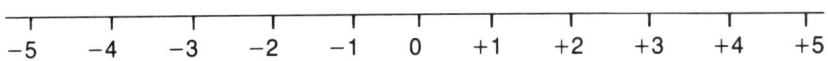

(*Figure 1   The number line*)

If a number is found on this line to be to the left of a second number, then the first is less than the second number; if to the right, then the first is greater than the second.

Example 1
Test whether the following expressions are true or false for the given values of A and B.

Values		Expression
A	B	
2	5	A>B
2	−5	A>B
−2	−5	A>B
−2	−1	A>B
−5	2	A<B
5	−2	A<B
−3	3	A=B

Solution
To do this we work out the value of each expression using the values given and then use the number line to decide whether or not the assertion is true or false *for those particular values*. So the solution is:

Values		Assertion		
A	B	Expression	Its value	Its logical state
2	5	A>B	2> 5	F
2	−5	A>B	2>−5	T
−2	−5	A>B	−2>−5	T
−2	−1	A>B	−2>−1	F
−5	2	A<B	−5< 2	T
5	−2	A<B	5<−2	F
−3	3	A=B	−3= 3	F

F=false T=true

SAQ 4
Complete the following table to determine whether the given expressions are true or false for the values given.

Values		Assertion		
A	B	Expression	Its value	Its logical state
3	7	A>B	3 > 7	F
5	3	A>B	5 > 3	T
−3	5	A>B	−3 > 5	F
8	5	A<B	8 < 5	F
3	9	A<B	3 < 9	T
8	−2	A<B	8 < −2	F

We are now in a position to use relationships to allow control of a program to jump to a new line when certain conditions are satisfied.

Example 2
In the following program segment after executing line 30, will the message be printed, or not?

```
10 LET A=-3
20 LET B=2
30 IF A+B>0 THEN PRINT "MESSAGE"
40 ...
```
Program 3

Solution
−3+2>0 is FALSE, so the message will not be printed, and control will pass straight to line 40.

SAQ 5
In the following program segments after executing line 30, will the message be printed, or will control pass directly to line 40?

(a)
```
10 LET A=7
20 LET B=-8
30 IF A-B<0 THEN PRINT "YES"
40 ...
```

(b)
```
10 LET X=-3
20 LET Q=3
30 IF X/Y=-1 THEN PRINT "YES"
40 ...
```

(c)
```
10 LET P=-1
20 LET Q=3
30 IF P+Q>Q THEN PRINT "YES"
40 ...
```

(d)
```
10 LET M=3
15 LET N=-4
20 LET P=-2
30 IF M-N<N-P THEN PRINT "YES"
40 ...
```

(e)
```
10 LET R=1
20 LET S=-2
30 IF R+S>-1 THEN PRINT "YES"
40 ...
```

BASIC also allows other relationships made up of $<$, $>$ and $=$.

>=   greater than or equal to
=<   less than or equal to
<>   not equal to

E.g.

```
5>=5     is TRUE
4=<5     is TRUE
5<>5     is FALSE
```

Note:

<= can be replaced by =<
=< can be replaced by <=

In both cases the order of the signs does not matter.

Using inequalities
Now you know how to see if a store location is less than a number, we will rewrite Program 2 so that it prints the message "young" for all ages under 10.

```
10 PRINT "INPUT YOUR AGE"
20 INPUT AGE
30 IF AGE<10 THEN PRINT "YOUNG"
40 END
```
Program 4

K Program 4

Exercise 1
(a) Write a program to input two numbers and to tell you whether the numbers are equal or not, and if not, which is the largest.

(b) Write another program to enter two numbers, but this time just to tell you whether they are equal or not.

A note on ELSE:
One extension to IF ... THEN ... is IF ... THEN ... ELSE .... The commands following THEN are acted upon if the condition is TRUE (you have just met this) and the commands following ELSE are acted upon if the condition is FALSE. For example:

```
IF A=B THEN PRINT "SAME" ELSE PRINT "DIFFERENT"
```

If the condition "A=B" is TRUE then the word "SAME" is printed, and if the condition "A=B" is FALSE then the word "DIFFERENT" is printed.

Although this is not used elsewhere in this book, you might like to include it in your own programs.

2.5 Repetitions and WHILE ... WEND ...
We are now going to introduce a method of repetition which has a lot in common with IF ... THEN .... We have seen that computers are very good at making decisions. They are also very good at repeating things a number of times. Because of the similarities with IF ... THEN ..., it seems appropriate that we

introduce WHILE . . . WEND . . . now, and leave the other methods of repetition until later.

WHILE . . . WEND . . . loops are one method of repeating actions until a condition is met. A WHILE . . . WEND . . . loop looks like this:

WHILE *condition*

actions to be repeated

WEND

From the previous sections on IF . . . THEN . . . and on Inequalities we saw how conditions worked, so we can make a start at programming the WHILE...WEND... loop straight away. The first line of the loop always starts with WHILE followed by the *condition*. Then come the lines of the program to be repeated. And to tell the computer where the end of the loop is we use WEND, meaning WHILE END. For example:

```
10 I=0
20 WHILE I<10
30 I=I+1
40 WEND
50 END
```
Program 5

When the computer comes to the WHILE statement it decides if the *expression* I<10 is TRUE. If it is, the computer does the action(s) inside the loop, which in Program 5 means incrementing I by 1. When the computer comes to the statement WEND it goes back to the top of the loop to see if the expression is still TRUE; i.e. is I still less than 10? If it is, the computer repeats the action(s) inside the loop again. And so on. If, however, the expression is not TRUE, i.e. I now has a value of 10, then when the computer comes to the WHILE line the computer skips the commands inside the loop, jumping straight to the statement WEND and then carrying on from there.

To help you learn this, type in and run Program 5. When the program has finished, type:

```
PRINT I
```

and you should get the result:

```
RUN
PRINT I
10
OK
```

To see what the program is doing, insert the following extra lines and run Program 5 again.

```
35 PRINT "AT LINE 35 I HAS THE VALUE", I
45 PRINT "AT THE END OF THE LOOP I HAS THE VALUE", I
```

and you get:

```
RUN
AT LINE 35 I HAS THE VALUE 1
AT LINE 35 I HAS THE VALUE 2
AT LINE 35 I HAS THE VALUE 3
AT LINE 35 I HAS THE VALUE 4
AT LINE 35 I HAS THE VALUE 5
AT LINE 35 I HAS THE VALUE 6
AT LINE 35 I HAS THE VALUE 7
AT LINE 35 I HAS THE VALUE 8
AT LINE 35 I HAS THE VALUE 9
AT LINE 35 I HAS THE VALUE 10
AT THE END OF THE LOOP I HAS THE VALUE 10
OK
```

So WHILE...WEND... loops are methods of repeating statements until a condition is met. This is especially useful when you need to repeat something until a job is done, but you don't know how many times you have to repeat the actions. With the WHILE...WEND... loops you can specify the condition, telling the computer when the job is finished (by setting the condition), and then let the computer work out how many times to repeat the actions. (If at all, i.e. the job may not need doing and if the condition is already met, the loop will not function at all. This will be introduced in full in Unit 8 when sorting is introduced.)

E.g.

```
10 INPUT NUMBER
20 COUNT=0
30 WHILE NUMBER>1
40 NUMBER=NUMBER/2
50 COUNT=COUNT+1
60 WEND
70 PRINT "NO.OF DIVISIONS=", COUNT
```

Program 6

The above program divides NUMBER by 2 until it gets to a number less than or equal to 1. But if you enter 1 in line 10 the loop will not function as the condition is already met by the time the computer comes to line 20.

SAQ 6
In the following program extracts, what value does NUMBER have to be for the loop to work?

(a)   WHILE NUMBER=5   (c)   WHILE NUMBER=4*5
         .
         .
         .
         WEND   WEND

(b)   WHILE NUMBER<6   (d)   WHILE NUMBER-5=7+1
         .
         .
         .
         WEND   WEND

(There is more than one value for NUMBER in part b)

Improved percentage program
Having introduced WHILE...WEND... we will now apply it to the percentage program:

Problem
It would be nice if instead of typing RUN to work out another percentage, the program would automatically ask for the next number and calculate another percentage. This would also mean that you only have to enter the total marks once. E.g.

Old program:

```
RUN
INPUT THE FIRST NUMBER
? 100
INPUT THE SECOND NUMBER
? 30
PERCENTAGE          30
OK

RUN
INPUT THE FIRST NUMBER
? 100
INPUT THE SECOND NUMBER
? 60
PERCENTAGE          60
OK
```

New program:

```
RUN
INPUT MAXIMUM MARKS
? 100
INPUT FIRST MARK
? 30
PERCENTAGE 30
INPUT NEXT MARK
? 55
PERCENTAGE 55
INPUT NEXT MARK
? 77
PERCENTAGE 77
INPUT NEXT MARK
.
.
```

and so on

As you can see, the program is going to go on and on for ever. To solve this, we will introduce a means of signalling that the end of the list has been reached.

Solution
One method is to end the list of numbers you enter in with a special number that will 'stick out like a sore thumb', e.g. -9999. We would hardly expect a pupil to obtain -9999 in any test! We want the program to run as normal when 'proper marks' are entered but to stop when the mark -9999 is entered.

So the program will have the following logical structure:

1. Start
2. Input the total marks
3. Input the first mark
4. WHILE the mark isn't -9999 do steps 5 to 9
5.   Calculate the percentage
6.   Print the percentage
7:     Input the next mark
8.   Go back to 4 (WEND)
9. End

Steps 5 to 8 are indented to show where the loop is.

To program this we have first to work out step 4. So far, we know how to use WHILE to repeat something when two numbers are the same, but not when they are different.

To do this we use the opposite of = (equals) which is <> (not equals). "<>" is made up of the "greater than" and "less than" signs. So step 4 will program like this:

```
60 WHILE MARK<>-9999
```

which means: while the mark isn't −9999, i.e. a 'proper' mark, do the following until you come to WEND.

So the program looks like this:

```
10  REM NEW PERCENTAGE PROGRAM
20  PRINT "ENTER MAXIMUM MARKS"
30  INPUT MAX
40  PRINT "ENTER FIRST MARK"
50  INPUT MARK
60  WHILE MARK<>-9999  ───────────── Start of loop
70  PERCENT=(MARK/MAX)*100
80  PRINT "PERCENTAGE",PERCENT
90  PRINT "ENTER NEXT MARK"
100 INPUT MARK
110 WEND  ─────────────────────── End of loop
120 END
```

Program 7

K enter and run Program 7.

A typical run: Line number

```
ENTER MAXIMUM MARKS                     20
? 80                                    30
ENTER FIRST MARK                        40
? 40                                    50
PERCENTAGE 50                           80
ENTER NEXT MARK                         90
? 55                                    100
PERCENTAGE 68.75                        80
ENTER NEXT MARK                         90
? -9999                                 100 ─────── 'terminating' mark
OK                                      120
```

How the computer sees the loop

Now let's look at the loop from the computer's viewpoint.

```
60  WHILE MARK<>-9999  ───────────── Start of loop
70  PERCENT=(MARK/MAX)*100
80  PRINT "PERCENTAGE",PERCENT
90  PRINT "ENTER NEXT MARK"
100 INPUT MARK
110 WEND  ─────────────────────── End of loop
```

The first line the computer comes across in the loop is line 60. If the number in the store location MARK is not −9999 then the computer carries on and does lines 70, 80, 90 and 100. When the computer gets to line 110 it finds the statement WEND which tells it to go back to the line with WHILE in it and carry on from there.

```
60                        WHILE line
70                        calculate percentage
80                        print percentage
90                        print prompt
100                       enter Mark
110                       WEND line
```

If, however, the value in the store location MARK is −9999 then when the computer gets to line 60 it looks down the program until it finds the statement WEND and carries on from there. So it does line 60 then 120, missing out the loop (lines 70 to 110).

```
60                        WHILE line
70
80
90
100
110                       WEND line
```

So when −9999 is entered the program does not give a percentage. Instead it leaves the program immediately. If the lines 90 and 100 were near the top of the WHILE . . . WEND . . . loop, then a percentage would be printed for −9999. Care must be taken when writing loops to make sure that they don't do anything other than what you want them to do. In Program 7 the first thing the computer does after a mark is entered, is to check that it is not −9999, so that the loop is 'terminated' as soon as the 'dummy' mark is entered.

Exercise 2
Write a program which asks the user to input height, width and depth for a box and then calculate the volume. (Volume=height*width*depth). If the user enters −9999 for height then the program should stop. To help you the steps are already given:

1. Set height to 0
2. Begin loop
3. Enter height, width and depth
4. Calculate volume
5. Print volume
6. End of loop
7. End

Step 1 is very important because the WHILE statement in step 2 will not know about the variable height which is introduced in step 3.

Exercise 3
If you enter zero for height in Program 13 (the answer to Exercise 2), then the computer still gives a volume. Change Program 13 so that volume is printed only if the height is not zero.

2.6 A note on GOTO

If you have had computing experience before studying this book, or if you have read computer magazines, you will almost certainly have come across the statement GOTO. In BASICA or GWBASIC there are very few occasions when using GOTO is necessary. In fact you won't find it used anywhere else in this book. We will explain how to use GOTO and show you how it is part of WHILE...WEND... loops, but we strongly recommend that you use it only when testing parts of a program and never in a finished program.

GOTO is a command allowing you to jump directly to another line without having any restrictions, e.g.

```
10 REM GOTO DEMO
20 PRINT "HELLO AT LINE 20"
30 GOTO 60
40 PRINT "HELLO AT LINE 40"
50 END
60 PRINT "HELLO AT LINE 60"
70 GOTO 40
```

Program 8

K Type in and run the above demo.

```
RUN
HELLO AT LINE 20
HELLO AT LINE 60
HELLO AT LINE 40
OK
```

As you can see, we jumped around the program without any restrictions. GOTO is very tempting to use for loops and to combine with IF statements, e.g. IF...THEN GOTO. Using GOTO like this allows your program to become messy and unstructured. Using WHILE...WEND... loops is far neater and helps enormously when you have to go through a program to find out why it doesn't work.

GOTO and WHILE...WEND...
Look at these two loops:

```
 90
100 WHILE I<10
110 I=I+1
120 WEND
130 .
```

```
 90
100 IF I>10 THEN GOTO 130
110 I=I+1
120 GOTO 100
130 .
```

Both loops do the same thing and you can see the similarities between them. The second program shows that WHILE...WEND... loops are made up of IF and GOTO. But the advantage of using WHILE...WEND... is that you can easily see where the loop begins and ends because it has two distinctive statements in it: WHILE and WEND. The other program has no distinctive commands, as IF will be very common in a large program.

One 'legitimate' use of GOTO is in very simple repetition:

```
100 I=I+1:IF I<10 THEN GOTO 100
```

(The colon allows you to put two commands on one line by acting as a marker telling the computer where one command ends and the other begins. It is explained more fully in Unit 6, Section 6.)

This section was included for interest only and not as a lesson on using GOTO. The rest of the book assumes no knowledge of GOTO and all exercises can be completed without using it.

2.7 Flowcharts

As we have said, the principal task for a programmer is to find a suitable way of expressing the solution strategy to solve a particular problem. At this stage we must introduce you to what must be the ugliest word in computer jargon: algorithm. This word is used to mean a general solution strategy, and is defined as a series of instructions or procedural steps for the solution of a specific problem. You will notice that in this case the computer is not mentioned. Apart from that, the definitions of program and algorithm are identical. A program then is an algorithm written for a computer.

There are three basic ways of stating an algorithm:

1. a description
2. BASIC coding
3. a flowchart

Flowcharts are a bit like blueprints and appeal to those of us who like to see events displayed in pictorial, chart or cartoon form.

We display the different functions within an algorithm by using differently shaped boxes.

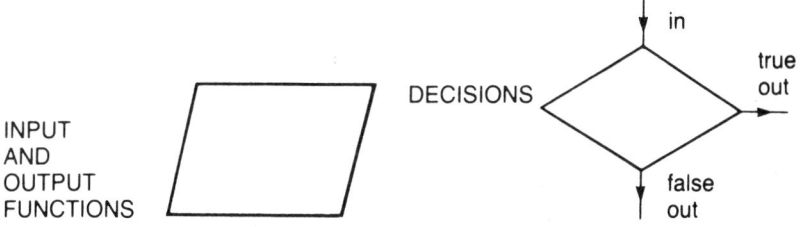

An → shows the sequence of the algorithm, and the boxes contain appropriate scripts.

The first program from Unit 1 can be expressed in flowchart form as follows:

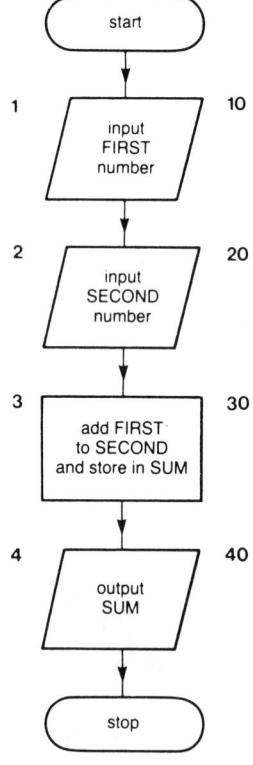

(Figure 2   Flowchart of Program 1 from Unit 1)

The descriptions of the functions in the boxes are in cryptic-English but could be followed by someone who has no knowledge of BASIC. In that respect we say that we try to keep these descriptions *language independent*. The numbers on the left-hand side of the boxes refer to the statements in the descriptive algorithm in Figure 4 of Unit 1, and the numbers on the right-hand side of the boxes refer to the statements in the BASIC program in Program 1 of Unit 1.

SAQ 7
Construct a flowchart for the percentage program (Program 10 of Unit 1).

The decision box
You have seen how decisions are effected in BASIC using the IF . . . THEN . . . statement. The logic is:

IF assertion is true THEN do something
otherwise (assertion is false) carry on to the next line

The basic idea of doing a statement or carrying on to the next line is depicted in a flowchart by two exit lines from a decision box. The following program line:

```
40 IF MARK=-9999 THEN PRINT "HELLO"
```

could be depicted in language independent form

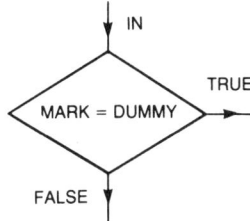

The assertion MARK=DUMMY may be expressed as a question

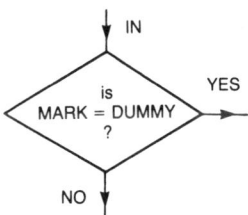

Flowchart style is up to you. The test of the effectiveness of a flowchart is whether or not you can follow the flowchart easily some time after its composition! Or, if you are trying to communicate your ideas to somebody else, whether they can follow your flowchart easily.

WHILE . . . WEND . . . loops can be treated as IF statements. The box at the top of the flowchart loop (Figure 3) has an IF in it. For the following program:

```
10 COUNT=0
20 WHILE COUNT<5
30 COUNT=COUNT+1
40 WEND
50 END
```

the flowchart starts with 'COUNT=5' and the YES branch going to END, and the NO branch going to COUNT=COUNT+1. Or you can have the first box with 'COUNT<5' and the NO branch going to END, and the YES branch going to COUNT=COUNT+1. Choose the method you like the most and the method you can understand best.

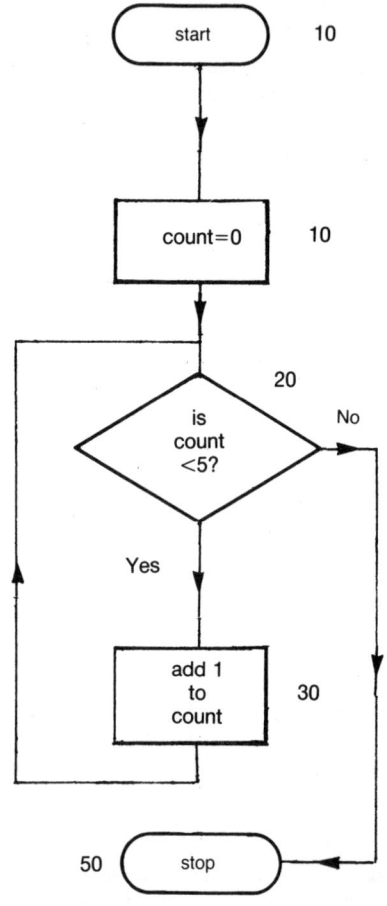

(Figure 3   Flowchart for IF demonstration)

The numbers on the right-hand side of the flowchart boxes refer to the statement numbers in the program.

SAQ 8
Write a flowchart for Program 8 in section 2.5

2.8 Counting

As we have said, computers are good at carrying out lots of repetitive procedures. If, however, we wish to control these activities, rather than just start and stop them, as we did in the last example, then we must use the computer to count the repetitions for us. If we carry out a specified number of repetitions of any activity, we start counting at the first activity, adding one for each subsequent activity, until we reach a predetermined limit. We can depict this procedure in flowchart form.

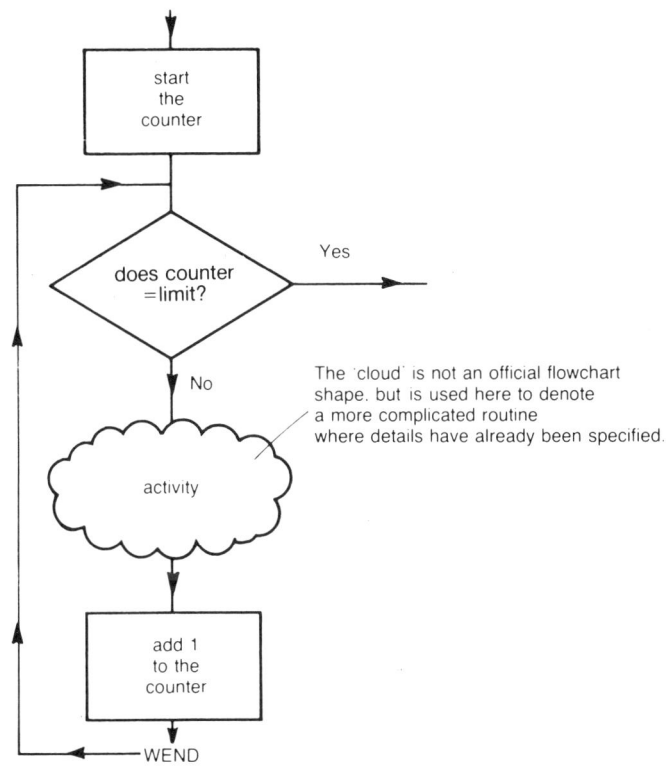

(Figure 4 A counter in a flowchart)

Notice that there are three parts to the counter:

1. the procedure that sets the counter to its initial value;
2. the procedure for adding 1 to the counter each time the activity is completed;
3. the procedure for stopping the counter and leaving the activity when it has been executed the required number of times.

SAQ 9
How many numbers will be inputted with the flowcharts?

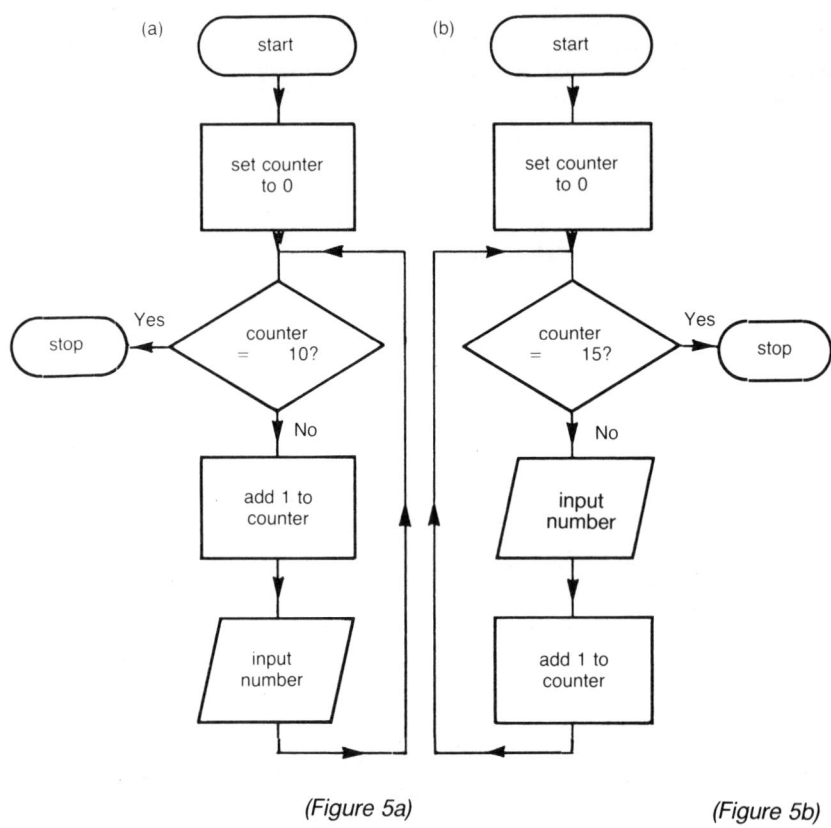

(Figure 5a) *(Figure 5b)*

SAQ 10
Make the following program read 5 numbers by completing the WHILE statement.

```
10 LET C=0
20 WHILE C<
30 INPUT NUMBER
35 C=C+1
40 WEND
50 END
```

Program 9

Example 3
Write a BASIC program to calculate and output the percentages for a group of five pupils.

Solution
If we assume that the 'activity' in the cloud in the flowchart of Figure 4 was

```
input the mark
calculate the percentage
output the percentage
```

then we can display the algorithm for this solution in flowchart form.

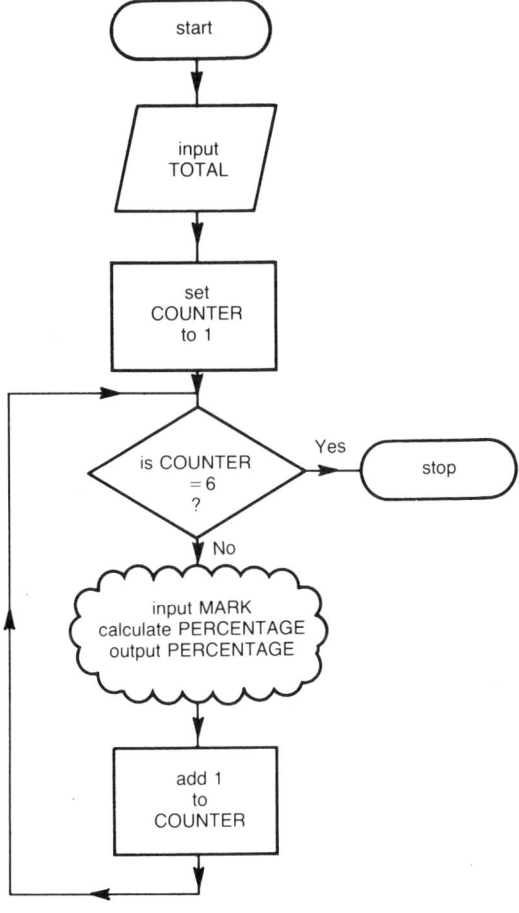

(Figure 6   Flowchart for percentage calculation on 5 marks)

This tells us the structure of the program that we need to write. The actual program can now be written by modifying Program 7 to incorporate the counter. So the required program is:

```
 10 REM NEW PERCENTAGE PROGRAM
 20 PRINT "ENTER MAXIMUM MARKS"
 30 INPUT MAX
 40 PRINT "ENTER FIRST MARK"
 50 INPUT MARK
 60 COUNT=1 ──────────────────── start the counter, "initialise"
 70 WHILE COUNT<6 ─────────────── counting complete?
 80 PRINT "COUNT HERE=",COUNT
 90 PERCENT=(MARK/MAX)*100
100 PRINT "PERCENTAGE",PERCENT
110 PRINT "ENTER THE NEXT MARK"
120 INPUT MARK
130 COUNT=COUNT+1 ─────────────── add 1 to the counter, "increment"
140 WEND
150 END
```

Program 10   Adding a counter to the percentage program

Typical run

```
ENTER MAXIMUM MARKS
? 75
ENTER FIRST MARK
? 57
COUNT HERE=    1
PERCENTAGE     76
ENTER THE NEXT MARK
? 62
COUNT HERE=    2
PERCENTAGE     82.66666
ENTER THE NEXT MARK
? 43
COUNT HERE=    3
PERCENTAGE     57.33333
ENTER THE NEXT MARK
? 39
COUNT HERE=    4
PERCENTAGE     52
ENTER THE NEXT MARK
? 70
COUNT HERE=    5
PERCENTAGE     93.33334
ENTER THE NEXT MARK
?
```

[K] Program 11

Exercise 4

In question 2 of Assignment 1, you wrote a program to calculate the cost of double-glazing a window. If you wanted to use the program to calculate the costs of double-glazing several windows, you would have to run the program again and again. This exercise asks you to modify the program to cover more than one window.

Notice that the 'activity' for repetition will be:

> input height and width of window
> calculate cost of installation of this window
> output the cost

(a) Draw a flowchart algorithm to calculate and output the cost of each of six windows.
(b) Code the algorithm in BASIC. [K] your answer and try a run for six windows on your microcomputer.
(c) Extend your program to cope with any chosen number of windows, to be specified at the beginning of the program.

Exercise 5
Extend the problem posed in question 1(b) of Assignment 1. The 'activity' for repetition will be:

> calculate the yield
> output the year and its yield
> calculate the deposit for the next year

(a) Draw a flowchart algorithm to calculate and output the yield for each year up to six years. Check your answer.
(b) Code this algorithm in BASIC in full detail. Check your answer. [K]
(c) Extend the algorithm to calculate and output the yield for each year up to any chosen number of years, to be specified at the beginning of the program. Check your answer. [K]

2.9 Comparisons

We have seen how the BASIC language allows us to compare two numbers. We often wish to decide whether a particular value is larger or smaller than another. This is a process which is fundamental to sorting items of data. Throughout the course we will consider sorting methods in some detail, so let's start with the simplest case.

Example 4
Devise an algorithm in descriptive form to input two numbers and to output the larger of the two.

Comment
We have expressed our algorithms as flowcharts throughout most of this Unit, so this time we will use the descriptive method introduced in Unit 1.

Solution
1. start
2. input first number
3. input second number
4. if first>second then output first
5. if second>first then output second
6. stop

This is not the neatest solution, but is close to the layman's 'first attempt' at the problem. We will seek neater solutions when we return to sorting methods in a later Unit.

Assignment 2

1. Devise a flowchart and write a BASIC program to input two numbers and output the smaller of the two. Modify the program so that it will process (a) five pairs of numbers, (b) any number of pairs of numbers.

2. Extend the 'mark–percentage' algorithm on page 41, and express it in the form of a flowchart and BASIC program:
   (a) to accommodate a class of any size;
   (b) to calculate the average percentage mark;
   (c) to pick out the highest mark.

Objectives of Unit 2

Now that you have completed this Unit, check that you are able to:

Combine literal printing and variable print in PRINT statements ☐

Use , to space PRINT statements ☐

Use WHILE . . . WEND . . . to repeat the use of a program ☐

Use a dummy value to terminate a program ☐

Use IF . . . THEN . . . [ELSE] ☐

Find the logical state of assertions including >, <, =, <>, =<, => ☐

Construct flowcharts ☐

Insert counters in flowcharts and programs to control the repeated use of part of a program or flowchart ☐

Answers to SAQs and Exercises

SAQ 1
(a) AREA 48
(b) LENGTH 8   WIDTH 6   AREA 48
(c) LENGTH   WIDTH   AREA
    8   6   48
(d) PRINT "LENGTH",B,"WIDTH",C

(e)   PRINT "LENGTH",B
       PRINT "WIDTH",C
       PRINT "AREA",A
(f)   PRINT "LENGTH","WIDTH"," ","AREA"

                                         └────── this prints a blank

SAQ 2
1.   FALSE
2.   FALSE
3.   TRUE
4.   TRUE
5.   TRUE

SAQ 3
(a)   IF FIRST=10 THEN SECOND=SECOND+5
(b)   IF NUMBER=AGE THEN INPUT TELNO

SAQ 4

Values		Assertion		
A	B	Expressions	Its value	Its logical state
3	7	A>B	3>7	F
5	3	A>B	5>3	T
-3	5	A>B	-3>5	F
8	5	A<B	8<5	F
3	9	A<B	3<9	T
8	-2	A<B	8<-2	F

If you got any of these wrong, look at them again on the number line

A	B	A to the left of B means A<B true
B	A	A to the right of B means A>B true

SAQ 5
(a)   CONTROL goes to LINE 40
(b)   "YES" is printed
(c)–(e) CONTROL goes to LINE 40

Exercise 1

Program to solve (a)

```
10 PRINT "ENTER TWO NUMBERS"
20 INPUT FIRST
30 INPUT SECOND
40 IF FIRST=SECOND THEN PRINT "THEY ARE EQUAL"
50 IF FIRST>SECOND THEN PRINT "FIRST IS LARGEST"
60 IF FIRST<SECOND THEN PRINT "SECOND IS LARGEST"
70 END
```

Program 11

Program to solve (b)

```
10 PRINT "ENTER TWO NUMBERS"
20 INPUT FIRST
30 INPUT SECOND
40 IF FIRST=SECOND THEN PRINT "THEY ARE EQUAL"
50 IF FIRST<>SECOND THEN PRINT "THEY ARE NOT EQUAL"
60 END
```

Program 12

SAQ 6
(a) NUMBER must be 5
(b) NUMBER can be any number less than 6, e.g. 1, 2, 3, 4, 5
(c) NUMBER must be 20
(d) NUMBER must be 13

Exercise 2

```
10 REM CALCULATES VOLUME
20 LET HEIGHT=0
30 WHILE HEIGHT<>-9999
40 PRINT "ENTER HEIGHT, WIDTH AND DEPTH"
50 INPUT HEIGHT
60 INPUT WIDTH
70 INPUT DEPTH
80 VOLUME=HEIGHT*WIDTH*DEPTH
90 PRINT VOLUME
100 WEND
```

Program 13

Exercise 3

```
10 REM CALCULATES VOLUME
20 LET HEIGHT=0
30 WHILE HEIGHT<>-9999
40 PRINT "ENTER HEIGHT, WIDTH AND DEPTH"
50 INPUT HEIGHT
60 INPUT WIDTH
70 INPUT DEPTH
80 VOLUME=HEIGHT*WIDTH*DEPTH
90 IF HEIGHT<>0 THEN PRINT VOLUME
100 WEND
```

Program 14

SAQ 7   **SAQ 8**

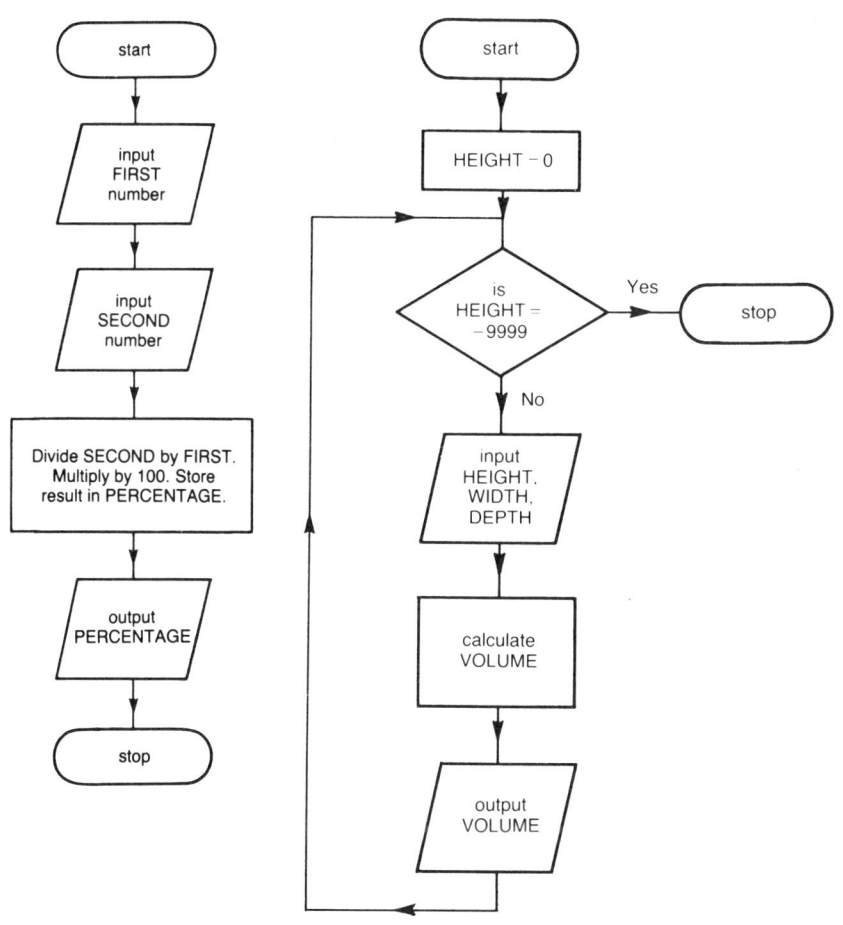

SAQ 9
(a) 10
(b) .15

SAQ 10

Line 20 should read

```
20 WHILE C<5
```

Exercise 4

(a)

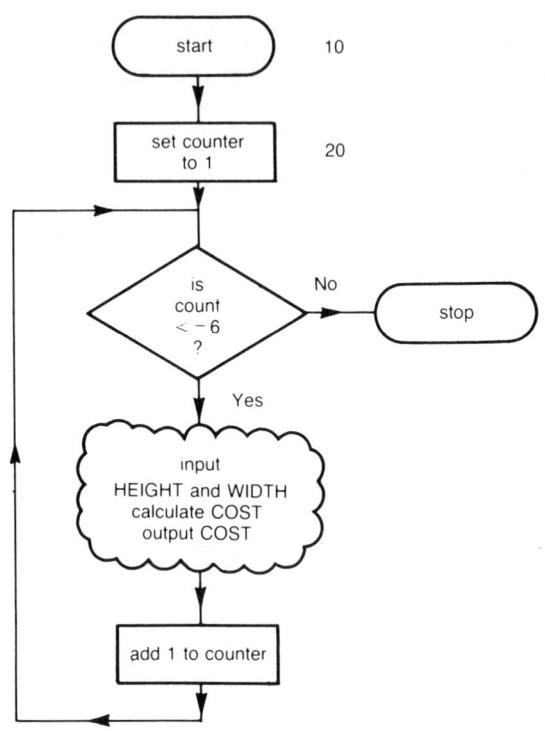

Program to solve (b)

```
 10 REM **COST OF DOUBLE GLAZING**
 20 LET COUNT=1
 30 WHILE COUNT=<6
 40 PRINT "ENTER HEIGHT IN METRES"
 50 INPUT HEIGHT
 60 PRINT "ENTER WIDTH IN METRES"
 70 INPUT AWIDTH
 80 LET COST=14*(HEIGHT+AWIDTH)+40*(HEIGHT*AWIDTH)+50
 90 PRINT "WINDOW",COUNT,"COST",COST
100 COUNT=COUNT+1
110 WEND
120 END
```

Program 15

```
RUN
ENTER HEIGHT IN METRES
? 1.5
ENTER WIDTH IN METRES
? 2
WINDOW    1    COST    219
ENTER HEIGHT IN METRES
? 1.5
ENTER WIDTH IN METRES
? 3
WINDOW    2    COST    293
ENTER HEIGHT IN METRES
? 1.5
ENTER WIDTH IN METRES
? 4
WINDOW    3    COST    367
ENTER HEIGHT IN METRES
?
```

Program to solve (c)

```
 10 **COST OF DOUBLE GLAZING**
 11 PRINT "ENTER NUMBER OF WINDOWS"
 12 INPUT NUMBER
 20 LET COUNT=1
 30 WHILE COUNT=<NUMBER
 40 PRINT "ENTER HEIGHT IN METRES"
 50 INPUT HEIGHT
 60 PRINT "ENTER WIDTH IN METRES"
 70 INPUT AWIDTH
 80 LET COST=14*(HEIGHT+AWIDTH)+40*(HEIGHT*AWIDTH)+50
 90 PRINT "WINDOW",COUNT,"COST",COST
100 COUNT=COUNT+1
110 WEND
120 END
```

Program 16

```
RUN
ENTER NUMBER OF WINDOWS
? 3
ENTER HEIGHT IN METRES
? 1.5
ENTER WIDTH IN METRES
? 1.25
WINDOW    1    COST    163.5
ENTER HEIGHT IN METRES
? 2
ENTER WIDTH IN METRES
? 1.6
WINDOW    2    COST    228.4
ENTER HEIGHT IN METRES
? 1.4
ENTER WIDTH IN METRES
? 1
WINDOW    3    COST    139.6

OK
```

Exercise 5

(a)

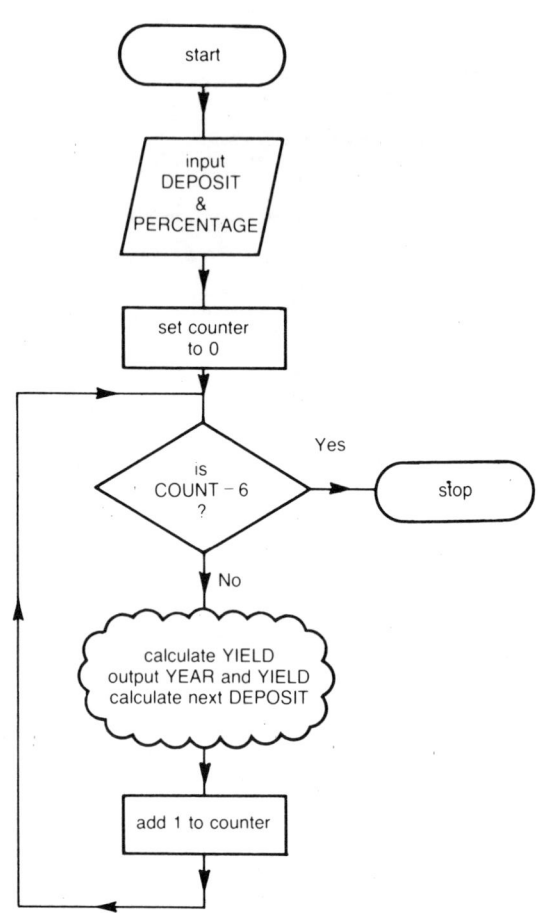

Program to solve (b)

```
10 REM**COMPOUND INTEREST**
20 PRINT "ENTER DEPOSIT"
30 INPUT DEPOSIT
40 PRINT "ENTER PERCENTAGE INTEREST"
50 INPUT PERCENT
60 LET COUNT=1
70 WHILE COUNT<=6
80 LET YIELD=(PERCENT*DEPOSIT)/100
90 PRINT "YEAR",COUNT,"YIELD",YIELD
100 LET DEPOSIT=DEPOSIT+YIELD
110 LET COUNT=COUNT+1
120 WEND
130 END
```

Program 17

```
RUN
ENTER DEPOSIT
? 500
ENTER PERCENTAGE INTEREST
? 12.5
YEAR     1     YIELD     62.5
YEAR     2     YIELD     70.3125
YEAR     3     YIELD     79.10156
YEAR     4     YIELD     88.98926
YEAR     5     YIELD     100.1129
YEAR     6     YIELD     112.627

OK
```

Program to solve (c)

```
 10 REM**COMPOUND INTEREST**
 20 PRINT "ENTER NUMBER OF YEARS"
 30 INPUT YEARS
 40 PRINT "ENTER DEPOSIT"
 50 INPUT DEPOSIT
 60 PRINT "ENTER PERCENTAGE INTEREST"
 70 INPUT PERCENT
 80 LET COUNT=1
 90 WHILE COUNT<=YEARS
100 LET YIELD=(PERCENT*DEPOSIT)/100
110 PRINT "YEAR",COUNT,"YIELD",YIELD
120 LET COUNT=COUNT+1
140 WEND
150 END
```

Program 18

```
RUN
ENTER NUMBER OF YEARS
? 4
ENTER DEPOSIT
? 1000
ENTER PERCENTAGE INTEREST
? 13.75
YEAR     1     YIELD     137.5
YEAR     2     YIELD     156.4063
YEAR     3     YIELD     177.9121
YEAR     4     YIELD     202.375

OK
```

UNIT 3
Strings

3.1	What is a string?	64
3.2	More about strings	66
3.3	PRINT . . .;. . .	66
3.4	INPUT". . .";. . .	68
3.5	Numbers and strings in PRINT statements	70
3.6	Standard letters	72
3.7	Patterns, files, READ with DATA	74
3.8	Sorting	80
	Assignment 3	83
	Objectives of Unit 3	84
	Answers to SAQs and Exercises	84

3.1 What is a string?

The first two units were concerned with processing numbers. The layman often sees the computer as a 'number cruncher' but this is certainly not the main function of a computer, especially in a commercial environment. In this Unit we will see how a computer *may be used to manipulate characters* using the BASIC language.

By *character* we mean the alphabet in capitals, the ten digits 0–9, punctuation marks and some special characters as follows:

@ A B C D E F G H I J K L M N O P Q R S T U
V W X Y Z [\ ] ← ↑ 0 1 2 3 4 5 6 7 8 9 : ; <
= > ? Space ! , # $ % & . ( ) + * − /

You have learnt to write programs using numbers (3, 57, −92, etc.) and variables (A, X, Z, etc.). BASIC also allows us to enter characters into the computer in groups.

These groups of characters are referred to as strings. Some examples of strings are:

```
CAT              (a word)
PYTHAGORAS       (a name)
Z9)?27           (a mixture of characters)
ABC 123W         (a car registration number)
```

i.e. *a string can be any mixture of characters* – even a space is a very important character in a string!

As far as BASIC is concerned, a number is treated as a number when it is to be used to do some arithmetic, otherwise it is considered to be a string of numeric characters. When we look at a car number or telephone number we see it as a group of numeric characters; we would not use this collection of digits to do any serious arithmetic.

Store location for strings

How then can we signal to the computer that the group of characters which we are entering should be treated as numbers for arithmetic purposes, or as just a string of characters? The distinction is made in BASIC by how we label the storage locations into which we put the characters. If a store location name is followed by the symbol $ then the characters which are entered into that location are treated as strings of characters.

So far we have used meaningful store location names, e.g. FIRST, SECOND, PERCENTAGE.

The store locations for strings can be just as meaningful and you can still use names of up to 40 characters in length, e.g. ANAME$, CAT$, TITLE$

You read these out loud as follows:

```
A$       A string        or    A dollar
B9$      B nine string   or    B nine dollar
```

Thus you can now think of a microcomputer as having two areas for store locations: one for numbers and one for characters. This is illustrated in Figure 1.

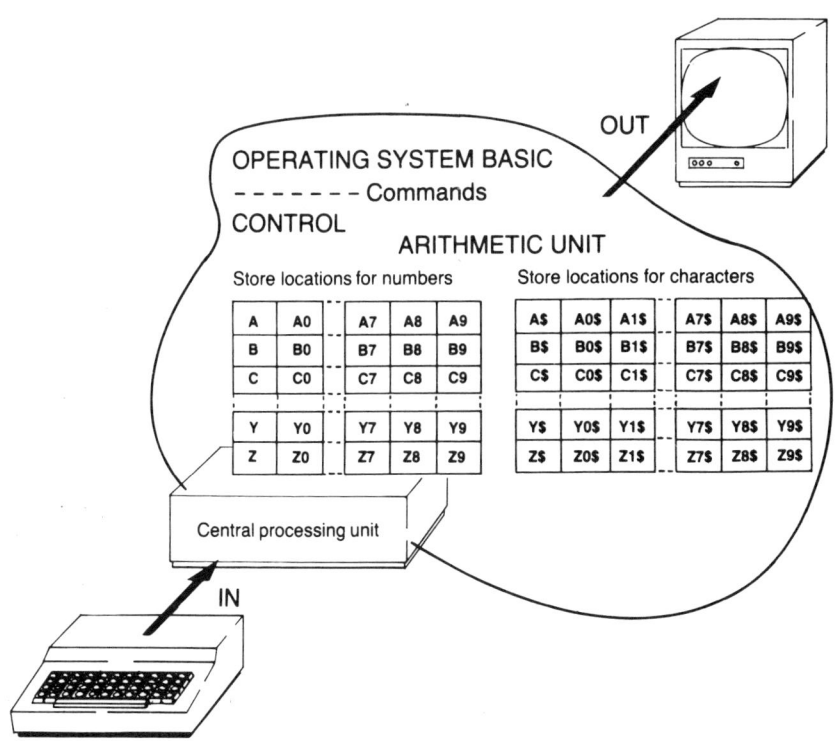

(Figure 1   A summary of our system so far)

" " with strings

Usually we have to show the computer that we want our string of characters to be treated as a string. To do this we put " " around the string. Thus we write

```
10 LET Q$="HELLO"
```

and

```
30 IF Q$="HELLO" THEN . . .
```

and so on

SAQ 1
Which of the following are correct BASIC statements?

```
(a)   LET A=87
(b)   LET B$="FRED"
(c)   LET M$=9583
(d)   LET K8="JAM POT"
(e)   LET L17=38
```

3.2 More about strings

'How long is a piece of string?' is a pertinent question here. In other words, how many characters can be input, stored or output as a single group? Initially in this course we will assume that a store location for strings will hold up to 80 characters, and that this restriction will apply to inputting and outputting strings. As most microcomputer screens are about 80 characters wide, this is a convenient restriction. So you must now think of a string memory location, not just as a labelled pigeon-hole, but as a location with 80 sub-divisions, as shown partly in Figure 2.

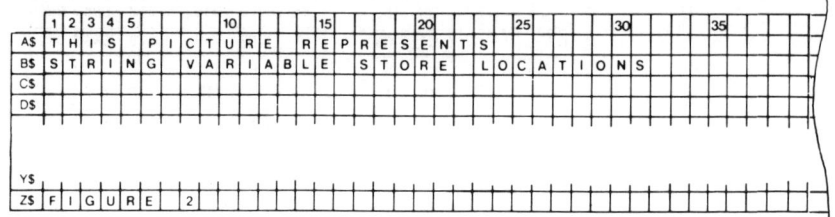

(Figure 2 Size of string store locations)

We have been discussing strings as if they were new but you have met them before in Unit 1. There we used the PRINT statement to output messages which were enclosed in quotation marks. We implied that the string enclosed in quotation marks was output *literally* character by character. Then we saw in Unit 2 how the commas between the elements of a PRINT statement caused the strings to be spaced out across the screen or printer.

3.3 PRINT . . .;. . .

From what we have covered so far you will realise that the layout of information on the screen is very important. This is just as true for strings as it is for numbers.

When handling textual information, i.e. strings of characters in the form of words or codes, we want the strings to be printed as in a sentence and not spaced out across the screen in print zones. The PRINT . . .;. . . statement achieves this effect for us. PRINT H$; T$ will take the characters in store location H$ and print them on the left-hand side of the output device, followed immediately by the characters from location T$.

In the next few pages we are going to simulate a data recording service of the not too distant future and use it to demonstrate the inputting and outputting of strings. Let's start by writing a program which simulates a telephone answering service.

```
 10 REM**TELE ANSWER**
 20 PRINT ──────────────── this prints a blank line
 30 PRINT "HELLO"
 40 PRINT "PLEASE STATE YOUR TELEPHONE NUMBER"
 50 INPUT TELNO$
 60 PRINT
 70 PRINT "HELLO",TELNO$
 80 PRINT
 90 PRINT "HELLO";TELNO$
100 PRINT
110 PRINT "HELLO ";TELNO$
120 PRINT
130 PRINT "HELLO";" ";TELNO$
140 END
```

Program 1   Printing strings

To help you analyse this program we have put below a 'trace' at the side of a typical run. The trace indicates which line in the program generates which line in the output.

```
RUN                                        Trace

                                           ...20
HELLO                                      ...30
PLEASE STATE YOUR TELEPHONE NUMBER         ...40
? 58632                                    ...50
                                           ...60
HELLO           58632                      ...70
                                           ...80
HELLO58632                                 ...90
                                           ...100
HELLO 58632                                ...110
                                           ...120
HELLO 58632                                ...130
OK
```

Comments

Trace 50   INPUT TELNO$ generated ?. Our response was 58632 which the computer treats as a string and not as a number. (If we wrote INPUT TELNO, then 58632 would be treated as a number.)

Trace 70   The PRINT . . .,. . . on line 70 prints the 5 of the telephone number at the 15th print position across the output line, whereas

Trace 90

The PRINT . . .;. . . of line 90 prints the 5 immediately adjacent to the O of HELLO.

Neither way is satisfactory, but:

Trace 110   Lines 110 and 130 show alternative ways of introducing the required spaces, either by printing HELLO▽(110) or by inserting the string ▽ in its own right into the output statement. (▽ indicates a space.)

K Program 1.

SAQ 2
Study this program and work out what the print output will be. Write down the output in the grid below.

```
 10 PRINT "PRINT LAYOUT"
 20 LET B$="BASIC"
 30 LET C$="COURSE"
 40 PRINT
 50 PRINT B$, C$
 60 PRINT
 70 PRINT B$;C$
 80 PRINT
 90 PRINT B$;" ";C$
100 END
```

Program 2

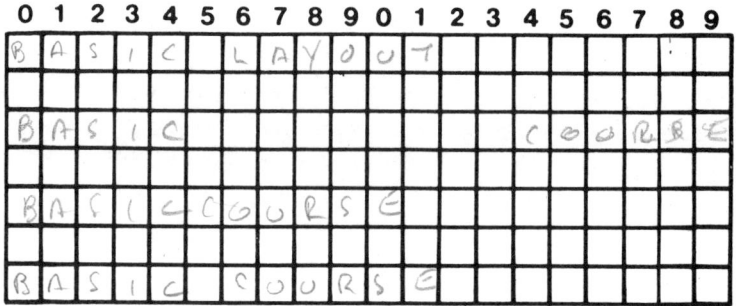

SAQ 3
Write a program which would print out the following:

0	1	2	3	4	5	6	7	8	9	0	1	2	3	4	5	6	7	8	9
B	A	S	I	C										B	A	S	I	C	
B	A	S	I	C	B	A	S	I	C	B	A	S	I	C	B	A	S	I	C
B	A	S	I	C		B	A	S	I	C		B	A	S	I	C			

3.4 INPUT"...";...

We have used PRINT"..." as a prompt for an INPUT statement in several of our programs so far. BASIC has a facility to allow us to combine these two into one statement. Thus in Program 1 (page 67) we could replace:

```
40 PRINT "PLEASE STATE YOUR TELEPHONE NUMBER"
50 INPUT TELNO$
```

with

```
40 INPUT "PLEASE STATE YOUR TELEPHONE NUMBER";TELNO$
```

The INPUT statement will always generate a ?, however, so in the next program we form the prompt into a direct question.

Also, in the last program we used the string "HELLO" several times. In the next program we will save a little typing by storing this string in location H$ at the start of the program.

```
 10 REM**TELE ANSWER 2**
 20 PRINT
 30 LET H$="HELLO"
 40 PRINT H$
 50 INPUT "WHAT IS YOUR TELEPHONE NUMBER";TELNO$
 60 PRINT
 70 PRINT H$,TELNO$
 80 PRINT
 90 PRINT H$;TELNO$          no question mark here
100 PRINT
110 PRINT H$;" ";TELNO$
120 END
```

Program 3   The computer asks the questions

```
RUN                                    computer response to line 50
HELLO
WHAT IS YOUR TELEPHONE NUMBER? 58632

HELLO            58632

HELLO58632

HELLO 58632

OK
```

K Program 3.

SAQ 4

What would appear on the screen when this program was run, assuming your name is John Smith and your age is 45?

```
10 LET T$="THANK YOU"
20 INPUT "WHAT IS YOUR NAME";N$
30 PRINT
40 INPUT "WHAT IS YOUR AGE";A$
50 PRINT
60 PRINT T$,N$,A$
```

Program 4

3.5 Numbers and strings in print statements

We could have entered the telephone number of the previous program into a numeric store location. We would of course soon run into problems if the numbers were too long, or contained spaces (e.g. 01 693 4539). Let's compare how BASIC would output this data from numeric and string store locations.

In this program note how we use the string of characters in S$ to print a scale across the output page.

```
10 REM**TELE ANSWER**
20 PRINT
30 LET H$="HELLO"
35 LET S$="12345678901234567890 12345"
40 PRINT H$
50 INPUT "WHAT IS YOUR TELEPHONE NO";TELNO$
55 INPUT "WILL YOU REPEAT THAT PLEASE";TELNO
60 PRINT S$
70 PRINT H$,TELNO$
75 PRINT H$,TELNO
80 PRINT S$
90 PRINT H$;TELNO$
95 PRINT H$;TELNO
100 PRINT S$
110 PRINT H$;" ";TELNO$
115 PRINT H$;" ";TELNO
120 END
```

Program 5 Printing strings and numbers

```
RUN
HELLO
WHAT IS YOUR TELEPHONE NUMBER? 58632
WILL YOU REPEAT THAT PLEASE? 58632
12345678901234567890 12345 ────────── 60
HELLO           58632
HELLO               58632 ──────────── 75
12345678901234567890 12345
HELLO058632
HELLO 58632                              95
12345678901234567890 12345
HELLO 58632
HELLO  58632                            115
OK

RUN
HELLO
WHAT IS YOUR TELEPHONE NUMBER?-58632
WILL YOU REPEAT THAT PLEASE?-58632
12345678901234567890 12345
HELLO          -58632
HELLO          -58632                    75
12345678901234567890 12345
HELLO-58632
HELLO-58632                              95
12345678901234567890 12345
HELLO -58632
HELLO -58632                            115
OK
```

Trace

60 | S$ numbers each print position across the page.
75 | Note that the first digit 5 is placed at the 16th position. The 15th is reserved for
95 | the sign (+ or −) of the number in TELNO, but if the sign is '+' it is not
115 | printed, but a space is left. A similar effect occurs in 95 and 115.

75 Note the effect when TELNO$ and TELNO both
95 hold −58632

115

K Program 5.

SAQ 5
Write a program to input your name as a string and your age as a number and to output the message, 'My name is   and I am   years old' with the normal spacing.

Data recording service
The following is a further example of how print layout is achieved in BASIC. We can imagine that in the not too distant future our TV set, telephone and computer will be linked together as an 'intelligent' terminal. On seeing an attractive advertisement we may 'dial' a number and the following dialogue might ensue.

```
                                                           Trace
HELLO                                                       30
THIS IS A DATA-RECORDING SERVICE                            40
                                                            50
PLEASE ENTER THE DETAILS AS REQUESTED                       60
                                                            70
YOUR NAME? C. A. SMITH                                      80
YOUR TELEPHONE NUMBER? 23685                                90
NUMBER OR NAME OF HOUSE? 77                                100
ROAD? CHALMERS ROAD                                        110
TOWN OR CITY? WORTHING                                     120
YOUR POSTAL CODE? BR7 9QY                                  130
                                                           140
                                                           150
                                                           160
THANK YOU FOR YOUR ENQUIRY                                 170
                                                           180
YOUR PERSONAL DETAILS HAVE BEEN RECORDED AS:               190
NAME C. A. SMITH TELEPHONE NO. 23685                       200
ADDRESS 77 CHALMERS ROAD                                   210
        WORTHING BR7 9QY                                   220
                                                           230
DETAILS OF OUR SERVICES AND PRODUCTS                       240
WILL BE SENT TO YOU                                        250
YOUR PERSONAL DETAILS WILL REMAIN CONFIDENTIAL             260
```

(Of course, instead of 'will be sent to you', it will eventually be 'will now be output to your terminal', and then the only detail needing to be input would be a subscriber code.)

This simulated dialogue was achieved by the following program.

```
 10 REM**DATA RECORD**
 20 PRINT
 30 PRINT "HELLO"
 40 PRINT "THIS IS A DATA-RECORDING SERVICE"
 50 PRINT
 60 PRINT "PLEASE ENTER THE DETAILS AS REQUESTED"
 70 PRINT
 80 INPUT "YOUR NAME";ANAME$
 90 INPUT "YOUR TELEPHONE NO";TELNO$
100 INPUT "NUMBER OR NAME OF HOUSE";HOUSE$
110 INPUT "ROAD";ROAD$
120 INPUT "TOWN OR CITY";CITY$
130 INPUT "YOUR POST CODE";POST$
140 PRINT
150 PRINT
160 PRINT
170 PRINT "THANK YOU FOR YOUR ENQUIRY"
```

```
180 PRINT
190 PRINT "YOUR PERSONAL DETAILS HAVE BEEN RECORDED AS:"
200 PRINT "NAME ";ANAME$;" TELEPHONE NO. ";TELNO$
210 PRINT "ADDRESS ";HOUSE$;" ";ROAD$
220 PRINT "        ";CITY$;" ";POST$
230 PRINT
240 PRINT "DETAILS OF OUR SERVICES AND PRODUCTS"
250 PRINT "WILL BE SENT TO YOU"
260 PRINT "YOUR PERSONAL DETAILS WILL REMAIN
    CONFIDENTIAL"
```

Program 6 Data recording service

[K] Program 6.

3.6 Standard letters

A data recording service, such as we have just looked at, may be in the future, but standard personalised letters are with us now. Such a letter would be composed on a word processor, but if your microcomputer does not have word processing facilities available, you could achieve modest results using BASIC. Your own choice of letter will be left to you in Exercise 2 (page 73).

Example 1
A bank recruiting office receives many enquiries about employment. Its policy is to interview suitable applicants initially at its local branch. A stereotyped letter is sent from the recruiting office to each applicant containing individual details of the proposed interview. Devise a BASIC program to write such a letter.

Solution
The following program would do this job.

```
 10 REM**LETTER WRITER**
 20 PRINT
 30 INPUT ANAME$
 40 INPUT ADATE$
 50 INPUT BNAME$
 60 INPUT ATIME$
 70 INPUT BDATE$
 80 INPUT LOCATION$
 90 INPUT CNAME$
100 PRINT
110 PRINT
120 PRINT "DEAR ";ANAME$;","
130 PRINT
140 PRINT "THANK YOU FOR YOUR LETTER OF ";ADATE$;"."
150 PRINT "WE INVITE YOU TO ATTEND FOR INTERVIEW WITH"
160 PRINT BNAME$;" AT ";ATIME$;" ON ";BDATE$
170 PRINT "AT OUR ";LOCATION$;" BRANCH"
180 PRINT
190 PRINT "YOURS SINCERELY,"
200 PRINT
210 PRINT
220 PRINT
230 PRINT CNAME$
240 PRINT
250 PRINT
260 END
```

Program 7 Bank interview letter

This would result in the following run:

```
RUN                                                   Trace
                                                       20
?MISS JONES                                            30
?13TH OCTOBER                                          40
?MR FELLOWS                                            50
?10.00AM                                               60
?20TH OCTOBER                                          70
?HIGH ST. SIDCUP                                       80
?C. A. SIDWELL                                         90
                                                      100
                                                      110
DEAR MISS JONES,                                      120
                                                      130
THANK YOU FOR YOUR LETTER OF 13TH OCTOBER.            140
WE INVITE YOU TO ATTEND FOR INTERVIEW WITH            150
MR FELLOWS AT 10.00 AM ON 20TH OCTOBER                160
AT OUR HIGH ST. SIDCUP BRANCH.                        170
                                                      180
YOURS SINCERELY,                                      190
                                                      200
                                                      210
                                                      220
C.A. SIDWELL                                          230
```

You might find the program difficult to use since all you get is a series of prompts ?. You might, therefore, make a skeletal aide-memoire to act as a reminder of the structure of the letter:

```
? A$
? B$
? C$
? D$
? E$
? F$
? G$

DEAR A$,

THANK YOU FOR YOUR LETTER OF B$.
WE INVITE YOU TO ATTEND FOR INTERVIEW WITH
C$ AT D$ ON E$
AT OUR F$ BRANCH.

YOURS SINCERELY,

G$
```

K Program 7

Exercise 1
An estate agent periodically sends out a letter to check whether clients on his books are still looking for a property, and that his details of their requirements (e.g. type of property, price range, etc.) are correct. Devise a BASIC program to write such a letter.

Exercise 2
We all write letters requesting things, e.g. details of a product, a service, a holiday, a job, etc. Devise a BASIC program to write a letter which will cover as wide a range of applications as possible, leaving you to fill in only the particular details of each enquiry.

3.7 Patterns, files, READ with DATA

READ with DATA
So far in this course we have entered data at the keyboard during the execution of a program as a response to an INPUT statement. Another way of introducing data into a program is to store it in DATA statements within the program itself and then to READ the items into the program from the DATA statements as required. Usually, data is stored at the end of a program, or program segment.

Every time the computer comes to a READ statement it takes the next item of data from the DATA queue* and places it in the location specified in the READ statement. *For a READ statement to be executed there must be a corresponding item of DATA available in the DATA queue.*

Thus in this program the following happens:

```
 10 READ A$
 20 READ B$
 30 READ C$
100 DATA TOM, DICK
110 DATA HARRY
```
Program 8

At 10, READ tells the computer to take the first item of DATA and put it in location A$. The first DATA item occurs in line 100 and is TOM, so TOM goes in location A$. At the next READ statement (20), the computer takes the next DATA item which is DICK, and so on. You can check that this has happened by putting:

```
40 PRINT A$
50 PRINT B$
60 PRINT C$
```

into the program.

SAQ 6
What is wrong with this program segment?

```
10 READ A$
20 READ B
30 READ C
40 READ D$
50 DATA PAUL, MARY, 63
```
Program 9

A more complex example is shown by this program segment:

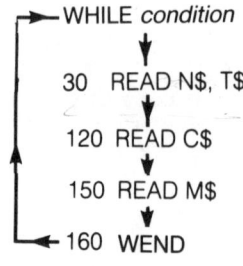

```
      WHILE condition
 30   READ N$, T$
120   READ C$
150   READ M$
160   WEND
```

---

*Items can be separated by a comma, e.g. DATA TOM,DICK has two items "TOM" and "DICK".

```
200 DATA    BENNY, COPPER, DRAPER
210 DATA    EDDIE, GWYNNE
220 DATA    HETTIE
230 DATA    MORLEY, PROSSER, SMYTHE, WEEKS
240 DATA    WILSON, WRIGHT
```

Here is what happens:

First time round the loop

N$	reads BENNY
T$	reads COPPER
C$	reads DRAPER
M$	reads EDDIE

Stores at end of first time round

N$	BENNY
T$	COPPER
C$	DRAPER
M$	EDDIE

Second time round loop

N$	reads GWYNNE	(i.e. next unread
T$	reads HETTIE	item of DATA)
C$	reads MORLEY	
M$	reads PROSSER	

Stores at end of second time round

N$	GWYNNE
T$	HETTIE
C$	MORLEY
M$	PROSSER

SAQ 7
What will be the final state of the stores when all the data has been read?

SAQ 8
What would the contents of locations A$, B$ and C$ be after this program segment has read all the DATA items?

```
 5 WHILE NUMBER<TOTAL
10 READ A$
20 READ B$
30 READ C$
40 WEND
50 DATA TINKER, TAILOR, SOLDIER
60 DATA SAILOR, RICH MAN
```

Program 10

Files and records

Quite often we want to record data which is of one kind, i.e. it makes up a file of information. A telephone directory is a good example of what in data processing is called a file, that is a collection of similar records. Each record has the form

Name	Address	Telephone number

and is said to consist of a number of *fields* – in this case three: name, address and telephone number. A *record* is then a collection of *fields* and a *file* is a collection of *records*. A telephone directory is arranged in alphabetical order of surnames which gives it a simple structure.

Comparing strings

We may wish to compare strings. Suppose, for example, we have a personal telephone directory in our microcomputer and we wish to find out whether SMITH is in our record. The computer will have to compare the string "SMITH" against all the strings in the name field of our directory. It can do this very easily because each letter is represented inside the computer by an ASCII code. (ASCII stands for American Standard Code for Information Interchange.) Thus:

A is 65
B is 66

and so on. (See Appendix A for a full list of binary codes.) So words placed in alphabetical order on paper will be represented in the computer by codes in numerical order.

Thus if

```
A$="CAT"
B$="DOG"
C$="CAT"
D$="FISH"
E$="CATS"

A$=C$
```

But `B$>A$` (it is further on in the alphabet)
and `E$>A$` (the extra S on CAT puts it after CAT in alphabetical order.)

We shall now use this facility in our examples.

Example 2

Set up a data file of names and associated telephone numbers. Write a BASIC program to search through the file to find a particular name, and if found then output the associated telephone number.

Solution
We could attempt a descriptive algorithm as follows:

1. Start
2. Input query name
3. Read first record from file (i.e. name & number)
4. Check for end of file and check for name = query. If either are TRUE then exit loop
5. Read next data items
6. Return to 4
7. Either print 'not found' or 'found'

However, BASIC does not generally allow statements as complicated as 3, 4 or 7, so we have to split up these statements as shown in the next algorithm:

1. Start
2. Input query name
3. Read first record from data file
4. If end of file is reached or name is found then exit loop
5. Read next bit of data
6. End loop
7. If name found then print 'found'
8. If name not found then print 'not found'
9. Stop

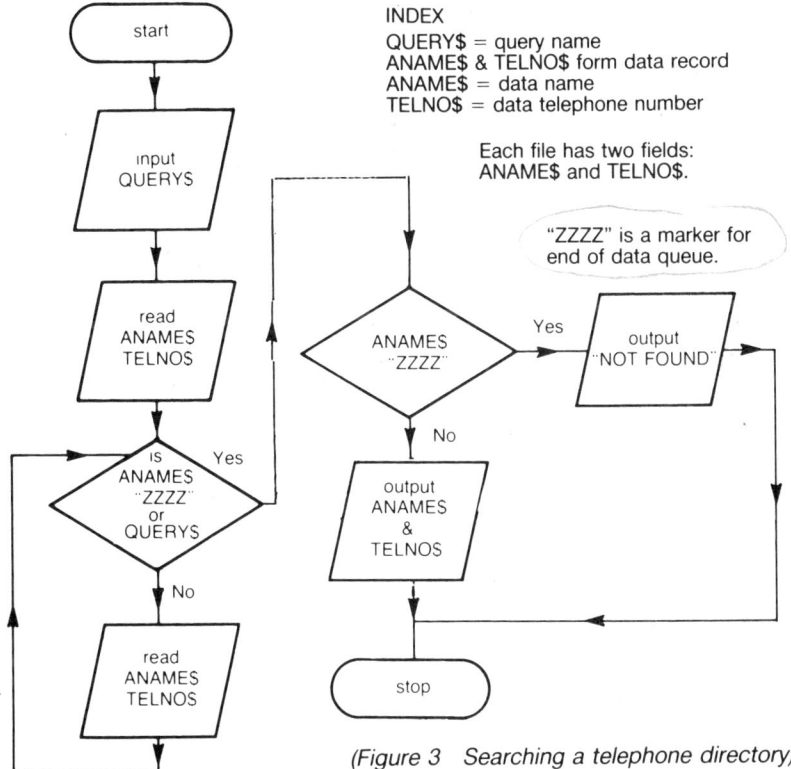

(Figure 3   Searching a telephone directory)

Now each record contains two fields on this occasion: name and number.

Field 1	Field 2
Name ANAME$	Telephone number TELNO$
BENNY	1234

e.g.

so each DATA item must contain information for each field. Thus the READ line will be:

READ ANAME$, TELNO$

and the DATA lines are of the form:

DATA BENNY,1234

Notice that the end-of-file number is a DATA item (line 220), so it has to have data to fill TELNO$ as well as ANAME$. Without this an error message (out of data) would appear on the screen. So we write:

DATA ZZZZ,END OF FILE

and not just

DATA ZZZZ

Looking at step 4 you will notice that the beginning of the WHILE . . . WEND . . . loop is checking for two things: the end of the data file and to see if the name has been found.

To code this double bit we use this:

40 WHILE ANAME$<>"ZZZZ" AND ANAME$<>QUERY$

The bits on both sides of the AND are exactly the same as the conditions we have already met so far. The computer continues with the loop only if the end of file hasn't been reached and if the name hasn't already been found. Or if you read it the other way round, the computer stops the loop if the end of file is reached or if the name is found in the data file.

You can also use AND in IF statements, e.g.

IF A>B AND C>D THEN . . .

Just think of AND as two separate conditions that both must be TRUE before control passes to the statements that follow.

```
10  REM**TELEPHONE DIRECTORY**
20  INPUT "SURNAME OF PERSON SOUGHT";QUERY$
30  READ ANAME$,TELNO$
40  WHILE ANAME$<>"ZZZZ" AND ANAME$<>QUERY$
50  READ ANAME$,TELNO$
60  WEND
70  IF ANAME$="ZZZZ" THEN PRINT QUERY$;" IS NOT IN
    DIRECTORY"
80  IF ANAME$=QUERY$ THEN PRINT QUERY$;"'S PHONE NUMBER
    IS ";TELNO$
90  END
100 REM DATA STARTS HERE
110 DATA BENNY,1234
120 DATA COPPER,9823
130 DATA DRAPER,1850
140 DATA EDDIE,7296
150 DATA GWYNNE,5821
160 DATA HETTIE,4539
170 DATA MORLEY,7830
180 DATA PROSSER,1383
190 DATA SMYTHE,1147
200 DATA WEEKS,5529
210 DATA WILSON,9936
220 DATA ZZZZ,END OF FILE
```

Program 11   Telephone directory

Typical run

```
RUN
SURNAME OF PERSON SOUGHT? MORLEY
MORLEY'S PHONE NUMBER IS 7830
OK

RUN
SURNAME OF PERSON SOUGHT? WEEK
WEEK IS NOT IN DIRECTORY
OK
```

In the second run we entered the name "WEEK" whereas the name "WEEKS" was actually in the file. The computer compares these patterns of characters and finds them unequal. If we were looking through a telephone directory we might realise that we were really looking for WEEKS rather than WEEK. We could of course re-run the program with a variety of spellings of a name, if we were in doubt.

[K] Program 11.

SAQ 9
In the last program we introduced AND into the WHILE statement. This SAQ is to help you understand AND.

(a) In the following program extracts, what values must A and B have for the loop to work?

(i)   WHILE A=6 AND B=7
      .
      .
      .
      WEND

(ii)   WHILE A=15 AND B=0
        .
        .
        .
    WEND

(iii)   WHILE A=6-1 AND B<8
        .
        .
        .
    WEND

(iv)   WHILE A-1=5 AND B+2=6
        .
        .
        .
    WEND

(b) Write a WHILE statement which will continue with the loop if the string in A$ is "HELLO" and the string in B$ is "GOODBYE".

3.8 Sorting

You will have noticed that the telephone directory data in Example 2 was in alphabetical order, as you would expect. It would be difficult for the user in normal practice if this were not so. However, our solution to this searching problem did not use this information; we just searched through the data file record by record until we found the name, or reached the end of the file. Our algorithm would have worked equally well had the data not been in alphabetical order. We shall spend some time later in the course sorting and searching data, at which point you will realise the advantages of sorting data into alphabetical order.

Let's make a modest start with this problem.

Example 3
Write a BASIC program to enter two names into the computer and output that name which would come first in alphabetical order.

Solution

Descriptive algorithm
1. Start
2. Input first name
3. Input second name
4. If first name<second name output first
5. If second name<first name output second
6. Stop

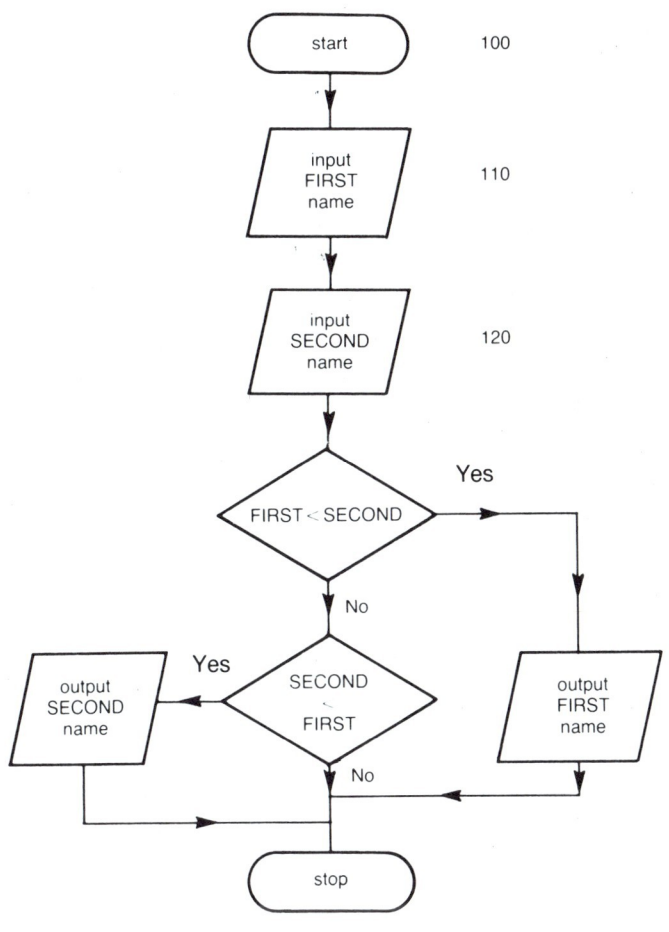

(Figure 4   Finding the first of two in alphabetical order)

```
100 REM**FIRST IN ALPHABETICAL ORDER**
110 INPUT "FIRST NAME";ANAME$
120 INPUT "SECOND NAME";BNAME$
130 IF ANAME$<BNAME$ THEN PRINT ANAME$;" IS FIRST"
140 IF BNAME$<ANAME$ THEN PRINT BNAME$;" IS FIRST"
```

Program 12

Typical run

```
RUN
FIRST NAME? BROWN
SECOND NAME? SMITH
BROWN IS FIRST
```

```
OK
RUN
FIRST NAME? SMITH
SECOND NAME? BROWN
BROWN IS FIRST
```

K Program 12

The 3-card trick

Suppose now that we wanted to input three names and output the name that comes first in alphabetical order. A standard solution to this would be to follow the approach in Figure 5.

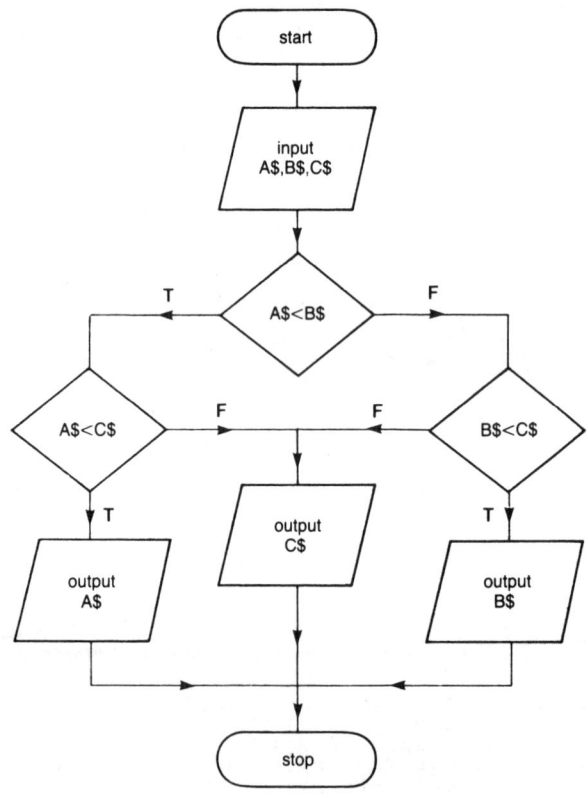

(Figure 5   Finding the first of three in alphabetical order)

When asked to solve this problem, most students present an answer similar to the algorithm in Figure 5. It is a perfectly good solution, but it bodes ill for the future. Future trouble stems from the fact that we have had to utilise 3 decision and 3 output functions. This method would overtax our patience and ingenuity if we tried to repeat it for 4, 5 . . . let alone 10 names. The fundamental problem is allowing each variable to retain its own individual storage location, and how we are best able to label that location.

A simpler method of solving this problem is to input the names one by one and to store *lowest-so-far* in A$. The program retains *only* lowest-so-far, destroying all the other discarded data. In the next Exercise we suggest you try this approach to solving the problem.

Exercise 3
Write a BASIC program to input three names and output that name which would come first in alphabetical order using the method discussed in the last few lines.

Exercise 4
A data file of European countries and their capital cities is suggested below. Write a BASIC program to use this file as the basis of a quiz with the user, presenting the user with the country and asking the user to name the capital city. Respond to the input by telling the user whether she or he is correct or not, and in the latter case giving the correct answer.

```
140 DATA FRANCE, PARIS
150 DATA WEST GERMANY, BONN
160 DATA THE NETHERLANDS, THE HAGUE
170 DATA POLAND, WARSAW
180 DATA ITALY, ROME
190 DATA SPAIN, MADRID
200 DATA PORTUGAL, LISBON
210 DATA HUNGARY, BUDAPEST
220 DATA DENMARK, COPENHAGEN
230 DATA NORWAY, OSLO
240 DATA ZZZZ, END OF FILE.
```

Assignment 3

1. Compose a descriptive algorithm and draw a flowchart to match the BASIC program in Program 15 (page 87).

2. Modify your program for Exercise 4 to count the numbers of correct and incorrect responses, and to give a summary of the marks at the end of the quiz.

3. Devise an algorithm and write a BASIC program to do the following task. Store several words as individual letters in DATA statements, e.g. the words 'algorithm' and 'flowchart' could be stored:

   ```
   900 DATA A,L,G,O,R,I,T,H,M
   910 DATA F,L,O,W,C,H,A,R,T
   ```

   Count the number of vowels and consonants contained in the words, and output the totals of these counts together with the ratio total number of vowels/total number of consonants.

Objectives of Unit 3

Now that you have completed this Unit, check that you are able to use the following in simple programs:

String storage locations ☐
PRINT...;... ☐
INPUT"...";... ☐
READ ☐
DATA (one field only) ☐
IF A$ = B$ THEN ... ☐
DATA (more than one field) ☐
Simple sorting procedure ☐

Answers to SAQs and Exercises

SAQ 1
(a), (b) and (e) are correct but (e) is not acceptable in minimal BASIC.
(c) is incorrect: M$ is a string location, so you need "9583"
(d) is incorrect: K8 is a number store location so the string "JAM POT" cannot be assigned to it.

SAQ 2

P	R	I	N	T		L	A	Y	O	U	T								
B	A	S	I	C										C	O	U	R	S	E
B	A	S	I	C	C	O	U	R	S	E									
B	A	S	I	C		C	O	U	R	S	E								

(Answer shown for standard print zones)

SAQ 3

```
10 LET B$="BASIC"
20 PRINT B$, B$
30 PRINT B$; B$; B$; B$
40 PRINT B$; " "; B$; " "; B$
50 END
```

Program 13

SAQ 4

```
WHAT IS YOUR NAME? JOHN SMITH
WHAT IS YOUR AGE? 45
THANK YOU     JOHN SMITH    45
```

SAQ 5

```
10 INPUT "WHAT IS YOUR NAME";N$
20 INPUT "WHAT IS YOUR AGE";A
30 PRINT "MY NAME IS ";N$;" AND I AM";" YEARS OLD"
40 END
```

Exercises 1 and 2

Exercises 1 and 2 are very similar in nature and an answer for Exercise 1 has not been included.

```
 10 REM**ENQUIRY LETTER**
 20 PRINT
 30 PRINT "DETAILS OF ADDRESSEE"
 40 PRINT
 50 INPUT "NAME...";ANAME$
 60 INPUT "STREET...";STREET$
 70 INPUT "TOWN...";TOWN$
 80 PRINT
 90 INPUT "DATE FOR THIS LETTER";ADATE$
100 PRINT
110 PRINT "DETAILS OF PRODUCT/SERVICE"
120 PRINT
130 PRINT "ITEM OF INTEREST"
140 INPUT ITEM$
150 PRINT "SOURCE OF INFORMATION"
160 INPUT SOURCE$
170 INPUT "DATE OF SOURCE";BDATE$
180 PRINT
190 PRINT
200 PRINT
210 PRINT ANAME$
220 PRINT STREET$
230 PRINT TOWN$
240 PRINT
250 PRINT
260 PRINT ADATE$
270 PRINT
280 PRINT
290 PRINT "DEAR SIR,"
300 PRINT
310 PRINT "WILL YOU KINDLY SEND ME DETAILS OF"
320 PRINT ITEM$;","
330 PRINT "AS ITEMISED IN THE"
340 PRINT SOURCE$
350 PRINT "DATED ";BDATE$;"."
360 PRINT
370 PRINT
380 PRINT "YOURS FAITHFULLY,"
390 PRINT
400 PRINT
410 PRINT
420 PRINT "O.L. SEYMOUR"
```

Program 14

Typical run

```
RUN

DETAILS OF ADDRESSEE

NAME...? E P SOFTWARE LTD
STREET...? EDGWARE ROAD
TOWN...? LONDON
```

```
DATE FOR THIS LETTER? 12TH OCTOBER 1980

DETAILS OF PRODUCT/SERVICE

ITEM OF INTEREST
?BUSINESS SOFTWARE PACKAGES
SOURCE OF INFORMATION
?MAGAZINE "MODERN COMPUTING"
DATE OF SOURCE? 10TH OCTOBER


E P SOFTWARE LTD
EDGWARE ROAD
LONDON

12TH OCTOBER 1980


DEAR SIR,

WILL YOU KINDLY SEND ME DETAILS OF
BUSINESS SOFTWARE PACKAGES,
AS ITEMISED IN THE
MAGAZINE "MODERN COMPUTING"
DATED 10TH OCTOBER.

YOURS FAITHFULLY,


O.L. SEYMOUR
```

SAQ 6

Line 20 will try to read the second DATA item which is MARY, which is a string, but the location in line 20 is a number location. The computer would stop and indicate a syntax error. To read "MARY", line 20 must be 20 READ B$.

Line 40 calls for a fourth DATA item but there are only three items in line 50.

SAQ 7

N$	SMYTHE
T$	WEEKS
C$	WILSON
M$	WRIGHT

SAQ 8

```
A$="SOLDIER"
B$="SAILOR"
C$="RICH MAN"
```

Notice that "RICH MAN" is read as one item since there is no comma between the two words. If you run this program you will get a message such as "out of data at line 50". Why?

SAQ 9

Answer for part (a):

(i) A must have the value 6 and B must have the value 7
(ii) A must have the value 15 and B must have the value 0
(iii) A must have the value 5 and B must be less than 8, e.g. 7,6,5, etc.
(iv) A must have the value 6 and B must have the value 4

Answer for part (b):

```
WHILE A$="HELLO" AND B$="GOODBYE"
 .
 .
 .
WEND
```

Remember: The parts on either side of the AND must both be true.

Exercise 3

A simple method of solving this problem is shown in Program 15. The names are input one by one. The new name is compared with the first so far in line 50. The first so far is stored in ANAME$, which means line 50 only changes ANAME$ if the new name is lower. The new name is inputted in the last line of the loop so it is checked immediately by the WHILE statement in line 40.

```
 10 REM**FIRST IN ALPHABETICAL ORDER*
 20 INPUT "FIRST NAME ";ANAME$
 30 INPUT "NEXT NAME ";BNAME$
 40 WHILE BNAME$<>"ZZZZ"
 50 IF BNAME$<ANAME$ THEN ANAME$=BNAME$
 60 PRINT "FIRST SO FAR IS ";ANAME$
 70 INPUT "NEXT NAME ";BNAME$
 80 WEND
 90 PRINT ANAME$;" WAS OVERALL FIRST"
100 END
```
Program 15

Typical run

```
RUN
FIRST NAME? TOM
NEXT NAME? SID
FIRST SO FAR IS SID
NEXT NAME? JOE
FIRST SO FAR IS JOE
NEXT NAME? PETE
FIRST SO FAR IS JOE
NEXT NAME? FRED
FIRST SO FAR IS FRED
NEXT NAME? BILL
FIRST SO FAR IS BILL
NEXT NAME? RON
FIRST SO FAR IS BILL
NEXT NAME? ALAN
FIRST SO FAR IS ALAN
NEXT NAME? ZZZZ
ALAN WAS OVERALL FIRST
OK
```

Exercise 4

```
 10 REM**EUROPEAN CAPITALS QUIZ**
 20 PRINT
 30 READ COUNTRY$,CAPITAL$
 40 WHILE COUNTRY$<>"ZZZZ"
 50 PRINT "WHAT IS THE CAPITAL OF ";COUNTRY$
 60 INPUT ANSWER$
 70 IF ANSWER$=CAPITAL$ THEN PRINT "THAT'S RIGHT"
 80 IF ANSWER$<>CAPITAL$ THEN PRINT "WRONG!
    IT'S ";CAPITAL$
 90 READ COUNTRY$,CAPITAL$
100 WEND
110 PRINT "END OF TEST"
120 END
130 DATA FRANCE,PARIS
140 DATA WEST GERMANY,BONN
150 DATA THE NETHERLANDS,THE HAGUE
160 DATE POLAND,WARSAW
170 DATA ITALY,ROME
180 DATA SPAIN,MADRID
190 DATA PORTUGAL,LISBON
200 DATA HUNGARY,BUDAPEST
210 DATA DENMARK,COPENHAGEN
220 DATA NORWAY,OSLO
230 DATA ZZZZ,END OF FILE
```

Program 16

Typical run

```
RUN
WHAT IS THE CAPITAL OF FRANCE
?PARIS
THAT'S RIGHT
WHAT IS THE CAPITAL OF WEST GERMANY
?BONN
THAT'S RIGHT
WHAT IS THE CAPITAL OF THE NETHERLANDS
?HAGUE
WRONG!IT'S THE HAGUE
WHAT IS THE CAPITAL OF POLAND
?WARSAW
THAT'S RIGHT
WHAT IS THE CAPITAL OF ITALY
?ROME
THAT'S RIGHT
WHAT IS THE CAPITAL OF SPAIN
?BONN
WRONG! IT'S MADRID
WHAT IS THE CAPITAL OF PORTUGAL
```

etc.

UNIT 4
Lists

4.1	Variables	90
4.2	Lists	90
4.3	List variables	90
4.4	List input and output	93
4.5	The FOR . . . NEXT . . . loop	96
4.6	Nested loops	102
4.7	Interchanging	105
	Assignment 4	109
	Objectives of Unit 4	109
	Answers to SAQs and Exercises	110

4.1 Variables

We have already seen how a memory location may store several different values during the course of a program's execution. Thus the value in a store location may vary during a run, and so we often refer to the location names as variables in a program.

NUMBER, ATIME, COUNT, THENAME

are called numeric variables, and their counterparts:

NUMBER$, ATIME$, COUNT$, THENAME$

are called string variables. The store labels are used in expressions in program statements just as mathematicians use variables in equations.

4.2 Lists

Lists and supermarkets seem inextricably linked. We go in with a list of items which we wish to buy, and emerge with the items and a list of prices in the form of a receipt. The list of prices results from the process of transferring the items from the basket to the counter. This is a fairly random process but we could have given the list a more meaningful order in a variety of ways. With a lot of effort we could have taken the items out of the basket in order of price, i.e. the cheapest first, the next cheapest, and so on, with the most expensive last, so that the till roll of prices would be in order of cost. Similarly, we could have taken them out of the basket in order of weight, the lightest first through to the heaviest last; and by so doing impose a completely different order on the receipt list. Being able to relate the position in a list in some way to the value of the item, is the most useful feature of lists, as we shall see by the end of this Unit.

4.3 List variables

Most of the data that we have considered so far can be classified into sets. We have considered sets of test marks, sets of names and associated telephone numbers, sets of countries and their capital cities. Most data can be classified in some way. If we are collecting data for some purpose, this very purpose gives the set of values common characteristics. There are obvious advantages to naming the storage locations for items in a set of data in a way which emphasises that all the items belong to one set. Even better, it would be useful if the storage location names identified the position of an item within the set.

For example, storage, or variable, notation; this emphasises that the values are in some way associated with each other, and allocates a position within the set. This is achieved in the following way.

Consider a set of marks in a teacher's mark book. They form a natural list and in BASIC we can allocate storage locations symbolised in the following way:

Item	Storage location symbol
Item	*Storage location symbol*
The first member of the M-list is 42	M(1)=42
The second member of the M-list is 67	M(2)=67
The third member of the M-list is 90	M(3)=90
etc. . . .	

M(1), M(2), M(3) are like separate memory locations. You can take any store location and put numbers in brackets after it to make list store locations, e.g.

List name	*List store locations in that list*
M(I)	M(1), M(2), M(3) . . .
A0(I)	A0(1), A0(2), A0(3) . . .
C$(I)	C$(1), C$(2), C$(3) . . .
Q6$(I)	Q6$(1), Q6$(2), Q6$(3) . . .

The number in the brackets (here shown as I*) is called the index of the list, and may be any positive integer up to a limit set by your computer. We advise that you use meaningful names for your list as you should do for all variables. E.g. ANAME$(1), ANAME$(2), etc.

String lists

As you can see from the table above, lists can be string lists as well as numeric lists. Thus if you name a list M(I) it is clearly a list of numbers, but M$(I) would be a list of strings, e.g. a list of names could be stored:

Index	Item	Variable name
1	Jones	N$(1), or ANAME$(1)
2	Alan	N$(2), or ANAME$(2)
3	Smith	N$(3), or ANAME$(3)
etc	etc	etc

(Figure 1   String list names)

List of arrays

A table of data, like that shown in Figure 1, is often referred to as *an array of data*. With the data displayed in rows and columns in this way (indexed by item), a table is often referred to as *a two-dimensional array*. A list (i.e. just one column of data) is similarly called a one-dimensional array. We will see how BASIC provides for two-dimensional arrays in a later Unit.

OPTION BASE n

When using arrays the first location can have an index number of 0 or 1. Before you define the length of an array, you must set the first location's index number using OPTION BASE:

---

* Throughout the remainder of the course the letter I (ninth in the alphabet) will be used for the index of lists. Please take care when entering programs not to confuse I with the lower case L.

OPTION BASE 0 – sets index to start at 0. E.g. ANAME(0), ANAME(1), ANAME(2), etc.
OPTION BASE 1 – sets index to start at 1. E.g. ANAME(1), ANAME(2), ANAME(3), etc.

The default state (the state when you first enter BASIC) is O, i.e. arrays start with the first index number as 0.

DIM or how long is a list?

As long as you choose! We said that the index may be any reasonable positive integer, and within the overall memory limitations of a particular computer, we can choose a list to be of any desired length, provided that we warn the system first. On the IBM you do not need to warn the computer of lists of 10 or fewer items but it is better to give advance warning of all lists. To do this you use a DIMENSION statement:

```
LINE NUMBER DIM A (LENGTH OF LIST)
```

which must appear in the program before you use the array A. So in this Unit we include DIM statements. Even if your computer does not need DIM statements for small arrays, it is all right to leave the DIM statements in your programs.

Items and index numbers

The following paper and pencil exercises should reinforce our understanding of what is meant by the terms item and index, and their often only fleeting relationship. They also prepare the ground for the interchange–sort procedure which we will consider in detail later in this Unit.

Example 1

Transfer the item of lowest value in the following list to position 1, by comparing in turn each of the values in the remainder of the list with the current value at position 1. Interchange the items if the one in the remainder of the list is lower than that at position 1. (It is easier to do than to describe!)

List: 3, 42, −8, 9, −11

Start		Compare & interchange stages			
position or index	item	1st run c	2nd run c&i	3rd run c	4th run c&i
1	3	3	−8	−8	−11
2	42	42	42	42	42
3	−8	−8	3	3	3
4	9	9	9	9	9
5	−11	−11	−11	−11	−8

(Figure 2   Sort to place lowest number first)

SAQ 1

Carry out the procedure in Example 1 for the following list of numbers:

6, 8, 4, 7, 3, 9, 1

4.4 List input and output

Before we can manipulate the items in a list, we have to get the list of items into the computer, and after processing usually get another list out.

Example 2
Write a BASIC program to input three numbers into a list and output the elements of the list in reverse order.

Solution
We will call the list ALIST(I). The required program is then:

```
10 REM*EXAMPLE 2**
20 OPTION BASE 1
30 DIM ALIST(3)
40 INPUT ALIST(1)
50 INPUT ALIST(2)
60 INPUT ALIST(3)
70 PRINT
80 PRINT
90 PRINT ALIST(3),ALIST(2),ALIST(1)
100 END
```
Program 1 Reversing the order of a list

Typical run

```
RUN
? 29
? 32
? -17

-17            32              29

OK
```

K Program 1.

We have done as requested in the question, but have not made a significant advance in programming technique since we could have done the job with the techniques of earlier Units simply by calling the variables P, Q and R and outputting them as R, Q and P. To do the job better we need to count the list as it is inputted so that we can use the counter in reverse order when we output the list. The next example adds this refinement.

Counting a list

Example 3
Write a program to input five numbers into a list, to display the items of the list and its index in the form of a table, and then output the elements of the list in reverse order.

Solution
As listed in the question, there are three main parts to the solution and we can display these in flowchart form as in Figure 3.

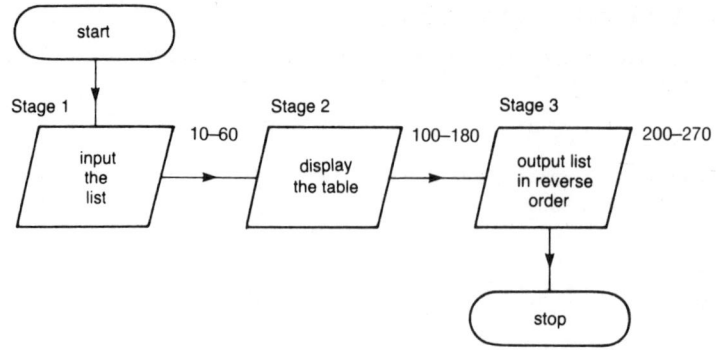

(Figure 3   Stages in solving Example 3)

Stage 1
We use the variable C to count the elements of the list on input, and to act as an index for the list.

```
10 REM**INPUT A LIST**
12 OPTION BASE 1
15 DIM ALIST(5)
20 LET C=1
30 WHILE C<=5
40 INPUT "ENTER THE NEXT NUMBER";ALIST(C)
50 LET C=C+1
60 WEND
```
Program 2   Counting a list on entry

Stage 2
The table will have the form you met in the answer to SAQ 1. A simple PRINT ..,.. will suffice to display the table.

```
100 REM**DISPLAY THE TABLE**
110 PRINT
120 PRINT
130 PRINT "INDEX","ITEM"
140 LET C=1                     ⎤
150 WHILE C<=5                  │
160 PRINT C,ALIST(C)            ├── prints the table
170 LET C=C+1                   │
180 WEND                        ⎦
```
Program 3   Printing the list in input order

Stage 3
Now we make C count from 5 down to 1 in order to print the list in reverse order.

```
200 REM**OUTPUT LIST IN REVERSE**
210 PRINT
220 PRINT
230 LET C=5                     ⎤
240 WHILE C<>0                  ├── prints list in reverse order
250 PRINT ALIST(C)              │
260 LET C=C-1                   │
270 WEND                        ⎦
```
Program 4   Printing in reverse order

We have shown the three program modules that provide the solution. All we have to do now is put them together as follows. The few changes (which don't affect what the program does) are explained in the comments.

Changes

```
 10 REM**INPUT A LIST**
 12 OPTION BASE 1
 15 DIM ALIST(5)
 20 LET C=1
 30 WHILE C<=5
 40 INPUT "ENTER THE NEXT NUMBER";ALIST(C)
 50 LET C=C+1
 60 WEND
 70 REM  }
 80 REM  }                                         REM statements to help
                                                   reader see the divisions
 90 REM**DISPLAY THE TABLE**                       in the program
100 PRINT
110 PRINT
120 PRINT "INDEX","ITEM"
130 LET D=1 ─────────────────────────────────      We've used D as an
140 WHILE D<=5                                     index to remind you
150 PRINT D,ALIST(D)                               that its name doesn't
160 LET D=D+1                                      matter – only its value.
170 WEND
180 REM  }
190 REM  }  ─────────────────────────────────      More REMs
200 REM**OUTPUT LIST IN REVERSE**
210 PRINT
220 PRINT
230 LET E=5 ─────────────────────────────────      And we've used E here.
240 WHILE E<>0
250 PRINT ALIST(E)
260 LET E=E-1
270 WEND
280 END ─────────────────────────────────────      END added.
```

Program 5   The full reverse list program

```
RUN
ENTER THE NEXT NUMBER? -8
ENTER THE NEXT NUMBER? 15
ENTER THE NEXT NUMBER? 23
ENTER THE NEXT NUMBER? -4
ENTER THE NEXT NUMBER? 19

INDEX          ITEM
1              -8
2              15
3              23
4              -4
5              19

19
-4
23
15
8
OK
```

K Program 5.

To solve the problem in Example 3 we've done quite a bit of programming but the program only works for a list of five numbers. A small reward for a great effort! But if we change statements 20–60 which counted the five items, we can make the program accept any number of items so long as we know the number before inputting.

But we need to make DIM depend on the number of items we are inputting.

Here is our solution. Note lines 20–30 which set the dimension of the array according to the number of items in the list.

```
10 REM**INPUT A LIST OF NUMBER ITEMS**
12 OPTION BASE 1
20 INPUT "HOW MANY ITEMS IN LIST";NUMBER
30 DIM M$(NUMBER)
40 LET C=1
50 WHILE C<=NUMBER
60 INPUT "ENTER THE NEXT ITEM"; M$(C)
70 LET C=C+1
80 WEND
```

Program 6

To be able to input *any* number of items of data into individual store locations with just half-a-dozen statements represents a significant improvement in programming technique. But, of course, we are never satisfied! Why should we bother to count the items, especially if the list is long, when we can get the computer to do it for us? The next exercise asks you to do this.

Exercise 1
Write a BASIC program to

(a) Input a list of numbers, the list being of unknown length; terminate the list with the dummy '–9999'. Call the list NUMBERS(C) and assume that the list will be 30 or less items. So DIM NUMBERS(30) will declare the list. Check your answer.

(b) Now modify your program to output those items whose index number is odd. *Hint:* use COUNT=COUNT+2 to skip even entries.

4.5 The FOR ... NEXT ... loop

As we have said repeatedly, a computer is good at lots of repetitive operations. In order to control these operations we usually have to count them. Since we introduced the idea of counting in Unit 2, we have used the following sequence of statements several times.

LET COUNT=1
WHILE COUNT<=LIMIT

activity

LET COUNT=COUNT+1
WEND

Program 7

These repetitive operations are so important in programming that special provision is made for them. In BASIC this is done by means of the FOR . . . NEXT . . . facility.

The sequence in Program 7 has three elements:

LET COUNT=1	which starts the count
COUNT<=LIMIT	which stops the counting process
LET COUNT=COUNT+1	which defines the incremental step

The same features occur in the FOR . . . NEXT . . . loop where the above sequence becomes:

```
                  start    finish    increment
FOR COUNT=1 TO LIMIT STEP (1)
    (activity)
NEXT COUNT
```

Program 8

Notice that NEXT COUNT returns control to the line FOR COUNT=1 to LIMIT STEP (1) without you having to put the line number of FOR COUNT . . . in the NEXT COUNT statement.

Arrays and FOR . . . NEXT . . . loops were made for each other. Together they form possibly the most potent facility of the BASIC language. Let's look in detail at how these loops work, and then repeat some of our earlier routines with lists using this new facility.

Examples of FOR . . . NEXT . . . loops in action

(a)
```
10 FOR I=4 TO 10 STEP (2)
20 PRINT I
30 NEXT I
RUN
4
6
8
10
OK
```

(b)
```
10 ·FOR K=11 TO 4 STEP (-2)
20 PRINT K
30 NEXT K
RUN
11
9
7
5
OK
```

(c)
```
10 FOR J=-3 TO 10 STEP (3)
20 PRINT J
30 NEXT J
RUN
-3
0
3
6
9
OK
```

(d)
```
10 FOR L=4 TO -5 STEP (-2)
20 PRINT L
30 NEXT L
RUN
4
2
0
-2
-4
OK
```

Programs 9–12

SAQ 2
Write out the lists of numbers printed out by the following loops.

(a)
```
10 FOR E=1 TO 9 STEP (2)
20 PRINT E
30 NEXT E
```

(b)
```
10 FOR F=-30 TO -18 STEP (3)
20 PRINT F
30 NEXT F
```

(c)
```
10 FOR G=8 TO -4 STEP (-5)
20 PRINT G
30 NEXT G
```

(d)
```
10 FOR H=-2 TO -11 STEP (-4)
20 PRINT H
30 NEXT H
```

Programs 13–16

FOR ... NEXT ... with STEP (1)
The above examples and SAQs had steps of 2, 3, −2, −4 and −5. Quite often, however, we simply want to use a step of 1. When that is the case, you can omit STEP (1) from the statement. Thus

FOR C=1 TO N

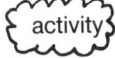

NEXT C

Program 17

is taken by the computer to mean a step of 1.

Input/output routines with FOR ... NEXT ...
Routines are made easier by the FOR ... NEXT ... facility. For example, we can rewrite Program 5 using these loops. Notice that at lines 20 and 150 we require a step of 1 so STEP (1) has been omitted.

Comparison with Program 5

```
10   REM**INPUT A LIST OF 5 NAMES**
12   OPTION BASE 1
15   DIM ANAME$(5)
20   FOR C=1 TO 5
30   INPUT "ENTER THE NEXT NAME";ANAME$(C)    } Replaces lines 20–60
40   NEXT C
50   REM
60   REM
100  REM**DISPLAY THE TABLE**
110  PRINT
120  PRINT
130  PRINT "INDEX","NAME"
140  PRINT
150  FOR D=1 TO 5
160  PRINT D,ANAME$(D)                        } ———————— Replaces lines 130–170
170  NEXT D
180  REM
190  REM
200  REM**OUTPUT LIST IN REVERSE**
210 ·PRINT
220  PRINT
230  FOR E=5 TO 1 STEP (-1)
240  PRINT E,ANAME$(E)                        } ———————— Replaces lines 230–260
250  NEXT E
260  END
```

Program 18 Using FOR ... NEXT ... to reverse a list

```
RUN
ENTER THE NEXT NAME? DICKENS
ENTER THE NEXT NAME? HARDY
ENTER THE NEXT NAME? SNOW
ENTER THE NEXT NAME? AUSTEN
ENTER THE NEXT NAME? ORWELL
```

```
INDEX        NAME

1            DICKENS
2            HARDY
3            SNOW
4            AUSTEN
5            ORWELL

5            ORWELL
4            AUSTEN
3            SNOW
2            HARDY
1            DICKENS
OK
```

K Program 18.

General FOR ... NEXT ... loop
The FOR ... NEXT ... loop can be expressed in quite general terms as

FOR I=S TO F STEP (J)

NEXT I

providing that S, F and J are given 'reasonable' values before the loop is executed. Unreasonable values would be something like

S=2, F=10, and STEP (−3)

since you can't get from 2 to 10 in steps of −3, in the normal course of events.

Exercise 2
In Exercise 5 of Unit 2 you wrote a program (Program 17) to calculate the yield on an investment for a period of years to be specified. Re-write lines 60 to 120 of the program using a FOR ... NEXT ... loop.

Exercise 3
If you are mathematically inquisitve, you might like to try the following which demonstrates the potential of the FOR ... NEXT ... loop. Write a program to tabulate the squares and cubes of the odd integers from 1 to 21 inclusive.

Output display
We always aim at a clear presentation of output data on the screen or printer. The FOR ... NEXT ... facility is used widely in presenting output routines.

Use to skip lines
As you saw in the layout of letters in Unit 3, Section 5, it is useful to 'print' blank lines. The following routine does this for you.

```
10 REM**FOR...NEXT**
20 REM**TO SKIP LINES IN A PRINT ROUTINE**
30 PRINT "HELLO"
40 FOR HELLO=1 TO 10
50 PRINT
60 NEXT HELLO
70 PRINT "HELLO FROM 11 LINES BELOW"
80 END
```
Program 19

```
RUN
HELLO




HELLO FROM 11 LINES BELOW
```

K Program 19.

Drawing a line
We may wish to print lines across the screen or page, e.g. to separate blocks of data or just to underline. The following routine does this.

```
10 REM**FOR...NEXT**
20 REM**TO DRAW LINES**
30 FOR M=1 TO 40
40 PRINT "*";         ──── instruction to print * 40 times
50 NEXT M
60 PRINT
70 END
```
Program 20

```
RUN

****************************************
OK
```

SAQ 3
Why does line 40 in Program 20 have ; at the end of the line? What happens if line 40 is 40 PRINT "*"?

K Program 20.

Loops in flowcharts

Loops are so important that they have a special flowchart symbol of their own:

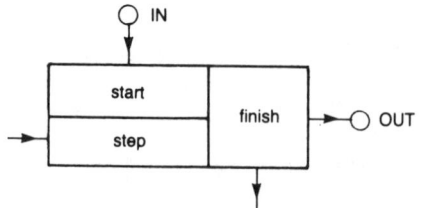

(Figure 4a   Flowchart symbol for a FOR ... NEXT ... loop)

The floating ends are the connections to the activity:

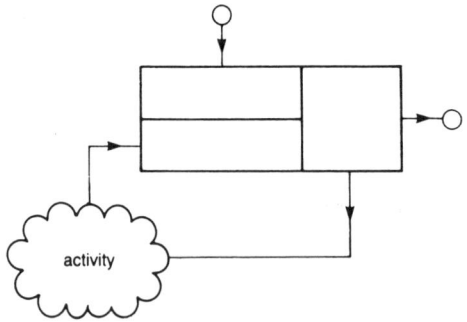

(Figure 4b   Flowchart symbol's relationship to activity)

4.6 Nested loops

Program 20 drew a line of 40 asterisks. We can rewrite the program so that we can specify in line 30 a number of asterisks and so vary the length of the line. So with the program:

```
10 REM**LINES OF DIFFERENT LENGTH**
20 LET N=1 ───────────────── number to go in line 30
30 FOR M=1 TO N
40 PRINT "*";
50 NEXT M
60 PRINT
70 END
```
Program 21

we get

RUN
*

OK

To vary the line length we simply key in

```
20 LET N=REQUIRED LENGTH
```

and key run:

```
20 LET N=2

RUN
**
OK

20 LET N=3

RUN
***
OK

20 LET N=4

RUN
****
OK

20 LET N=8

RUN
********
OK

20 LET N=16

RUN
****************
OK

20 LET N=32

RUN
********************************
OK
```

K Program 21.

Nested FOR... NEXT... loops
You have seen in Program 21 how you can control the effect of the FOR... NEXT... loop of lines 30–50 by changing the value of N. We hope by now that the 'obvious' question springs to your mind: 'Why not control the value of N by using another FOR... NEXT... loop?' The following program does just that. The M-loop of lines 30–50 is itself controlled by the N-loop of lines 20–70. The M-loop is said to be 'nested' within the N-loop.

```
10 REM**NESTED FOR...NEXT...LOOPS**
20 FOR N=1 TO 16
30 FOR M=1 TO N
40 PRINT "*";
50 NEXT M
70 NEXT N
80 END
```

Inner loop: controls number of * in each row (lines 30–50)

Outer loop: controls the rows (lines 20–70)

Program 22   Nested loops

```
RUN
*
* *
* * *
* * * *
* * * * *
* * * * * *
* * * * * * *
* * * * * * * *
* * * * * * * * *
* * * * * * * * * *
* * * * * * * * * * *
* * * * * * * * * * * *
* * * * * * * * * * * * *
* * * * * * * * * * * * * *
* * * * * * * * * * * * * * *
* * * * * * * * * * * * * * * *
OK
```

It is important that you understand how this works. For example, when the computer has just finished printing the 9th row of asterisks N will be 9. It leaves the inner loop (line 50) and control goes to the outer loop (line 70). N then increases to its next value of 10. Control reverts to the inner loop at line 30. The computer then goes round the inner loop (lines 30–50) ten times before exiting again to line 70.

K Program 22.

More print patterns from loops

If generating print patterns with loops appeals to you, here is another one plus two Exercises.

```
10 REM**NESTED FOR...NEXT...LOOPS**
15 P=1
20 FOR N=1 TO 5
25 LET P=2*P ——————————— Multiplies current value of
30 FOR M=1 TO P              P by 2 for each pass
40 PRINT "*";                around loop.
50 NEXT M
60 PRINT
70 NEXT N
80 END
```

Program 23

```
RUN
* *                                          P=2

* * * *                                      P=4

* * * * * * * *                              P=8

* * * * * * * * * * * * * * * *              P=16

* * * * * * * * * * * * * * * * * * * * * * * * * * * * * * * *   P=32


OK
```

K Program 23.

Exercise 4
Write a program using nested loops to print out the 7, 8 and 9 multiplication tables.

Exercise 5
Write a program using nested loops to print out rectangles of asterisks of dimensions to be chosen by you.

4.7 Interchanging

We considered in Unit 2 the problem of finding the smaller of 2 numbers, and in Unit 3 the smallest of 3. In this Unit we have done exercises on interchanging items of a list, in preparation for writing an interchange program.

We have been comparing the items of a list with the item at position 1, and interchanging if the item in the list is smaller than that at position 1. When you did this in SAQ 1, you did it manually, and we have not yet looked at the problems of writing a program to perform the interchange. We can't just say

Copy A into B and then B into A

since the first transaction 'copy A into B' overwrites and destroys what's in B, giving us copies of A in A and in B. Instead we have to put the contents of B away in some safe, temporary store *before* we overwrite B with A. We can show the process diagrammatically:

```
      ↓
┌─────────────┐
│ TEMP ← B    │
│ B ← A       │
│ A ← TEMP    │
└─────────────┘
      ↓
```

Where ← means place the number in the right-hand store into the left-hand store.

Suppose, for example, you want to sort a list of names N$-list and you want to interchange the first name, N$(1) with some other name N$(K) at position K. This can be done using a temporary store location T$:

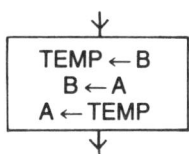

Remember that it is the contents of N$(1) and N$(K) that are being swapped. Suppose N$(1)=FRED and N$(K)=JIM then this is what is happening:

	Store locations		
	N$(1)	N$(K)	T$
start	FRED	JIM	
next stage	FRED	JIM	JIM
next stage	FRED	FRED	JIM
end	JIM	FRED	JIM

(The fact that T$ still has JIM in it doesn't matter; we have achieved the object which is to swap the locations of FRED and JIM.)

Flowchart for name sort

In the number sort (SAQ 1) we wanted to put the lowest number at the top of the list. We can do the same with a list of names, e.g. if we wish to put the first in alphabetical order at the top of the list. So we test each name in turn against the one currently at the top of the list and interchange only if the name under test comes before the one at the top of the list. A flowchart for this is:

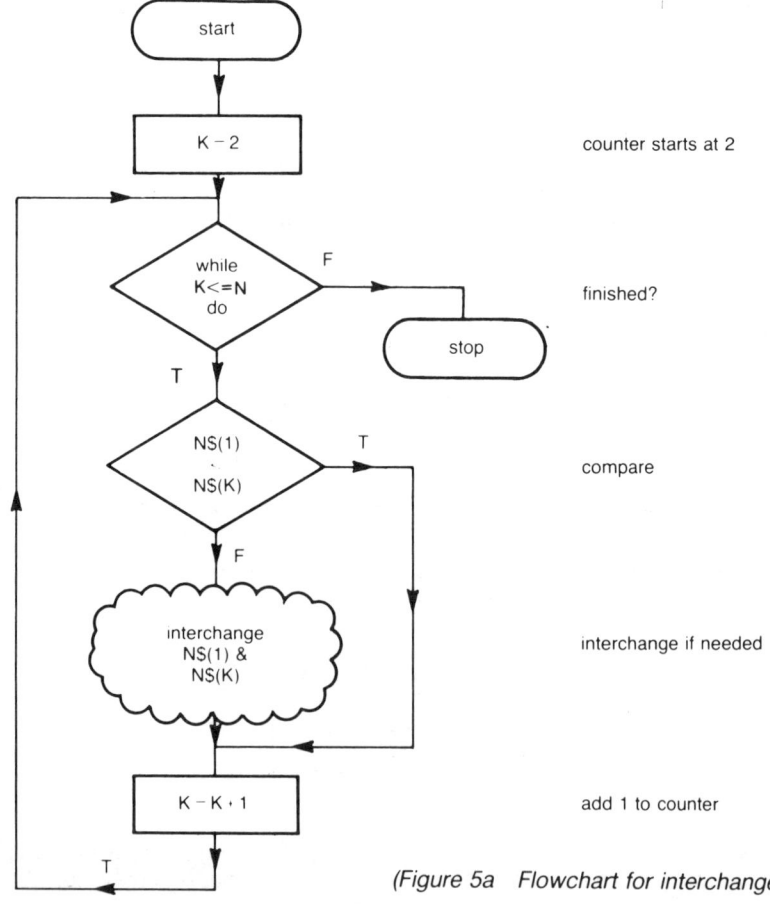

(Figure 5a   Flowchart for interchange)

Or, if we want to use the special flowchart symbol for FOR . . . NEXT . . ., it would look like this:

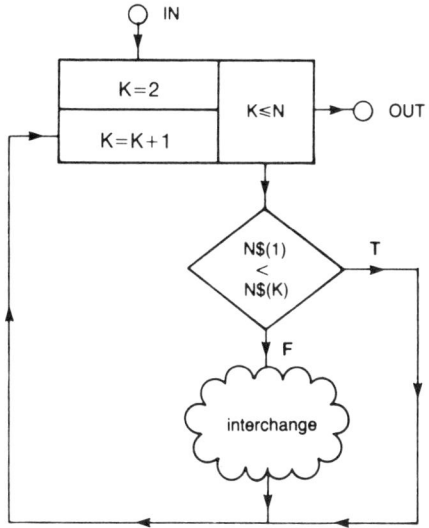

(Figure 5b   Flowchart for interchange with FOR . . . NEXT . . . symbol)

This new routine can now be used to construct a program.

Example 4
Write a program to enter a list of names, the list being of unknown length, into an array. Print out this list with index in input order. By means of the interchange routine place the name of lowest alphabetic value in position 1 in the list, and output the new list.

Solution

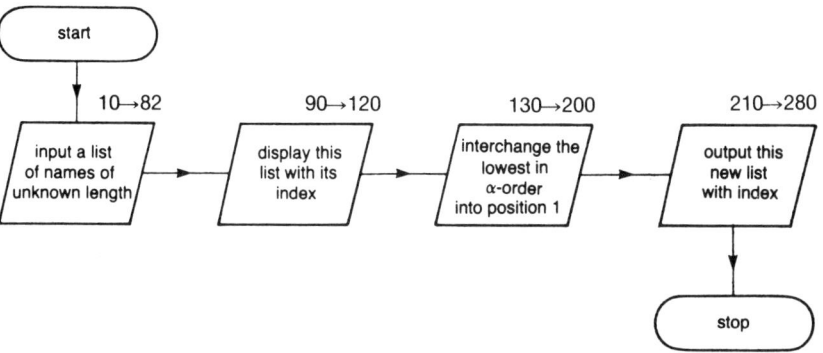

(Figure 6   Flowchart for Example 4)

Interchange program

```
10 REM**FIRST IN ALPHABETICAL ORDER**
15 OPTION BASE 1
20 DIM ANAME$(30)
30 INPUT "ENTER THE FIRST NAME";ANAME$(1)
40 LET C=1
50 WHILE ANAME$(C)<>"ZZZZ"
60 C=C+1
70 INPUT "NEXT NAME";ANAME$(C)
80 WEND
81 REM**DON'T WANT ZZZZ IN LIST**
82 C=C-1
90 REM**PRINT LIST**
100 FOR I=1 TO C
110 PRINT ANAME$(I)
120 NEXT I
130 REM**INTERCHANGE ROUTINE**
140 FOR K=2 TO C
150 WHILE ANAME$(1)>ANAME$(K)   2
160 REM**IN WRONG ORDER SO CHANGE**
170 LET TEMP$=ANAME$(K)
180 LET ANAME$(K)=ANAME$(1)
190 LET ANAME$(1)=TEMP$
195 WEND
200 NEXT K
210 REM**SORTED SO LIST 'EM**
220 PRINT
230 PRINT "LIST AFTER INTERCHANGE"
240 PRINT
250 PRINT "INDEX","ITEM"
260 FOR L=1 TO C
270 PRINT L,ANAME$(L)
280 NEXT L
290 END
```

Program 24 Finding the first item in alphabetical order

```
RUN
ENTER THE FIRST NAME? JONES
NEXT NAME? PRICE
NEXT NAME? DAVIES
NEXT NAME? EVANS
NEXT NAME? ZZZZ
JONES
PRICE
DAVIES
EVANS

LIST AFTER INTERCHANGE

INDEX           ITEM
1               DAVIES
2               PRICE
3               JONES
4               EVANS
OK
```

A note on WHILE...WEND...

In the last program, lines 150 to 195 make up a WHILE...WEND... loop. Instead of the loop we could have used:

```
IF ANAME$(1)>ANAME$(K) THEN LET TEMP$=ANAME$(K)
IF ANAME$(1)>ANAME$(K) THEN LET ANAME$(K)=ANAME$(1)
IF ANAME$(1)>ANAME$(K) THEN LET ANAME$(1)=TEMP$
```

This would have done the same job as the WHILE ... WEND ... loop but it is neater to use a loop as the condition is stated only once. A list of IF lines, all with the same condition, can only be replaced by a loop if the condition is no longer TRUE after the IF lines have acted. In Program 24 the condition is no longer TRUE when the computer comes to line 195 because the strings have been put in order, so the loop does not repeat endlessly.

If a print routine is inserted into the interchange procedure as below (lines 196–199), then we can look at the effect of each pass round the loop.

```
130 REM**INTERCHANGE ROUTINE**
140 FOR K=2 TO C
150 WHILE ANAME$(1)>ANAME$(K)
160 REM**IN WRONG ORDER SO CHANGE**
170 LET TEMP$=ANAME$(K)
180 LET ANAME$(K)=ANAME$(1)
190 LET ANAME$(1)=TEMP$
195 WEND
196 FOR L=1 TO C
197 PRINT ANAME$(L);" ";
198 PRINT
199 NEXT L
200 NEXT K
```

K Program 24 with new lines 196 to 199.

Assignment 4

1. It will probably have occurred to you by now that, having placed the item of lowest value into position 1, we could repeat the procedure by placing the item of lowest value in the remainder of the list into position 2, and so on for the rest of the list. To sort the complete list in this way demands nested FOR ... NEXT ... loops.

   Modify Program 24 to sort a complete list into alphabetical order.

2. Input a file of names and associated telephone numbers into two lists, ANAME$(I) and TELNO$(I) respectively. Use the index I to search through the file to find a particular name, and if found then to output the associated telephone number.

Objectives of Unit 4

Now that you have completed this Unit, check that you are able to write simple programs using:

List store location names

    to input lists ☐

    to print lists ☐

Counters to count the number of items in a list ☐
FOR ... NEXT ... loops
    to print a list ☐
    to input a list ☐
    to print * layouts ☐
Nested loops
    to print * layouts ☐
Interchange routine ☐

Answers to SAQs and Exercises

SAQ 1

The six stages of the procedure are shown here in the following program run:

```
RUN
ENTER A LIST OF NAMES ONE BY ONE
END THE LIST WITH ZZZZ

NEXT NAME? 6
NEXT NAME? 8
NEXT NAME? 4
NEXT NAME? 7
NEXT NAME? 3
NEXT NAME? 9
NEXT NAME? 1
NEXT NAME? ZZZZ

INDEX      ITEM
1          6
2          8
3          4
4          7
5          3
6          9
7          1

6  8  4  7  3  9  1
4  8  6  7  3  9  1
4  8  6  7  3  9  1
3  8  6  7  4  9  1
3  8  6  7  4  9  1
1  8  6  7  4  9  3

LIST AFTER INTERCHANGE

INDEX      ITEM
1          1
2          8
3          6
4          7
5          4
6          9
7          3

OK
```

Exercise 1

```
  5 OPTION BASE 1
 10 DIM NUMBERS(30)
 20 REM**A LIST OF NUMBERS OF UNKNOWN LENGTH**
 30 INPUT "FIRST NUMBER";NUMBERS(1)
 40 LET COUNT=1
 50 WHILE NUMBERS(COUNT)<>-9999
 60 LET COUNT=COUNT+1
 70 INPUT "NEXT NUMBER";NUMBERS(COUNT)
 80 WEND
 90 REM************
100 REM REMEMBER COUNT COUNTED -9999 AS AN ITEM
110 LET N=COUNT-1
120 REM************
130 REM
140 REM**OUTPUT THE NUMBERS WHOSE INDEX IS ODD**
150 LET C=1
160 PRINT
170 PRINT
180 PRINT "ODD INDEX","ITEM"
190 WHILE C<=N
200 PRINT C,NUMBERS(C)
210 C=C+2
220 WEND
230 END
```

Program 25

```
RUN
FIRST NUMBER? 1
NEXT NUMBER? 2
NEXT NUMBER? 3
NEXT NUMBER? 4
NEXT NUMBER? 5
NEXT NUMBER? 6
NEXT NUMBER? 7
NEXT NUMBER? 8
NEXT NUMBER? 9
NEXT NUMBER? -9999

ODD INDEX      ITEM
 1              1
 3              3
 5              5
 7              7
 9              9
OK
```

SAQ 2
(a)   1, 3, 5, 7, 9
(b)   −30, −27, −24, −21, −18
(c)   8, 3, −2
(d)   −2, −6, −10

Exercise 2

```
10 REM**COMPOUND INTEREST**
20 PRINT "ENTER YEARS,DEPOSIT,%INTEREST"
30 INPUT YEARS ,DEPOSIT , INTEREST
40 REM***********************
50 FOR C=1 TO YEARS
60 LET YIELD=(INTEREST*DEPOSIT)/100
70 PRINT "YEAR ";C;"YIELD ";YIELD
80 LET DEPOSIT=DEPOSIT+YIELD
90 NEXT C
100 REM***********************
110 END
```
} The FOR ... NEXT ... loop

Program 26

```
RUN
ENTER YEARS, DEPOSIT, %INTEREST
? 5,500,11.25
YEAR          1         YIELD        56.25
YEAR          2         YIELD        62.57813
YEAR          3         YIELD        69.61816
YEAR          4         YIELD        77.4502
YEAR          5         YIELD        86.16336
OK
```

Exercise 3

```
10 REM**SQUARES AND CUBES**
20 PRINT"NUMBER","SQUARE","CUBE"
30 FOR I=1 TO 21 STEP (2)
40 LET S=I*I
50 LET C=I*I*I
60 PRINT I,S,C
70 NEXT I
80 END
```

Program 27

```
RUN
NUMBER       SQUARE      CUBE
1            1           1
3            9           27
5            25          125
7            49          343
9            81          729
11           121         1331
13           169         2197
15           225         3375
17           289         4913
19           361         6859
21           441         9261
```

SAQ 3

; suppresses the print return so that the print head stops after printing *. Thus the next * will be printed on the same line. Without ; the asterisks would be printed in a column 40 print lines deep.

Exercise 4

```
 10 REM**MULTIPLICATION TABLES**
 40 FOR T=7 TO 9
 50 FOR K=1 TO 12
 60 LET P=K*T
 70 PRINT K;" TIMES";T;"=";P
 80 NEXT K
 90 PRINT
100 NEXT T
110 END
```
Program 28

```
RUN
 1 TIMES 7=7
 2 TIMES 7=14
 3 TIMES 7=21
 4 TIMES 7=28
 5 TIMES 7=35
 6 TIMES 7=42
 7 TIMES 7=49
 8 TIMES 7=56
 9 TIMES 7=63
10 TIMES 7=70
11 TIMES 7=77
12 TIMES 7=84

 1 TIMES 8= 8
 2 TIMES 8=16
 3 TIMES 8=24
 4 TIMES 8=32
 5 TIMES 8=40
 6 TIMES 8=48
 7 TIMES 8=56
 8 TIMES 8=64
 9 TIMES 9=72
10 TIMES 8=80
11 TIMES 8=88
12 TIMES 8=96
```
— we still have a lot to learn about 'tabulation'

```
 1 TIMES 9=9
 2 TIMES 9=18
 3 TIMES 9=27
 4 TIMES 9=36
 5 TIMES 9=45
 6 TIMES 9=54
 7 TIMES 9=63
 8 TIMES 9=72
 9 TIMES 9=81
10 TIMES 9=90
11 TIMES 9=99
12 TIMES 9=108

OK
```

Exercise 5

```
10 INPUT "LENGTH OF RECTANGLE";L
20 INPUT "WIDTH OF RECTANGLE";W
30 FOR I=1 TO W
40 FOR J=1 TO L
50 PRINT "*";
60 NEXT J
70 PRINT
80 NEXT I
```

UNIT 5
An end to strings and PRINT

5.1	Introduction	116
5.2	Length of a string of characters	116
5.3	Frequency tables	117
5.4	Frequency diagrams	120
5.5	Tabulation	123
5.6	Cutting up strings	127
5.7	VAL	132
	Assignment 5	135
	Objectives of Unit 5	136
	Answers to SAQs and Exercises	136

5.1 Introduction

The earlier units were concerned with introducing topics; new ideas came thick and fast. This Unit is mainly concerned with strings, but you will meet the TAB and LOCATE statements which are important additions to your printing repertoire. The title of this Unit is a slight exaggeration, but by the end of the Unit you will have met most of the main string and print functions of the BASIC language.

5.2 Length of a string of characters

In Unit 3 we asked the qustion 'How long is a piece of string?'. At the time it may have seemed a rather facetious question, but the number of characters contained in a particular string storage location is often a vital piece of information. This is especially so if we are trying to use the memory allocation of a particular computer as efficiently as possible.

In BASIC the operation LEN(A$) gives the length of A$ as a number of characters.

Thus:

If A$="FRED" then LEN (A$)=4
If B$="I" then LEN (B$)=1

SAQ 1
What are the values of the following:

(a) LEN (C$) where C$="ANN"
(b) LEN (D$) where D$="A"
(c) LEN (E$) where E$="72"
(d) LEN (F$) where F$="CAT 123"

Example 1
Write a BASIC program to input a list of words, ending with ZZZZ, and to print out the length of each word.

Solution
We have arranged the program to read in the words from a DATA statement in order to reduce the inputting time needed. Each word read from DATA is held in WORD$ (line 100) and its length stored in LENGTH (line 80). Then the result is printed out at line 90.

```
10 REM**LENGTH OF A WORD**
20 REM********************
30 REM**READ WORDS FROM A DATA LIST ONE BY ONE**
40 REM**OUTPUT THEIR LENGTHS**
50 REM********************
60 READ WORD$
70 WHILE WORD$<>"ZZZZ"
80 LET LENGTH=LEN(WORD$)
90 PRINT WORD$;" HAS ";LENGTH;" LETTERS'
100 READ WORD$
110 WEND
120 END
```

lines 60–100: read word, calculate length and print

```
130 DATA DEVISE,AN,ALGORITHM,AND,WRITE,A,BASIC,PROGRAM
140 DATA ZZZZ
```
Program 1   Measuring word lengths

```
RUN
DEVISE HAS 6 LETTERS
AN HAS 2 LETTERS
ALGORITHM HAS 9 LETTERS
AND HAS 3 LETTERS
WRITE HAS 5 LETTERS
A HAS 1 LETTERS
BASIC HAS 5 LETTERS
PROGRAM HAS 7 LETTERS
```

boxed(K) Program 1.

5.3 Frequency tables

Measuring the frequency with which something occurs is commonly needed in handling numerical information. For example, a knowledge of the frequency with which certain letters occur in normal language usage is an important factor in code-breaking activities. In order to measure frequencies it is useful to be able to use the simple technique used in statistical analysis of tally marks. This first paper and pencil example introduces this.

Tally marks

Example 2
Find the frequency with which each vowel occurs in the words in the following DATA statements.

```
900 DATA THE,HORSE,STOOD,STILL,TILL,HE,HAD,FINISHED,THE,
    HYMN
910 DATA WHICH,JUDE,REPEATED,UNDER,THE,SWAY,OF,A,
    POLYTHEISTIC
920 DATA FANCY,THAT,HE,WOULD,NEVER,HAVE,THOUGHT,OF,
    HUMOURING
930 DATA IN,BROAD,DAYLIGHT,ZZZZ
```

Solution
There are two ways to approach the problem:

(a)   Go through crossing out and counting up all the As, and then through again counting the number of Es, etc. This would involve five passes through the data for fairly sparse information (i.e. for a low hit-rate);

(b)   Draw up a table as below and take each vowel in sequence:

THE̸: put a *tally mark* in the E row;

HO̸RSE̸: put a mark in the O row, followed by another in the E row;

STO̸O̸D: put two more marks in the O row.

Vowel	Count				Total count or frequency
A	1111	1111			9
E	1111	1111	1111	1	16
I	1111	1111			10
O	1111	1111			10
U	1111	1			6

```
900 DATA THE,HORSE,STOOD,STILL,TILL,HE,HAD,FINISHED,THE,
    HYMN
910 DATA WHICH,JUDE,REPEATED,UNDER,THE,SWAY,OF,A,
    POLYTHEISTIC
920 DATA FANCY,THAT,HE,WOULD,NEVER,HAVE,THOUGHT,OF,
    HUMOURING
930 DATA IN,BROAD,DAYLIGHT,ZZZZ
```

(Figure 1   Completed tally count)

SAQ 2
Use the tally method to draw up a frequency table of the lengths of words for the data in Example 2.

Getting the computer to count
Having found a paper and pencil method of counting frequencies, we now need a method of getting the computer to do the counting of a list. The power of lists is derived from an apt use of the index. In question 2 of Assignment 4 we saw how the items of two lists of data (name and telephone number lists) were linked by a common index. The third member of the number-list was the telephone number for the third name in the name-list, etc. Generally the I-th member of the name-list is linked with the I-th member of number-list.

Suppose we want to count the number of times the digits 0, 1, 2 . . . 9 occur in a sequence. We can use 10 counters:

```
C(0), C(1), C(2)...C(9)
```

each of which will be zero at the start. To count the digits in 473808 we take the first digit in the sequence: 4. 1 is added to C(4) and so on:

Digits entered	Counters after entry									
	C(0)	C(1)	C(2)	C(3)	C(4)	C(5)	C(6)	C(7)	C(8)	C(9)
start	0	0	0	0	0	0	0	0	0	0
4	0	0	0	0	1	0	0	0	0	0
7	0	0	0	0	1	0	0	1	0	0
3	0	0	0	1	1	0	0	1	0	0
8	0	0	0	1	1	0	0	1	1	0
0	1	0	0	1	1	0	0	1	1	0
8	1	0	0	1	1	0	0	1	2	0

So the idea is that when I is entered at the key-board, increment C(I) by 1. This can be achieved in just two BASIC statements.

```
120 INPUT I
140 LET C(I)=C(I)+1
```
⎯ A list counter

SAQ 3
The sequence

```
10 INPUT N
20 LET C(N)=C(N)+1
```

is used to count the number of 0s, 1s, 2s, etc. in the following input data: 3, 1, 0, 5, 9, 9, 6, 6, 6, 0, 4, 4, 2, 4, 1, 2, 1, 3, 0, 2, 1, 3. What are the values of the following?

(a) C(3) after 3 numbers have been inputted.
(b) C(9) after 12 numbers have been inputted.
(c) C(1) after all the numbers have been inputted.
(d) C(0) after all the numbers have been inputted.

We will now use this method of counting a list in an example.

Example 3
Write a program to input a sequence of single digits and to output the frequency with which each digit occurs.

Solution
A digit is one of the set of 10 numbers 0, 1, 2, 3 . . . 9. We will enter these one by one, with the sequence being terminated by −9999. So far, very routine!

The counting list will have 10 counters:

C(0), C(1), C(2)... C(9)

The program to solve the complete problem has two parts. (i) The input and increment routine incorporates the two statements (70 and 90) discussed above. (ii) The output routine is driven by a FOR . . . NEXT . . . loop, with index J running from 0 to 9.

```
  5 OPTION BASE 0          ⎯ This statement is optional
                             as the default is 0
 10 REM**COUNT THE NUMBER OF TIMES EACH DIGIT IS
    ENTERED**
 20 REM**AND STORE IN A COUNT LIST COUNT(I)**
 30 REM*****************
 40 DIM COUNT(10)
 50 PRINT "ENTER A SERIES OF SINGLE DIGITS"
 60 PRINT "ENDING THE LIST WITH -9999"
 70 INPUT "FIRST DIGIT";DIGIT
 80 WHILE DIGIT<>-9999
 90 LET COUNT(DIGIT)=COUNT(DIGIT)+1
100 INPUT "NEXT DIGIT";DIGIT
110 WEND
```

```
120 REM***************
130 PRINT
140 PRINT "DIGIT","COUNT"
150 PRINT
160 FOR J=0 TO 9
170 PRINT J,COUNT(J)
180 NEXT J
190 END
```

Program 2   Counting with a list counter Count(l)

Typical output
(after entering 3, 7, 6, 4, 9, 1, 4, 9, 2, 7, 8, 0, 1, 5, 2, 7, −9999.)

DIGIT	COUNT
0	1
1	2
2	2
3	1
4	2
5	1
6	1
7	3
8	1
9	2

K Program 2.

Frequency table for string lengths
We have written two programs so far in this Unit: the first to find the lengths of strings, and the second to build up a frequency table.

In the following exercise we want you to combine these two ideas to build up a frequency table of lengths of words. If you wish you can use the words in the DATA statements already used in Example 2. Assume that the words will not be longer than 15 characters, so the length-list will have elements:

L(1), L(2), L(3)...   L(15).

Exercise 1
Write a program to read in a set of words and to display a frequency table of their lengths.

5.4 Frequency diagrams

Frequency diagram for number of vowels
The picture of tally marks in Figure 1 makes a more immediate impact on us and somehow gives us more information about the distribution of frequencies of the vowels than just the column of figures. So why not get the computer to print a picture for us? You saw how to print rows of asterisks in Unit 4 by driving the print head across the page (or screen) with a FOR . . . NEXT . . . loop of variable range.

SAQ 4
What will appear on the screen as a result of the following program?

```
 10 READ A
 20 WHILE A<>-9999
 30 FOR I=1 TO A
 40 PRINT "*";
 50 NEXT I
 60 PRINT
 70 READ A
 80 WEND
 90 END
100 DATA 5,5,4,3,2,1,-9999
```
Program 3

We can do the same thing using the frequencies from Figure 1 to determine the range and thus the number of asterisks printed across the page. This will generate a picture of the distribution.

Example 4
Write a program to print out a frequency diagram for the distribution of vowels given in Example 2.

Solution
Notice that the program draws the diagram from the frequencies we have already calculated. We have stored these frequencies in line 250.

We read the frequencies (lines 60 to 100) with a counter AFREQ(K) where AFREQ(1) is the number of As, AFREQ(2) the number of Es, etc.

Then we print the asterisks across the page according to the value of AFREQ(K) (lines 170 to 230).

```
  5 OPTION BASE 1
 10 REM**FREQUENCY DISTRIBUTION**
 20 REM**PREPARATION PICTURE**
 30 REM**FREQUENCY LIST IS AFREQ(K)**
 40 DIM AFREQ(18)
 50 LET K=1
 60 READ AFREQ(K)
 70 WHILE AFREQ(K)<>-9999         reading the frequencies and
 80 LET K=K+1                     storing them in AFREQ(1), AFREQ(2)...
 90 READ AFREQ(K)
100 WEND
110 REM*****************
120 REM**DON'T ADD -9999**
130 LET N=K+1
140 PRINT**PRINT ROUTINE**
150 PRINT
160 FOR X=1 TO N
170 WHILE AFREQ(X)<>0
180 FOR Y=1 TO AFREQ(X)
190 PRINT "*";                    printing * across
200 NEXT Y                        the page
210 REM**CHANGE AFREQ(X) TO FOOL LOOP**
```

```
220 AFREQ(X)=0
230 WEND
240 PRINT
250 PRINT
260 NEXT X
270 REM***************
275 DATA 0,1
280 DATA 1,5,4,6,9,0,1,3,1,0,0,1,0,0,0,-9999
```

Program 4 Drawing a frequency distribution

K Program 4.

Frequency diagram for length of words

If we want to draw a diagram of the frequencies with which the word lengths occurred in SAQ 2, we need to modify Program 4. Two modifications are necessary:

First, the frequency list contains more items. There are 17 frequencies (1 to 17) plus −9999, so that's 18 items and we add 40 DIM AFREQ(18) to Program 4.

Second, the print routine at line 170 will run into problems when the frequency is zero. We can't drive the FOR... NEXT... loop from 1 to 0! So we must prevent the program going into the FOR... NEXT... loop when the frequency is zero. To do this we add a WHILE... WEND... loop.

So the program is

```
  5 OPTION BASE 1
 10 REM**FREQUENCY DISTRIBUTION**
 20 REM**PREPARATION PICTURE**
 30 REM**FREQUENCY LIST IS AFREQ(K)**
 40 DIM AFREQ(18)
 50 LET K=1
 60 READ AFREQ(K)
 70 WHILE AFREQ(K)<>-9999
 80 LET K=K+1
 90 READ AFREQ(K)
100 WEND
110 REM***************
120 REM**DON'T ADD -9999**
130 LET N=K-1
140 REM**PRINT ROUTINE**
150 PRINT
160 FOR X=1 TO N
170 WHILE AFREQ(X)<>0
180 FOR Y=1 TO AFREQ(X)
190 PRINT "*";
200 NEXT Y
210 REM**CHANGE AFREQ(X) TO FOOL LOOP**
220 AFREQ(X)=0
230 WEND
240 PRINT
250 PRINT
260 NEXT X
```

```
270 REM****************
275 DATA 0,1
280 DATA 1,5,4,6,9,0,1,3,1,0,0,1,0,0,0,-9999
```

modified Program 4

A run of the modified Program 4 produces:

```
*
*****
****
******
*********

*
***
*

*
```
───────────────▶─────────── print out ends about here!

(Figure 2 Frequency diagram of modified Program 4)

K Program 4 (modified).

5.5 Tabulation

We've got the essential ingredients of a picture, but it is still far from being a meaningful diagram. It will help if we have the facility to move the print head across the page or screen to any pre-determined position. This is called tabulation (to arrange in tabular or table-form). In BASIC the TAB function does this for us.

We take the same approach as we did in Unit 3, namely to write a snippet of program which explains itself – an approach well worth cultivating!

First, look at what happens if you number print positions across the screen:

```
50 PRINT "123456789012345678901234567890 1234567890"
60 PRINT "A";TAB(5);"E";TAB(7);"I";TAB(19);"O";TAB(31);"U"

RUN
123456789012345678901234567890 1234567890
A   E I           O           U
OK
```

Program 5

You can see that TAB(5) printed E at the *sixth position*. Why? Because the machine counts print positions from position 0. This is demonstrated by Program 6 where the scale across the screen goes from 0:

```
50 PRINT"01234567890123456789012345678901234567 89"
60 PRINT"A";TAB(5);"E";TAB(7);"I";TAB(19);"O";TAB(31);"U"

RUN
01234567890123456789012345678901234567 89
A    E I            O              U
OK
```

Program 6

Now TAB(5) goes to the position labelled 5, but it is still in the sixth position across the screen.

SAQ 5
Write a program to print COL 1, COL 2, COL 3 across the screen with COL 1 starting at position 0, COL 2 at position 10 and COL 3 at position 20.

Variable TAB and its effects
We can drive line 60 of the vowel print with a FOR ... NEXT ... loop to produce an actual table.

```
50 FOR I=1 TO 7
60 PRINT "A";TAB(5);"E";TAB(7);"I";TAB(19);"O";
   TAB(31);"U"
70 NEXT I
```

Program 7

```
RUN
A    E I            O              U
A    E I            O              U
A    E I            O              U
A    E I            O              U
A    E I            O              U
A    E I            O              U
A    E I            O              U
OK
```

Here is an example which shows how we can drive TAB with a variable. If we use TAB(V) where V is a variable, we can drive the print head to different positions across the screen. The program

```
30 FOR A=1 TO 10
40 PRINT TAB(A);"HELLO"  ——— Value of A in TAB(A) is determined by
50 NEXT A                     the loop variable A
60 END
```

Program 8

produces:

```
RUN
  HELLO
   HELLO
    HELLO
     HELLO
      HELLO
       HELLO
        HELLO
         HELLO
          HELLO
           HELLO
OK
```

We can go one step further and combine these two effects in one program:

```
50 FOR I=1 TO 7
60 PRINT TAB(0+I);"A";TAB(5+I);"E";TAB(7+I);"I";
65 PRINT TAB(19+I);"O";TAB(3ı+I);"U"
70 NEXT I
80 END
```

Program 9

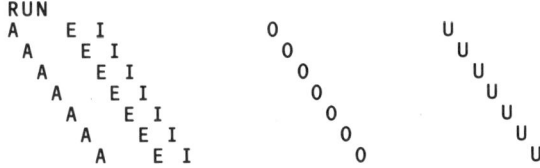

SAQ 6
Write a program segment to input three numbers of the user's choice which will place the string "HEADING" at three different positions across the same output line.

TAB and the frequency diagram
We are now in a position to set out the frequency diagram of Figure 2 in a more attractive manner.

The print routine of the modified Program 4 (lines 150 to 280) was:

```
150 PRINT
160 FOR X=1 TO N
170 WHILE AFREQ(X)<>0
180 FOR Y=1 TO AFREQ(X)
190 PRINT "*";
200 NEXT Y
210 REM**CHANGE AFREQ(X) TO FOOL LOOP**
220 AFREQ(X)=0
230 WEND
240 PRINT
250 PRINT
260 NEXT X
```

125

```
270 REM****************
275 DATA 0,1
280 DATA 1,5,4,6,9,0,1,3,1,0,0,1,0,0,0,-9999
```

Program 4 (modified)

We can now add the following new lines:
line 160 to print column headings
line 170 to print a rule across the screen
line 180 to start the column divides (the rest of the divides we printed by the following loop)
line 200 (in the loop) prints X and AFREQ(X) across the page plus the column divides. This line ends in ";" which makes the next PRINT instruction (line 230) appear on the same line.

You will probably have to study this carefully to see all the detail in it:
(lines 5 to 130: see Program 4.)

```
140 REM**PRINT ROUTINE**
150 PRINT
160 PRINT "LENGTH";TAB(8);"AFREQ";TAB(18);"TALLY"
170 PRINT " _____ "
180 PRINT TAB(7);"I";TAB(12);"I"
190 FOR X=1 TO N
200 PRINT TAB(2);X;TAB(7);"I";TAB(9);AFREQ(X);
    TAB(12);"I";TAB(14);
210 WHILE AFREQ(X)<>0
220 FOR Y=1 TO AFREQ(X)
230 PRINT "*";
240 NEXT Y
241 AFREQ(X)=0
242 WEND
250 PRINT
260 NEXT X
270 REM*****************************
280 DATA 1,5,4,6,9,0,1,3,1,0,0,1,0,0,0,-9999
```

Program 10

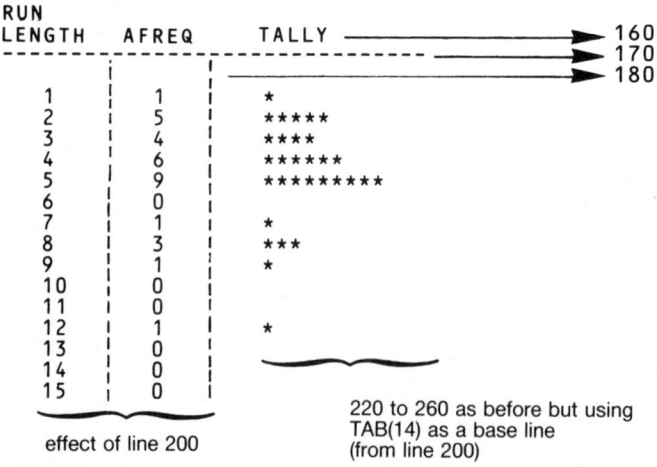

220 to 260 as before but using TAB(14) as a base line (from line 200)

effect of line 200

K Program 10.

Exercise 2

Modify Program 4 to give a printout similar to that developed for Program 10 and to include the following points:

(a) an appropriate change of headings;
(b) a printout of the letters A,E,I,O and U as appropriate in the left-hand column;
(c) an appropriate scale at the base of the diagram.

5.6 Cutting up strings

Let's now look at a string which, though being an entity in its own right, contains more than one item of information. For example, 23 June 1971 is a single date but there are occasions when we want to look at only part of it, e.g. the month.

Filing dates

How many times have you been faced with a box on a form like this?

Date						
	D	D	M	M	Y	Y

If we look at D D M M Y Y the presentation has problems. Compare

    23 June 1971, or 230671

with

    14 Sept 1973, or 140973

The later date has the smaller number. Whereas with

    4 July 1933, or 040733

and

    15 Jan 1967, or 150167

the later date has the larger number. Clearly then D D M M Y Y is not very useful for filing dates.

The solution is to put the dates in the form Y Y M M D D. This makes the four dates above:

330704, 670115, 710623, and 730914

giving date and number consistency.

Dates are usually stored as numbers in the machine for use in calculations but are entered as strings to allow checking procedures to occur before they are stored.

If we are interested in a salary increment, then the year and month parts of the number would be important. If we are a music centre and send out reminders to our clients every three months to have their pianos tuned, then only the month may be important. The whole data-string is important in its own right, but we can see that there may be valid reasons for cutting it up.

LEFT$(X$,I) and RIGHT$(X$,I)

If we want to consider part of a string, then we need a statement that will do this for us. We will start with two such statements.

LEFT$(X$,I) gives the left-most I characters of the string X$.

e.g. if X$="CUTTING"
then LEFT$(X$,3)=CUT

RIGHT$(X$,I) gives the right-most I characters of X$.

RIGHT$(X$,4)=TING

Let's get the machine to tell us its own story. We enter a 6-character string and use the index I of the FOR . . . NEXT . . . loop to peel off sub-strings of lengths 1 to 6. The scale (line 30) helps you to identify what's happening.

```
10 REM**STRING TEST**
20 INPUT "ENTER A 6-CHARACTER STRING";X$
30 PRINT TAB(10);"1234567890"
40 FOR I=1 TO 6
50 LET A$=LEFT$(X$,I)
60 PRINT I;TAB(10);A$
70 NEXT I
```

Program 11

Left string run

```
RUN
ENTER A 6-CHARACTER STRING? 123456
          1234567890
1         1
2         12
3         123
4         1234
5         12345
6         123456
OK
```

Now if we change line 50 of Program 11 to

`50 LET A$=RIGHT$(X$,I)`

and enter the string ABCDEF, the result is:

Right string run

```
RUN
ENTER A 6-CHARACTER STRING? ABCDEF
          1234567890
1         F
2         EF
3         DEF
4         CDEF
5         BCDEF
6         ABCDEF
OK
```

[K] Program 11. Then change line 50 for RIGHT$.

SAQ 7
If A$="1A2B3C4D", what are the following?

(a) LEFT$(A$,1)
(b) LEFT$(A$,4)
(c) RIGHT$(A$,3)
(d) RIGHT$(A$,4)

Cutting up strings of variable length
Program 11 is a bit awkward because we had to specify (in line 40) how long the string was to be: 6 characters. But we might want to input strings of any length. This is easily done by modifying Program 11 so that the computer measures the length of the string we input and runs that length to control the FOR ... NEXT ... loop. The modifications required are:

```
10 REM**STRING TEST**
20 INPUT "ENTER A STRING";X$
30 PRINT TAB(10);"1234567890"
40 FOR I=1 TO LEN(X$) ———————— LEN(X$) acts as the upper limit of the loop.
50 LET A$=LEFT$(X$,I)
60 PRINT A$
70 NEXT I
80 END
```
Program 12

```
RUN
ENTER A STRING? HAMSTRING
          1234567890
1         H
2         HA
3         HAM
4         HAMS
5         HAMST
6         HAMSTR
7         HAMSTRI
8         HAMSTRIN
9         HAMSTRING
OK
```
[K] Program 12.

Exercise 3
Write a program to output those words in the DATA statements in Example 2 (page 117) which begin with a vowel.

Exercise 4
Write a program to change the output of the RIGHT$ run of Program 11 to:

```
     F
    EF
   DEF
  CDEF
 BCDEF
ABCDEF
```

MID$(X$,I,J)

We have used LEFT$ and RIGHT$ to cut sections off either end of a string, but we might want a section in the middle of a string, e.g. MM in YYMMDD. There is another BASIC statement that will give us a section of this type:

```
MID$(X$,I,J)
```

This will cut a sub-string of length J, starting from position I:

```
MID$(X$,I,J)
```
          └── length of sub-string from position I
              └── position in the string

e.g. IF X$="POSITION"

MID$(X$,5,2)=TI

and MID$(X$,2,4)=OSIT

We will use the computer again to demonstrate MID$ at work by a further modification to Program 11. We have already adapted Program 11 to allow us to input a string of any length. This gave us Program 12. If we now change line 50 of Program 12 to

```
50 LET A$=MID$(X$,I,1)
```

and input SHOESTRING we get:

```
10 REM**STRING TEST**
20 INPUT "ENTER A STRING";X$
30 PRINT TAB(10);"1234567890"
40 FOR I=1 TO LEN(X$)
50 LET A$=MID$(X$,I,1)
60 PRINT I;TAB(10);A$
70 NEXT I
80 END
```
Program 13

```
RUN
ENTER A STRING? SHOESTRING
          1234567890
1         S
2         H
3         O
4         E
5         S
6         T
7         R
8         I
9         N
10        G
OK
```

Here MID$ is looking at all possible sub-strings of length 1.

If we now use

```
50 LET A$=MID$(X$,I,2)
```

and input STRINGENT we get:

```
RUN
ENTER A STRING? STRINGENT
              1234567890
1             ST
2             TR
3             RI
4             IN
5             NG
6             GE
7             EN
8             NT
9             T  ─────────────  'null' string
OK
```

[K] Program 13.

The last sub-string caused problems. We can't get a sub-string 2 characters long from a string of 9 characters starting at the 9th character. In trying to do so we enter a default state, and are given a null-string as a reward. There must always be enough characters left of the original string to take out the sub-string.

Generally, if we wish to take out J characters we will not be able to start this sub-string beyond the (LEN(X$)−J+1)th position.

Yes, +1.

e.g. if LEN(X$)=10 and J=3, then LEN(X$)−J=7.

but we can get a sub-string of length 3 from a string of length 10 if we start at 8, i.e. character positions 8, 9, 10 of the original string.

SAQ 8
Write a program to accept as input London telephone numbers in the form 01 XXX XXXX and output the exchange codes only. (Remember that the spaces are characters just as much as the digits.)

Mid-string program
As you have probably spotted, MID$ can cut left sub-strings and right sub-strings if we want it to. In other words, it can give us every possible sub-string. Here is a program that makes it do that for us. First it prints out all sub-strings of length 1, then all of length 2 and so on until it prints the whole word which is the only sub-string of the same length as the word itself!

```
 10 REM**STRING TEST**
 20 INPUT "ENTER A STRING";X$
 30 PRINT " J";TAB(5);" I";TAB(10);"1234567890"
 40 FOR J=1 TO LEN(X$)
 50 FOR I=1 TO LEN(X$)-J+1
 60 LET A$=MID$(X$,I,J)
 70 PRINT J;TAB(5);I;TAB(10);A$
 80 NEXT I
 90 PRINT " "                    J is the length of the sub-string,
100 NEXT J                       starting at I.
110 END
```

Program 14

```
RUN
ENTER A STRING? STRING
```

J	I	1234567890	Note headings and scale
1	1	S	
1	2	T	
1	3	R	
1	4	I	
1	5	N	
1	6	G	
2	1	ST	
2	2	TR	
2	3	RI	
2	4	IN	
2	5	NG	
3	1	STR	
3	2	TRI	
3	3	RIN	
3	4	ING	
4	1	STRI	
4	2	TRIN	
4	3	RING	
5	1	STRIN	
5	2	TRING	
6	1	STRING	

OK

K Program 14.

5.7 VAL

Having found a method of cutting up strings, we now need a method of examining what we have got. One such method is to use VAL(A$) which looks at the numeric value of A$.

VAL(A$) gives us the numerical value of the string A$ provided A$ starts with +, − or a digit. In all other cases, VAL(A$)=0.

Program to demonstrate VAL
In the following program we input seven strings (123456, 12345A, ... ABCDEF) and look at VAL for the string, VAL for the left-string of 2 characters and VAL of the mid-string of 2 characters starting from the third character.

You will see that if the left-most character of the string (or sub-strings) is a digit, then a value will be given, even if the rest of the string contains non-numeric characters.

```
10 REM**THE VAL FUNCTION**
20 INPUT "FIRST STRING";N$
30 WHILE N$<>"ZZZZ"
40 LET N=VAL(N$)
50 LET P=VAL(LEFT$(N$,2))
60 LET Q=VAL(MID$(N$,3,2))
70 PRINT " "
80 PPINT N,P,Q
90 PRINT " "
```

```
100 INPUT "NEXT STRING";N$
110 WEND
120 END
```

Program 15

```
RUN
FIRST STRING?    123456
123456           12         34

NEXT STRING?     12345A
12345            12         34

NEXT STRING?     1234AB
1234             12         34

NEXT STRING?     123ABC
123              12         3

NEXT STRING?     12ABCD
12               12         0

NEXT STRING?     1ABCDE
1                1          0

NEXT STRING?     ABCDEF
0                0          0
```

VAL still gives the value of the left-most digits, even though the string contains AB–non-numeric characters.

A is now at position 3, so VAL(N$)=0

K Program 15.

SAQ 9
(a) VAL(A$) where A$=54
(b) VAL(B$) where B$=76XY
(c) VAL(C$) where C$=A3
(d) VAL(D$) where D$=−132
(e) VAL(LEFT$(E$,2)) where E$=593
(f) VAL(LEFT$(F$,1)) where F$=8AM
(g) VAL(LEFT$(G$,2)) where G$=Z35
(h) VAL(RIGHT$(H$,1)) where H$=593
(i) VAL(RIGHT$(I$,2)) where I$=8AM
(j) VAL(RIGHT$(J$,2)) where J$=Z35

Date string check
We are now in a position to see how VAL can be put to practical use, in this case to check the accuracy of dates keyed into a computer. This is typical of what happens in computers all the time. We know errors will frequently happen when data is keyed in so, wherever possible, we try to use the computer to detect the errors.

Example 4
Write a program to carry out data checks on the 3 fields of a 6-digit date-string.

Solution
The date-string ADATE$ has three fields in the form:

YY   MM   DD — RIGHT$(ADATE$,2)
            MID$(ADATE$,3,2)
      LEFT$(ADATE$,2)

We are going to consider the year 1988 only; so:

VAL(LEFT$(ADATE$,2)) should be 88,
VAL(MID$(ADATE$,3,2)) should have a range of 1–12,
VAL(RIGHT$(ADATE$,2)) should have a range of 1–31.

This is a fairly complex process so we first need to decide on the steps involved. These are given in the following flowchart:

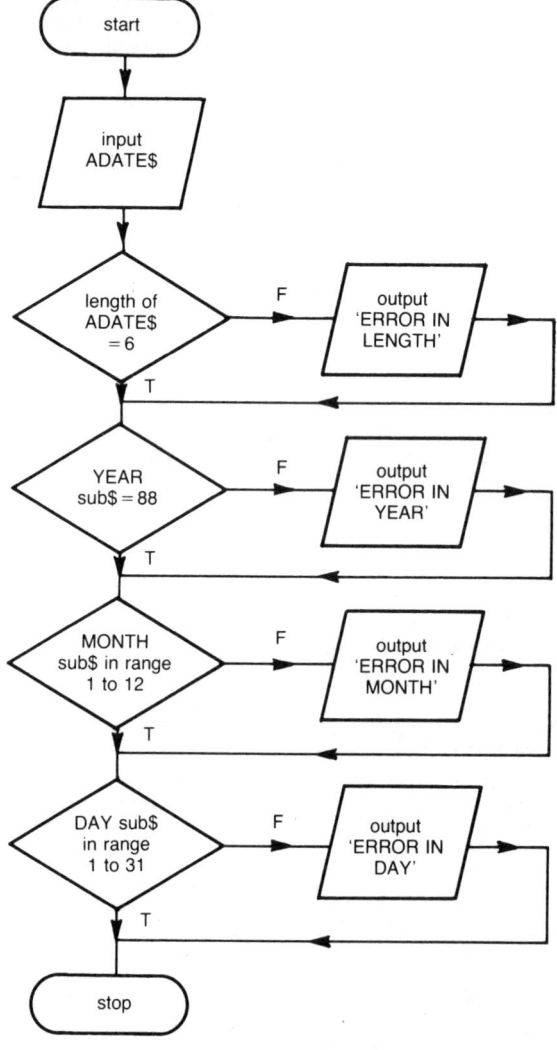

(Figure 3 Flowchart showing the four checks on YYMMDD)

The program is fairly straightforward as it goes through each of the four checks. If any check fails, the program prints an error message and carries on.

```
10 REM**DATE CHECK**
20 INPUT "FIRST DATE";ADATE$
30 WHILE ADATE$<>"ZZZZ"
40 IF LEN(ADATE$)<>6 THEN PRINT "ERROR IN LENGTH"
50 IF VAL(LEFT$(ADATE$,2))<>88 THEN PRINT
   "ERROR IN YEAR"
60 IF VAL(MID$(ADATE$,3,2))<1 THEN PRINT
   "ERROR IN MONTH"
70 IF VAL(MID$(ADATE$,3,2))>12 THEN PRINT
   "ERROR IN MONTH"
80 IF VAL(RIGHT$(ADATE$,3,2))<1 THEN PRINT
   "ERROR IN DAY"
90 IF VAL(RIGHT$(ADATE$,2))>31 THEN PRINT
   "ERROR IN DAY"
100 PRINT
110 INPUT "NEXT DATE";ADATE$
120 WEND
130 END
```

Program 16

Typical run

```
RUN
FIRST DATE? 1234567
ERROR IN LENGTH
ERROR IN YEAR
ERROR IN MONTH
ERROR IN DAY

NEXT DATE? 123456
ERROR IN YEAR
ERROR IN MONTH
ERROR IN DAY

NEXT DAY? 883456
ERROR IN MONTH
ERROR IN DAY

NEXT DATE? 881256
ERROR IN DAY

NEXT DATE? 881204

NEXT DATE?
```

K Program 16.

Assignment 5

1. Write a program to find the frequency with which each vowel occurs in the words in the JUDE data of Example 2, giving also a summary of the total number of vowels and consonants which occur in these words.

2. Write a program to input a string of characters and to output this string in reverse order

Objectives of Unit 5

Check that you are now able to write simple programs:

Using LEN(A$) ☐

Using LET C(I)=C(I)+1 to count frequencies ☐

To print a frequency diagram ☐

Using TAB to print in columns ☐

Using TAB to print a frequency table with headings and scale ☐

Using LEFT$(X$,I) and RIGHT$(X$,I) ☐

Using MID$(X$,I,J) ☐

Using VAL(A$) ☐

Answers to SAQs and Exercises

SAQ 1
(a) 3;
(b) 1;
(c) 2 (not 72 – LEN counts the number of characters);
(d) 7 (LEN counts the characters regardless of whether they are numbers, letters or spaces).

SAQ 2
Your answer should be:

Word length	Count	Total
1	1	1
2	1111̶	5
3	1111	4
4	1111̶ 1	6
5	1111̶ 1111	9
6		0
7	1	1
8	111	3
9	1	1
10		0
11		0
12	1	1
13		0
14		0
15		0

SAQ 3
(a) C(3)=1 (not 3! C(3) has counted the number of 3s inputted.)
(b) C(9)=2
(c) C(1)=4
(d) C(0)=3

Exercise 1

The solution appears in the following text (modified Program 4, page 122).

SAQ 4

```
*****
*****
****
***
**
*
```

SAQ 5

```
10 PRINT "COL1";TAB(10);"COL2";TAB(20);"COL3"
```

SAQ 6

```
10 INPUT A,B,C
20 PRINT TAB(A);"HEADING";TAB(B);"HEADING";TAB(C);
   "HEADING"
```

Program 17

Exercise 2

```
  5 OPTION BASE 1
 10 REM**FREQUENCY DISTRIBUTION**
 20 REM**PEPARATION PICTURE**
 30 REM**FREQUENCY LIST IS AFREQ(K)**
 40 DIM VOWEL$(5)
 50 DIM AFREQ(5)
 60 FOR I=1 TO 5          ⎤
 70 READ VOWEL$(I)         ├────── reads vowels
 80 NEXT I                 ⎦
 90 FOR I=1 TO 5          ⎤
100 READ AFREQ(I)          ├────── reads frequency
110 NEXT I                 ⎦
111 N=I-1 ──────────────────────── gets rid of -9999
120 REM****************
130 REM**PRINT ROUTINE**
140 PRINT
150 PRINT "VOWEL";TAB(8);"AFREQ";TAB(18);"TALLY"
160 PRINT "-------"
170 FOR X=1 TO N
180 PRINT TAB(2);VOWEL$(X);TAB(7);"I";TAB(10);AFREQ(X);
    TAB(14);"I";TAB(16);
190 FOR Y=1 TO AFREQ(X)
200 PRINT "*";
210 NEXT Y
220 PRINT
230 NEXT X
240 PRINT "...SCALE...";TAB(15);"0....5....0....5....0"
250 REM*******
260 DATA A,E,I,O,U
270 DATA 9,16,10,10,6
```

Program 18

```
VOWEL   AFREQ   TALLY
---------------------------------
  A       9     *********
  E      16     ****************
  I      10     **********
  O      10     **********
  U       6     ******
....SCALE....0....5....0....5....0
```

K Program 18.

SAQ 7
(a) 1;
(b) 1A2B;
(c) C4D;
(d) 3C4D.

Notice that LEFT$ and RIGHT$ treat all characters in a string in the same way. It doesn't matter whether they are numbers or letters, they still get counted.

Exercise 3

```
 10 REM**IS LEFT-MOST CHARACTER A VOWEL?**
 20 READ WORD$
 30 WHILE WORD$<>"ZZZZ"
 40 LET ALETTER$=LEFT$(WORD$,1)
 50 IF ALETTER$="A" THEN PRINT WORD$
 60 IF ALETTER$="E" THEN PRINT WORD$
 70 IF ALETTER$="I" THEN PRINT WORD$
 80 IF ALETTER$="O" THEN PRINT WORD$
 90 IF ALETTER$="U" THEN PRINT WORD$
100 READ WORD$
110 WEND
120 END
130 DATA THE,HORSE,STOOD,STILL,TILL,HE,HAD,FINISHED,THE,
    HYMN
140 DATA WHICH,JUDE,REPEATED,UNDER,THE,SWAY,OF,A,
    POLYTHEISTIC
150 DATA FANCY,THAT,HE,WOULD,NEVER,HAVE,THOUGHT,OF,
    HUMOURING
160 DATA IN,BROAD,DAYLIGHT,ZZZZ
```
Program 19

```
RUN
UNDER
OF
A
OF
IN

OK
```

K Program 19.

Exercise 4
```
10 REM**STRING TEST**
20 INPUT "ENTER 6-CHARACTER STRING";X$
30 PRINT TAB(10);"1234567890"
40 FOR I=1 TO 6
50 LET A$=RIGHT$(X$,I)
```

```
60 PRINT I;TAB(16-I);A$
70 NEXT I
```

Program 20

```
RUN
ENTER 6-CHARACTER STRING? ABCDEF
                1234567890

1                    F
2                   EF
3                  DEF
4                 CDEF
5                BCDEF
6               ABCDEF

OK
```

K Program 20.

SAQ 8

```
10 INPUT "FIRST TELEPHONE NUMBER";N$
20 WHILE N$<>"ZZZZ"
30 PRINT MID$(N$,4,3)
40 INPUT "NEXT TELEPHONE NUMBER";N$
50 WEND
60 END
```

Program 21

K Program 21.

SAQ 9

(a) 54;
(b) 76 (stops at letters);
(c) 0 (starts with a letter. Therefore 0);
(d) −132;
(e) 59;
(f) 8;
(g) 0 (starts with a letter);
(h) 3;
(i) 0 (starts at A which is a letter);
(j) 35.

UNIT 6
Mainly about dice and games

6.1	Random numbers	**142**
6.2	The RND function	**143**
6.3	Random number postscript	**150**
6.4	Two examples	**151**
6.5	Keeping scores	**155**
6.6	Short cuts in program writing	**157**
6.7	Concatenation	**159**
6.8	STR$	**160**
	Assignment 6	**161**
	Objectives of Unit 6	**162**
	Answers to SAQs and Exercises	**162**

6.1 Random numbers

The programming function which allows us to inject a sense of fun into a program is the one which generates *random numbers*. This function is at the heart of many of the game-playing and simulation programs which are available for microcomputers.

You will have met random numbers when playing games; games that involve tossing a coin or throwing dice, or drawing numbers out of a hat. These domestic games have become institutionalised in casinos, bingo clubs, the ritualistic draw for the FA Cup competition, and, of course, on a larger scale, the monthly draw for premium bonds. Although we all have an intuitive idea of what we mean by a sequence of random numbers, it is quite difficult to define the idea clearly. Let's have a look at some number sequences to try to clarify this idea.

Here are three 'thought experiments' each of which involves throwing a six-sided die fifteen times. Imagine that in the first experiment the uppermost values of the die had those values shown in sequence A in Figure 1. The second experiment generated the numbers shown in sequence B and the third experiment gave us the numbers shown in sequence C.

Sequence A

5, 1, 2, 4, 6, 3, 2, 1, 6, 3, 5, 4, 3, 4, 2

Sequence B

6, 6, 6, 6, 6, 6, 6, 6, 6, 6, 6, 6, 6, 6, 6,

Sequence C

1, 2, 3, 4, 5, 6, 1, 2, 3, 4, 5, 6, 1, 2, 3

(Figure 1   Random sequences?)

Most of us would be quite happy that sequence A represented a typical sequence of numbers generated by throwing a die fifteen times. This number sequence shows no definable patterns or repetitions and each number occurrence would seem to be 'equally likely'. We are not surprised at the appearance of any of the sub-sequences in this main sequence. By contrast, however, sequence B is quite unreasonable. We would certainly not expect to have thrown fifteen sixes with fifteen consecutive throws of the die. We would be highly suspicious had this happened and we would blame a weighted die. Intuitively, we would be prepared to accept that sequence A had occurred 'by chance' but would not be prepared to accept that this was so for sequence B.

Another feature about random number sequences which we learn by experience is that, in long sequences, localised 'unfair' occurrences iron themselves out. What we mean by this is that after, say, a hundred throws, we would expect on average about sixteen ones, about sixteen twos, sixteen threes and so on. In other words, over a longer sequence we expect the 'laws of chance' to apply. If we now consider sequence C with its emerging pattern '... 6, 1, 2, 3, 4, 5, 6, 1 ...' continued for a hundred throws then this long-term averaging-out effect would be satisfied. But once again this sequence would not be intuitively acceptable to us as random because we would not expect this sequential pattern to persist over a hundred throws by chance alone.

These concepts of 'statistical averaging' over a sequence of throws, and of the 'reasonableness' of the patterning of the numbers in sequence are intuitively acquired from games of chance. There are statistical techniques to test these two features of a random number sequence but we will not be concerned with those techniques here.

A computer is a very determinate machine. You will therefore not be surprised to learn that quite special features have to be programmed into the machine to achieve a sequence of random numbers. For our uses, however, we will assume that a table of random numbers is very long and generation would have to occur for a long time before the sequence repetition became apparent. To achieve a different random number sequence from one program execution to another, all that a machine has to do is to start reading this table of random numbers from a different point. This starting point is often referred to as the 'seed' and we talk about random number sequences as starting from different seeds. Because the computer has to 'contrive' random number sequences, the numbers produced are usually referred to as *pseudo-random numbers*.

6.2 The RND function

To get random numbers on a microcomputer you use the function RND.

RND is a function that requires an argument. That is a number in brackets after it:

$$RND(A)$$

the argument of RND

'A' might be negative, zero or positive and the following program explores the effects of different values for A.

```
10 REM**THE RND FUNCTION**
20 INPUT "NEXT ARGUMENT FOR RND";A
30 FOR I=1 TO 10
40 LET B=RND(A)
50 PRINT B
60 NEXT I
70 END
```

Program 1   Effect of A on RND

```
RUN
NEXT ARGUMENT FOR RND? -1
.8188288
.8188288
.8188288
.8188288
.8188288        Negative A seems to fix the random number
.8188288
.8188288
.8188288
.8188288
.8188288
OK
```

```
RUN
NEXT ARGUMENT FOR RND? 0
.3116351
.3116351
.3116351
.3116351
.3116351        Zero A also seems to fix the random number
.3116351
.3116351
.3116351
.3116351
.3116351
OK

RUN
NEXT ARGUMENT FOR RND? 1
.7151002
.683111
.4821425
.9992938
.6465093        These look more like a sequence of random numbers
.1322918
.3692191
.5873315
.1345934
.9348853
OK

RUN
NEXT ARGUMENT FOR RND? 2
.7151002
.683111
.4821425
.9992938
.6465093        And so do these but they are the same as those with RND(1)
.1322918
.3692191
.5873315
.1345934
.9348853
OK
```

[K] Program 1 to see the effect of A on your microcomputer.

The RANDOMISE function

As far as generating useful random numbers is concerned, we will ignore arguments other than 1. But the RND(1) function returns the same sequence of random numbers each time the program is run. (This may seem a little strange, but it is a very useful feature if, when testing a program, we wish to re-run it using the same sequence of random numbers.) To change the 'seed', i.e. to start the generator at a random point in the sequence, we use the RANDOMISE command.

The 'seed' sets the sequence of random numbers the computer will generate. If we want a different set of random numbers each time, then we must set the seed to a different number each time. If you use just the command RANDOMISE on its own then the computer will prompt you, e.g.

```
RANDOMISE
RANDOM NUMBER SEED (-32768 TO 32767)?
```

and you have to enter a number for the seed. This is inconvenient, so it would be much better if we could automatically give the computer a different number each time. One way of doing this is to use the computer's clock. To see this, type:

```
PRINT TIME$
09:30:15
OK
```

which tells you it's 9.30 and 15 seconds! So we could use the seconds for our seed because unless you run the program at exactly the same number of seconds into the minute each time you will never get the same seed.

We want only the seconds of TIME$ which we can extract using RIGHT$:

```
RIGHT$(TIME$,2)
```

but RANDOMISE wants a number, so we use VAL to get a numeric variable from the string:

```
VAL(RIGHT$(TIME$,2))
```

giving us:

```
RANDOMISE VAL(RIGHT$(TIME$,2))
```

which we will use from now on as our seed.

```
10 REM**RANDOMISE**
20 RANDOMISE VAL(RIGHT$(TIME$,2))
30 FOR I=1 TO 10
40 LET B=RND(1)
50 PRINT B
60 NEXT I
70 END
```

Program 2 RANDOMISE to vary the sequence

```
RUN
.625387
.631877
.5735278
.9120885
.3355542
.7594321
.4166924
.6465105
.3874152
.8619056
OK
```

```
RUN
.1891687
.9405318
.6358446
.7251378
.8964062
7.687591E-02*
.4760797
.4566301
.9453376
.1764197
OK

RUN
.9457606
.6941938
.3865771
.4729406
.652998
.830538
.2268121
.2161516
.7019294
.9183631
OK
```

K Program 2.

RND(1)

What the above investigation demonstrates is that

```
RND(1)
```

will give random numbers within the range 0–1.

Changing the argument (A) doesn't seem to extend the range, so how can we get other random numbers? Quite simply by multiplying RND(1) by another number. So:

RND(1) gives a random number in the range 0–1;
6*RND(1) gives a random number in the range 0–6;
and 52*RND(1) gives a random number in the range 0–52:
etc.

```
 10 REM**RND AS A CONVERSION FACTOR**
 20 RANDOMISE VAL(RIGHT$(TIME$,2))
 30 PRINT " I","RND(1)","6*RND(1)","52*RND(1)"
 40 PRINT "---","------","------","------"
 50 FOR I=1 TO 10
 60 LET B=RND(1)
 70 LET C=6*B
 80 LET D=52*B
 90 PRINT I,B,C,D
100 NEXT I
110 END
```

Program 3 RND(1) as a conversion factor

* The 'E' will be explained in Section 7.6.

```
RUN
 I        RND(1)        6*RND(1)       52*RND(1)
---       ------        --------       ---------
 1        .1356409      .8138454       7.053327
 2        .1245527      .7473163       6.476741
 3        .0720629      .4323774       3.747271
 4        .4164831      2.498898       21.65712
 5        .8340893      5.004536       43.37265
 6        .2638266      1.58296        13.71898
 7        .9152276      5.491366       47.59184
 8        .150905       .9054299       7.84706
 9        .8859504      5.315703       46.06942
10        .3545814      2.127488       18.43823
OK


RUN
 I        RND(1)        6*RND(1)       52*RND(1)
---       ------        --------       ---------
 1        .7588099      4.55286        39.45812
 2        .2550459      1.530275       13.26239
 3        .704021       4.224126       36.60909
 4        .5440465      3.264279       28.29042
 5        .4631177      2.778706       24.08212
 6        .3884604      2.330763       20.19994
 7        .5413263      3.247957       28.14897
 8        .2726091      1.635655       14.17568
 9        .5091194      3.054716       26.47421
10        .4850745      2.910447       25.22388
OK
```

K Program 3.

SAQ 1
Write a program to print out 6 random numbers in the range 0 to 5.99999.

The RND+1 function
If you look again at the output of Program 3 on another run with 6*RND(1), the numbers were:

```
RUN
.0660427
2.990725
5.702153
4.759885
4.29189
3.861524
4.725985
3.13126
4.5679
4.370897
OK
```

Look now at the numbers before the decimal point. They are:

0, 2, 5, 4, 4, 3, 4, 3, 4, 4

i.e. members of the set

(0, 1, 2, 3, 4, 5)

But, if we were throwing dice we would generate members of the set (1, 2, 3, 4, 5, 6). All we have to do, then, is to add 1 to each member of the first set to get the second.

Now in games we frequently want to throw a die (outcomes 1, 2, 3, 4, 5, 6) or use a pack of cards (52 outcomes), so we are particularly interested in the functions:

6*RND(1)+1 and 52*RND(1)+1

The following program allows us to explore these.

```
 10 REM**RND AS A CONVERSION FACTOR**
 20 RANDOMISE VAL(RIGHT$(TIME$,2))
 30 PRINT " I","RND(1)","6*RND(1)+1","52*RND(1)+1"
 40 PRINT "---","------","------","------",
 50 FOR I=1 TO 10
 60 LET B=RND(1)
 70 LET C=6*B+1
 80 LET D=52*B+1
 90 PRINT I,B,C,D
100 NEXT I
110 END
```

Program 4   6*RND(1)+1 and 52*RND(1)+1

```
RUN
I            RND(1)       6*RND(1)+1    52*RND(1)+1
---          ------       ------        ------
 1           .3849085     3.309451      21.01524
 2           .37675       3.2605        20.591
 3           .3271899     2.963139      18.01387
 4           .662821      4.976926      35.46669
 5           .0833569     1.500141      5.334559
 6           .5160239     4.096143      27.83324
 7           .1703545     2.022127      9.858436
 8           .3972429     3.383458      21.65663
 9           .135218      1.811308      8.031334
10           .6067786     4.640672      32.55249
OK
```

K Program 4. (You may have to adjust the print pattern to fit your screen.)

The INT function

If you now look at the columns in the runs of Program 4 you will see that we have generated the random numbers we needed. Column 3 has numbers from 1 to 6 and column 4 has numbers from 1 to 52.

But what about all the excess numbers to the right of the decimal point? Well, we have a function to get rid of those: the INT function.

The effect of INT(X) is to give the whole number (or integer part) of the number X, i.e. the largest integer which is not larger than X. The effect of INT is to 'chop' down to the next lowest whole number:

INT(5.6)=5
INT(3.9)=3
INT(-3.2)=-4
INT(2)=2

If INT(-3.2)=-4 surprises you, look at the number line and remember that *INT always chops down to the next whole number.* It doesn't 'round' numbers.

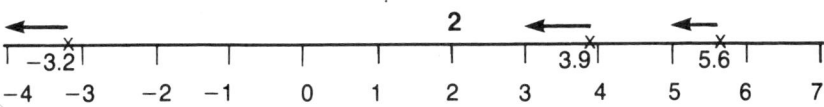

SAQ 2
What are the values of the following?
(a)   INT(4.5)
(b)   INT(9.1)
(c)   INT(-2.5)
(d)   INT(-0.99)
(e)   INT(1.01)

Now, with INT, we can at last generate the whole numbers from 1 to 6 and from 1 to 52 to use as dice or cards. All we need is

INT(6*RND(1)+1)

and

INT(52*RND(1)+1)

The following program prints out the values of these two functions:

```
 10 REM**THE INT FUNCTION**
 20 RANDOMISE VAL(RIGHT$(TIME$,2))
 30 PRINT " I","RND(1)","INT(6*...+1)","INT (52*...+1)"
 40 PRINT "---","------","------","------"
 50 FOR I=1 TO 10
 60 LET B=RND(1)
 70 LET C=INT(6*B+1)
 80 LET D=INT(52*B+1)
 90 PRINT I,B,C,D
100 NEXT I
110 END
```

Program 5   INT to give whole numbers

```
RUN
 I         RND(1)        INT(6*...+1)   INT(52*...+1)
---        ------        ------         ------
 1         .6283167       4              33
 2         .6230879       4              33
 3         .5764575       4              30
 4         .9150182       6              48
 5         .3384839       3              18
 6         .7623618       5              40
 7         .4196221       3              22
 8         .6494402       4              34
 9         .3903449       3              21
10         .8531165       6              45
OK


RUN
 I         RND(1)        INT(6*...+1)   INT(52*...+1)
---        ------        ------         ------
 1         .8805139       6              46
 2         .8782148       6              46
 3         .8227953       5              43
 4         .1642858       1               9
 5         .5906811       4              31
 6         .0174887       1               1
 7         .66596         4              35
 8         .8987078       6              47
 9         .6425422       4              34
10         .1082435       1               6
OK
```

K Program 5.

6.3 Random number postscript

The following program simulates the tossing of a die 100 times.

```
 10 REM**100 TOSSES OF A DIE**
 20 RANDOMISE VAL(RIGHT$(TIME$,2))
 30 FOR I=1 TO 10
 40 FOR J=1 TO 10
 50 LET X=INT(6*RND(1)+1)
 60 PRINT X," ";
 70 NEXT J
 80 PRINT
 90 NEXT I
100 END
```

Program 6 Die toss

```
RUN
 4      1      6      6      4      3      2      4      3      1
 6      6      2      2      5      3      6      5      2      2
 3      3      6      3      4      2      6      1      2      6
 6      1      4      3      5      2      2      2      1      6
 6      3      1      1      6      3      4      5      2      5
 6      1      4      2      2      4      5      1      2      4
 6      6      5      4      3      4      5      5      1      5
 3      5      4      3      5      3      6      6      6      6
 1      5      3      4      3      1      1      4      2      1
 6      3      6      1      6      1      6      5      3      1
OK
```

K Program 6.

Just to make sure that you understand the INT function, try the following questions.

SAQ 3
The program:

```
10 **REM SAQ**
20 FOR X=-3.8 TO -1.8 STEP(.2)
30 LET Y=INT(X)
40 PRINT X,Y
50 NEXT X
60 END
```

Program 7

prints out 11 pairs of numbers. What are they?

SAQ 4
The program:

```
10 REM**SAQ**
20 FOR X=1.6 TO 3.4 STEP(.2)
30 LET Y=INT(X)
40 PRINT X,Y
50 NEXT X
60 END
```

Program 8

prints out 10 pairs of numbers. What are they?

6.4 Two examples

This section is made up of two lengthy examples. We suggest that you try to treat them as exercises first and then compare your solution with ours.

Example 1
Write a program to simulate tossing a coin 100 times. Count and output the number of times the coin falls heads and tails.

Solution
The heart of the solution is a random number generator which produces a 1 or a 2.

We will use 1 to represent tails and 2 to represent heads. Using this approach, a descriptive algorithm for the solution to the problem is:

1. Start
2. Set heads and tails counters to zero
3. Start loop counter
4. Had 100 goes? If so goto 9
5. Generate random number (1 or 2)
6. If random number is 1, add 1 to tails counter
7. If random number is 2, add 1 to heads counter
8. End loop (goto 4)
9. Output totals for heads and tails
10. Stop

(Figure 2   Descriptive solution to coin toss)

Alternatively you may prefer a flowchart description of the solution:

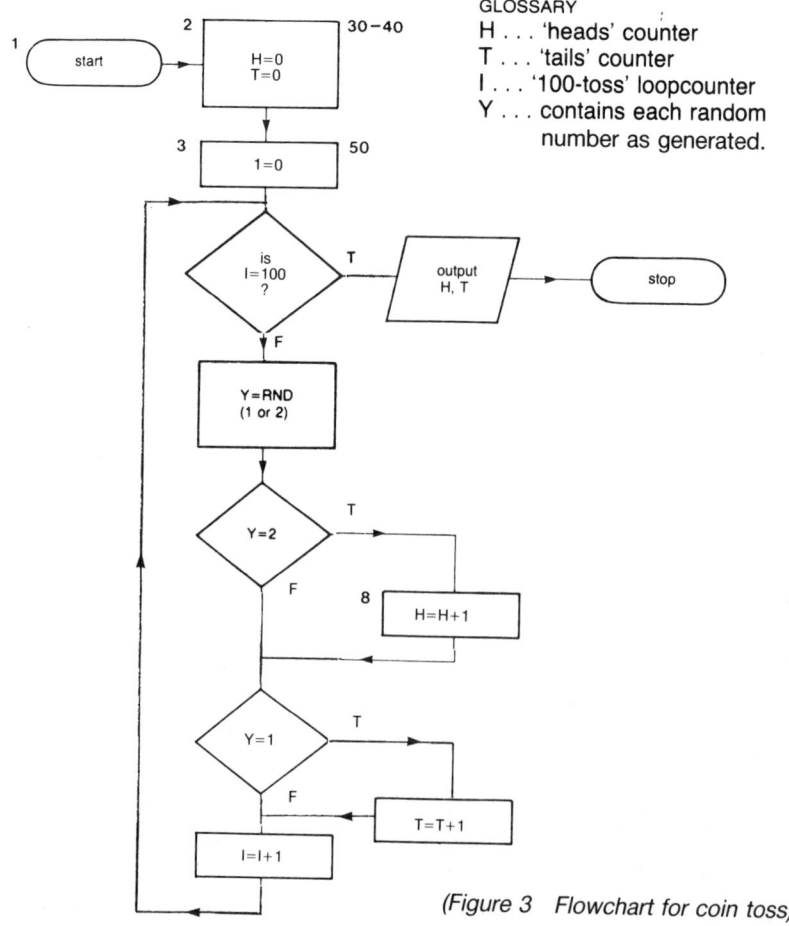

(Figure 3   Flowchart for coin toss)

And, finally, the program:

```
10 REM**TOSS 1 COIN 100 TIMES**
20 RANDOMISE VAL(RIGHT$(TIME$,2))
30 LET HEADS=0
40 LET TAILS=0
50 LET GOES=0                      ——————— 'I' is used instead of 'GOES' in flowchart
60 WHILE GOES<100
70 LET THROW=INT(2*RND(1)+1)
80 IF THROW=1 THEN TAILS=TAILS+1
90 IF THROW=2 THEN HEADS=HEADS+1
100 GOES=GOES+1
110 WEND
120 PRINT "HEADS","TAILS"
130 PRINT HEADS,TAILS
140 END
```

Program 9

```
RUN
HEADS           TAILS
54              46
OK
RUN
HEADS           TAILS
52              48
OK
RUN
HEADS           TAILS
58              42
OK
RUN
HEADS           TAILS
51              49
OK
```

K Program 9.

Example 2
Write a program to simulate tossing two coins 100 times. Count and output the number of times that the outcome of this imaginary experiment is: head-head (HH), tail-tail (TT), and head-tail or tail-head (HT or TH).

Solution
We use the same scoring rules: 1 for a tail and 2 for a head but we are now tossing two coins. We store the score from the first coin in TOSS1 and the score from the second coin in TOSS2. Then we add TOSS1 and TOSS2 to give the total score for that throw:

SCORE=TOSS1+TOSS2

SCORE can be 2, 3 or 4:

outcome	score
TT	1+1=2
TH or HT	1+2=2+1=3
HH	2+2=4

Then we count how many 2s we get, how many 3s, and how many 4s.

Counter for 2s   T2
Counter for 3s   M1   (M for Mix of Hs and Ts)
Counter for 4s   H2

The flowchart of the solution is:

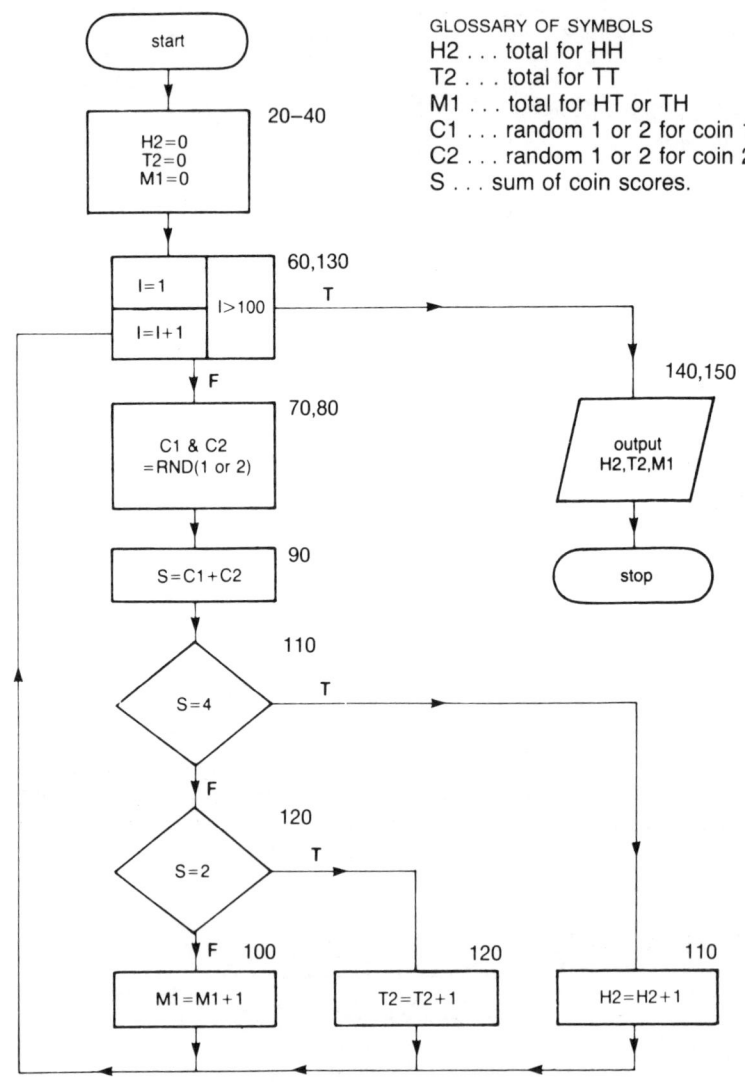

(Figure 4   Flowchart for two coin toss

And the program is:

```
10 REM**TOSS 2 COINS 100 TIMES**
20 LET HEADS2=0
30 LET TAILS2=0
40 LET MIX=0
50 RANDOMISE VAL(RIGHT$(TIME$,2))
60 FOR I=1 TO 100
70 LET TOSS1=INT(2*RND(1)+1)
80 LET TOSS2=INT(2*RND(1)+1)
90 S=TOSS1+TOSS2
100 IF S=3 THEN MIX=MIX+1
110 IF S=4 THEN HEADS2=HEADS2+1
120 IF S=2 THEN TAILS2=TAILS2+1
130 NEXT I
140 PRINT "TT","HT","HH"
150 PRINT TAILS2,MIX,HEADS2
160 END
```

Program 10   Two coin toss

```
RUN
TT          HT          HH
22          54          24
OK

RUN
TT          HT          HH
24          52          24
OK

RUN
TT          HT          HH
22          48          30
OK
```

6.5 Keeping scores

You may have noticed that we have used some ungainly variable names, such as TAILS2, HEADS2 and MIX. Perhaps you have been thinking, 'What about lists? Couldn't they be as useful here as they were with frequency tables?' Indeed they could, so let's try a score list SCORES(I) for the coin-tossing. So we say:

If the score is 2, add 1 to the number in SCORES(2)
If the score is 3, add 1 to the number in SCORES(3)
if the score is 4, add 1 to the number in SCORES(4)
Generally:
If the score is S, add 1 to the number in SCORES(S)

Application to tossing two coins
The line which increments the scores will be:

```
110 LET SCORES(SCORE)=SCORES(SCORE)+1
```

So the program is:

```
  5 OPTION BASE 1
 10 REM**TOSS 2 COINS 100 TIMES**
 20 DIM SCORES(4)
 30 FOR I=1 TO 4
 40 SCORES(I)=0
 50 NEXT I
 60 RANDOMISE VAL(RIGHT$(TIME$,2))
 70 FOR I=1 TO 100
 80 LET TOSS1=INT(2*RND(1)+1)
 90 LET TOSS2=INT(2*RND(1)+1)
100 LET SCORE=TOSS1+TOSS2
110 LET SCORES(SCORE)=SCORES(SCORE)+1
120 NEXT I
130 PRINT "TT","HT","HH"
140 PRINT SCORE(2),SCORES(3),SCORES(4)
150 END
```

Program 11

```
RUN
TT            HT          HH
23            52          25
OK


RUN
TT            HT          HH
25            53          22
OK


RUN
TT            HT          HH
22            57          21
OK


RUN
TT            HT          HH
24            50          26
OK
```

K Program 11.

Score lists for dice
The score list for throwing one die would be:

SCORES(1), SCORES(2), SCORES(3) . . . SCORES(6).

and for throwing two dice:

SCORES(2), SCORES(3), SCORES(4) . . . SCORES(12).

Exercise 1
Write a program to simulate throwing a die 100 times. Count and output the number of times each score occurs.

Exercise 2
Modify the program written for Exercise 1 to simulate the throwing of two dice 100 times.

Exercise 3
Write a program to display the data obtained from the program in Exercise 2, in the form of a frequency diagram.

6.6 Short cuts in program writing

Our programs are becoming quite long and the longer they are, the longer they take to key in on the computer. There are short cuts which help to speed up keying. We have deliberately avoided short cuts up to this point, feeling that intelligibility of coding is more important than speed. We will abbreviate some of our coding at times to show you what can be achieved, but will generally continue our policy of clarity of interpretation. If you are sending assignments to a tutor for marking, then please use short cuts sparingly.

The principal short cuts are:

1. The word LET may be omitted from assignment statements. Thus:

    ```
    20 LET A=B
    ```

    can be written

    ```
    20 A=B
    ```

2. More than one statement per line is allowed; the statements must be separated by :
    Thus:

    ```
    10 LET A=7
    20 LET B=8
    30 PRINT A+B
    ```

    can be written:

    ```
    10 LET A=7:LET B=8:PRINT A+B
    ```

    or, using the first short cut as well:

    ```
    10 A=7:B=8:PRINT A+B
    ```

    (This short cut speeds up program execution as well as keying time. Computers take up time interpreting each line number, so the fewer the line numbers, the quicker will be the execution.)

3. The word PRINT may be replaced by ?. However, when you ask the computer to list your program you find that ? is replaced by the full word PRINT. E.g. if you key in

   ```
   10 A=7:B=8:?A+B
   ```

   and then ask for LIST you get

   ```
   10 A=7:B=8:PRINT A+B
   ```

4. *You can include expressions in PRINT statements.* These expressions will be executed. We've already done this above where we said PRINT A+B.

But, be careful.

(a) Don't cram statements on a line just for the sake of doing so.

(b) Be very careful with transfer of control statements, e.g. GOTO ..., IF ... THEN ..., and later on GOSUB .... Remember, the lines referred to must exist and program control goes to the beginning of the line in the GOTO statement.

(c) Most programs spend 80% of their time in 20% of their coding. So, concentrate on abbreviating (and therefore speeding up) those statements which work the hardest, e.g. lines 70 to 120 in the solution to Exercise 3.

(d) The line number associated with a REM statement takes up run time so it is useful to tack a :REM ... on to the end of other statements. We do so in programs later in this Unit. They don't all look as tidy as they ought to, though.

(e) Take care to distinguish clearly between : and ; in the listings of programs: yours, ours and especially those in computer magazines. The pairs (,< and),> are often barely distinguishable in some listings.

Some examples of short cuts

First Program 2 (page 145), which was 7 lines, can be written in 4 lines:

3 statements on line 30, separated by colons

```
10 REM**RANDOMISE**
20 RANDOMISE VAL(RIGHT$(TIME$,2))
30 FOR I=1 TO 10: PRINT RND(1):NEXT I
40 END
```

RND is evaluated in a PRINT statement
was typed as ? but was listed as PRINT

Program 12

Second, Program 11, which was 16 lines, can be written in 11 lines:

3 assignment statements without LET

```
 5 OPTION BASE 1
10 REM**TOSS 2 COINS 100 TIMES**
20 DIM SCORES(4):SCORES(2)=0:SCORES(3)=0:SCORES(4)=0
30 RANDOMISE VAL(RIGHT$(TIME$,2))
40 FOR I=1 TO 100
```

```
50 TOSS1=INT(2*RND(1)+1):TOSS2=INT(2*RND(1)+1)
60 SCORE=TOSS1+TOSS2:SCORES(SCORE)=SCORES(SCORE)+1
70 NEXT I
80 PRINT "TT","TH","HH"
90 PRINT SCORES(2),SCORES(3),SCORES(4)
100 END
```

not worth condensing, because it is executed only once per run

this is where the work is being done, 50 to 60 are executed 100 times

Program 13

6.7 Concatenation

Having gone to a lot of trouble in Unit 5 to cut up strings, we will now spend some time putting them back together. The second ugliest word in the computing repertoire, concatenation, means to chain or link together. Program 14 shows us what is happening.

```
10 INPUT A$
20 INPUT B$
40 PRINT A$+B$
50 END
```

Program 14 Concatenation

```
RUN
?GET
?TOGETHER
GETTOGETHER

RUN
?CONCATE
?NATION
CONCATENATION
```

SAQ 5
Write a program to input a word and output its plural assuming that all words only need s adding to make their plurals.

Program 15 shows how we can use concatenation to build up a string from a list of symbols. We have stored the letters in line 120 (DATA) and in the loop 80 to 110 we add a new letter to the string on each pass around the loop.

```
  5 OPTION BASE 1
 10 REM**CONCATENATION**
 20 REM**SET UP DIRECTORY**
 30 DIM A$(10)
 40 FOR I=1 TO 10
 50 READ A$(I)
 60 NEXT I
 70 C$=" "
 80 FOR J=I TO 10
 90 C$=C$+A$(J)
100 PRINT J,C$
110 NEXT J
120 DATA A,B,C,D,E,F,G,H,I,J
130 END
```

Program 15

```
RUN
 1      A
 2      AB
 3      ABC
 4      ABCD
 5      ABCDE
 6      ABCDEF
 7      ABCDEFG
 8      ABCDEFGH
 9      ABCDEFGHI
10      ABCDEFGHIJ
```

K Program 15.

This process is of great value in textual analysis, but we will use it for codes and games.

6.8 STR$

This function has the reverse effect to that of the VAL-function. The VAL-function gives the numerical value of a string, and the STR$-function turns a number into just a string of characters.

STR$(X) gives the string representation of the value of X.

Printing STR$
STR$(N) looks very much like N itself, as the following program shows:

```
10 REM**THE STR$ FUNCTION**
20 INPUT "NEXT NUMBER";NUMBER
30 PRINT "01234567890123456 7890"
40 PRINT NUMBER,STR$(NUMBER)
50 END
```

Program 16

```
RUN
NEXT NUMBER? 17
01234567890123456 7890
 17             17
RUN
NEXT NUMBER?-17
01234567890123456 7890
-17            -17
RUN
NEXT NUMBER? 99.34
01234567890123456 7890
 99.34          99.34
RUN
NEXT NUMBER?-99.34
01234567890123456 7890
-99.34         -99.34
```

K Program 16.

In the next program we make use of the fact that STR$(8) treats 8, say, as a string, so that we add the character 8 (as opposed to its value) onto the end of a string.

```
10 REM**STR$ AGAIN**
20 C$=" "
30 REM HAVE EMPTIED C$
40 FOR J=1 TO 10
50 C$=C$+STR$(J)
60 PRINT J,C$
70 NEXT J
80 END
```

Program 17

```
RUN
 1      1
 2      12
 3      123
 4      1234
 5      12345
 6      123456
 7      1234567
 8      12345678
 9      123456789
10      12345678910
```

K Program 17.

Exercise 4
Write a program to input a word from the keyboard, to code each letter as a number and output the code as a sequence of numbers.

Guidance if required: set up a directory-list as in Program 15 but for the whole alphabet. Remember the DIM statement. Take each letter of the word and compare it with the items of the directory-list. When found in the directory, add that index, in string form, to the code string.

Exercise 5
Write a program to generate 20 random 3-letter words. (It's interesting to see how many times you have to run this program until you generate a bona fide word.)

Assignment 6

1. Write a program to deal a hand of cards, the size of which is left to you. Print out the hand in the form 1D,KC,8H,6S . . ., where D=diamonds, C=clubs, etc. 1=ace, T, J, Q, and K stand for ten, jack, queen and king. Remember that when a card has been dealt it cannot be dealt again.

    Guidance if required: write a program in sections:
    (a) set up the deck (we have previously called it a directory);
    (b) deal (using the RND generator 1–52 is easiest);
    (c) output.

    When a card has been dealt, put a marker (e.g. a *) in that position to signal that it cannot be used again.

2. Write a program to simulate a game of snakes and ladders using a 4×4 board and one die.

Guidance if required: though the board is square it can be represented in memory by a list B(l):
i.e. B(1), B(2), B(3) ... B(16)
B(3)=+4 could be a ladder going up 4 places.
B(9)=−7 could be a snake going down 7 places, etc.

Don't forget that your last throw has to give the right number to complete the board at exactly 16.

Suggestions (not part of the Assignment for your tutor): play the game a few times and estimate the average number of throws needed to run the board. Change the layout of the board and try some more runs. Design a bigger board, etc.

Objectives of Unit 6

When you have finished this Unit, check that you are able to:

Use RND to generate random numbers between 0 and 1 ☐

Use INT and RND to generate integer random numbers between 0 and a given integer N ☐

Simulate the tosses of a coin ☐

Simulate the tosses of two coins ☐

Simulate the throw of a die ☐

Simulate the throws of two dice ☐

Use score lists ☐

Abbreviate programs with ? and multiple statement lines ☐

Concatenate strings ☐

Use STR$(X) ☐

Answers to SAQs and Exercises
SAQ 1

```
10 RANDOMISE VAL(RIGHT$(TIME$,2))
20 FOR I=1 TO 6
30 LET N=6"RND(1)
40 PRINT N
50 NEXT I
60 END
```

Program 18

SAQ 2
(a) 4
(b) 9
(c) −3
(d) −1
(e) 1

SAQ 3

```
RUN
-3.8    -4
-3.6    -4
-3.4    -4
-3.2    -4
-3      -3
-2.8    -3
-2.6    -3
-2.4    -3
-2.2    -3
-2      -2
-1.8    -2
```

SAQ 4

```
RUN
1.6     1
1.8     1
2       2
2.2     2
2.4     2
2.6     2
2.8     2
3       3
3.2     3
3.4     3
```

Exercise 1

Descriptive algorithm for one die toss
1. Start
2. Set the 6 total store locations to zero
3. Start the 100-throws loop
4. Generate a random score from the set (1, 2, 3, 4, 5, 6)
5. Increment the total linked with this score
6. If loop counter <=100 *then* go to statement 4 *otherwise* go on to statement 7
7. Output score and total for each score value
8. Stop

```
 5 OPTION BASE 1
10 REM**THROW 1 DIE 100 TIMES**
20 DIM SCORES(6)
30 FOR J=1 TO 6
40 LET SCORES(J)=0
50 NEXT J
60 RANDOMISE VAL(RIGHT$(TIME$,2))
70 FOR I=1 TO 100
80 LET SCORE=INT(6*RND(1)+1)
```

```
 90 LET SCORES(SCORE)=SCORES(SCORE)+1
100 NEXT I
110 PRINT
120 PRINT "SCORE","FREQUENCY"
130 FOR K=1 TO 6
140 PRINT K,SCORES(K)
150 NEXT K
160 END
```

Program 19

```
RUN
SCORE          FREQUENCY
1              12
2              20
3              16
4              18
5              16
6              18

OK
RUN

SCORE          FREQUENCY
1              9
2              20
3              19
4              18
5              14
6              20


OK
RUN

SCORE          FREQUENCY
1              14
2              28
3              17
4              18
5              15
6              8

OK
RUN

SCORE          FREQUENCY
1              15
2              19
3              18
4              17
5              17
6              14
OK
```

K Program 19.

Exercise 2

```
 5 OPTION BASE 1
10 REM**THROW 1 DIE 100 TIMES**
20 DIM SCORES(6)
30 FOR J=1 TO 6
```

```
 40 LET SCORES(J)=0
 50 NEXT J
 60 RANDOMISE VAL(RIGHT$(TIME$,2))
 70 FOR I=1 TO 100
 80 LET SCORE=INT(6*RND(1)+1)
 90 LET SCORES(SCORE)=SCORES(SCORE)+1
100 NEXT I
110 PRINT
120 PRINT "SCORE","FREQUENCY"
130 FOR K=1 TO 6
140 PRINT K,SCORES(K)
150 NEXT K
160 END
```

Program 20

```
RUN
SCORE           FREQUENCY
2               1
3               5
4               10
5               13
6               11
7               19
8               16
9               5
10              10
11              5
12              5
OK
```

K Program 20.

How about 1000 throws? Well, just change line 70 to

`70 FOR I=1 TO 1000`

(forget what the REM line says!) and you will get a run such as:

```
RUN
SCORE           FREQUENCY
2               31
3               59
4               74
5               118
6               151
7               173
8               118
9               100
10              89
11              61
12              26

OK
```

Suggestions for further programs
1. How would you cope with printing a frequency diagram for this data, as 151 and 173 . . . would 'want to print' off the end of the line?
2. We need a general 'scaling' routine which adjusts to differing line widths, but makes best use of the full width of the page or screen.

Exercise 3

```
  5 OPTION BASE 1
 10 REM**FREQUENCY DIAGRAM**
 20 DIM SCORES(15)
 30 FOR J=2 TO 12
 40 LET SCORES(J)=0
 50 NEXT J
 60 RANDOMISE VAL(RIGHT$(TIME$,2))
 70 FOR I=1 TO 100
 80 LET TOSS1=INT(6*RND(1)+1)
 90 LET TOSS2=INT(6*RND(1)+1)
100 LET SCORE=TOSS1+TOSS2
110 LET SCORES(SCORE)=SCORES(SCORE)+1
120 NEXT I
130 PRINT
140 PRINT "FREQUENCY DIAGRAM"
150 PRINT
160 FOR K=2 TO 12
170 PRINT K;TAB(5);SCORES(K);TAB(10);
180 WHILE SCORES(K)<>0
190 FOR L=1 TO SCORES(K)
200 PRINT "*";
210 NEXT L
220 SCORES(K)=0
230 REM**FOOL LOOP**
240 WEND
250 PRINT
260 NEXT K
270 END
```

Program 21

RUN

FREQUENCY DIAGRAM

```
 2      4          ****
 3      6          ******
 4      6          ******
 5      8          ********
 6     19          *******************
 7     21          *********************
 8     10          **********
 9     11          ***********
10      8          ********
11      4          ****
12      3          ***
```

K Program 21.

SAQ 5

```
10 REM**PLURALS**
20 LET A$="S"
30 INPUT B$
40 PRINT B$+A$
50 END
```

Program 22

Exercise 4

```
  5 OPTION BASE 1
 10 REM**SIMPLE CODE**
 20 DIM ALETTERS$(26)
 30 FOR I=1 TO 26
 40 READ ALETTERS$(I)
 50 NEXT I
 60 INPUT "ENTER WORD FOR CODING";WORD$
 70 LENGTH=LEN(WORD$)
 80 FOR J=1 TO LENGTH
 90 I=1
100 WHILE MID$(WORD$,J,1)<>ALETTERS$(I)
110 I=I+1
120 WEND
130 CODE$=CODE$+STR$(I)+" "
140 NEXT J
150 PRINT
160 PRINT CODE$
170 END
180 DATA A,B,C,D,E,F,G,H,I,J,K,L,M,N,O,P,Q,R,S,
    T,U,V,W,X,Y,Z
```
Program 23

```
RUN
NEXT WORD FOR CODING? COMPUTING

3 15 13 16 21 20 9 14 7

OK
RUN
NEXT WORD FOR CODING? PARLIAMENT

16 1 18 12 9 1 13 5 14 20

OK
RUN
NEXT WORD FOR CODING? PROFESSIONALS

16 18 15 6 5 19 19 9 15 14 1 12 19

OK
```

K Program 23.

Exercise 5

```
  5 OPTION BASE 1
 10 REM**RANDOM 3 ALETTER WORDS**
 20 DIM ALETTER$(26)
 30 FOR I=1 TO 26
 40 READ ALETTER$(I)
 50 NEXT I
 60 RANDOMISE VAL(RIGHT$(TIME$,2))
 70 FOR WORDS=1 TO 20
 80 REM**EMPTY WORD$**
 90 WORD$=" "
100 REM**START OF WORD LOOP**
110 FOR LENGTH=1 TO 3
120 NUMBER=INT(26*RND(1)+1)
130 WORD$=WORD$+ALETTER$(NUMBER)
140 NEXT LENGTH
150 REM**END OF WORD**
```

```
160 PRINT WORD$
170 NEXT WORDS
180 REM**END OF WORDS LOOP**
190 END
200 DATA A,B,C,D,E,F,G,H,I,J,K,L,M,N,O,P,Q,R,
    S,T,U,V,W,X,Y,Z
```

Program 24

Too many REMs spoil a program's appearance; do they add to its intelligibility?

```
RUN
PDY
XNM
HPI
EVW
EFT
KZT
IGM
KWL
QHW
AIY
ZBQ
MSH
FFA
ZYJ
BBX
JPT
FSV
BPG
GNR
EEP
OK
```

How many times must you run to get a 'proper' word?

[K] Program 24.

UNIT 7
Handling numbers

7.1	Introduction	170
7.2	Averages and the arithmetic mean	170
7.3	Range	173
7.4	Number crunching	175
7.5	Dry running	178
7.6	The representation of numbers	180
7.7	The ABS-function	182
7.8	Iteration	183
	Assignment 7	187
	Objectives of Unit 7	187
	Answers to SAQs and Exercises	188

7.1 Introduction

We have demonstrated that computers are not just number crunchers but in this Unit we take a closer look at their arithmetic capacity. We concentrate on fairly straightforward arithmetic, so don't worry about finding it difficult. We're sure that you will be able to cope. We shall continue the 'let's see what happens if . . .' approach, and 'let's get the machine to tell us what is going on'. We hope that you will adopt the same approach with the machine that you use.

7.2 Averages and the arithmetic mean

'How long have you been taking over each Unit of the course, so far?' 'Well, on average, about 3 hours.' If we asked you how long it took you to complete a regular journey, such as going to work, you would answer in a similar manner. Sports enthusiasts use the terms 'goal average' and 'batting average', atlases abound with pictures of average rainfalls for the months of the year. We talk of average marks in a test or the average age of a group of people, etc.

If we wished to calculate the average or arithmetic mean of the ages of a particular group of people, we would add up the ages for all of the members of the group and divide that sum by the total number of people in the group. *To find the arithmetic mean, then, involves: adding up, counting and then dividing the sum by the count.*

Example 1
Find the arithmetic mean of the following set of numbers:

6, 7, 2, 5, 4, 4, 9, 8

Solution
Their sum=6+7+2+5+4+4+9+8=45.
There are 8 numbers.
So their arithmetic mean=45/8=5.625.

SAQ 1
Find the arithmetic mean of the following set of numbers:

8, 4, 2, 6, 1, 7, 6, 1, 4

Arithmetic mean

Example 2
Devise an algorithm and write a program to find the arithmetic mean of the numbers stored in these DATA statements, as follows:

```
130 DATA 56,47,52,65,24,34,59,37,49,66
140 DATA 38,24,62,76,31,47,66,61,74,45
150 DATA 66,44,55,67,36,56,54,54,50,43
160 DATA 18,83,23,79,29,-9999
```

Solution
We will express the algorithm first of all in a descriptive form:

1. Start
2. Set counter to 1

3. Set sum to 0
4. Input the first mark
5. WHILE ... WEND ... loop starts. If mark is −9999 then exit loop.
6. Add mark to sum
7. Increment counter
8. Input next mark
9. Loop back to 5
10. Calculate average
11. Output average

(Figure 1   Descriptive algorithm for arithmetic mean)

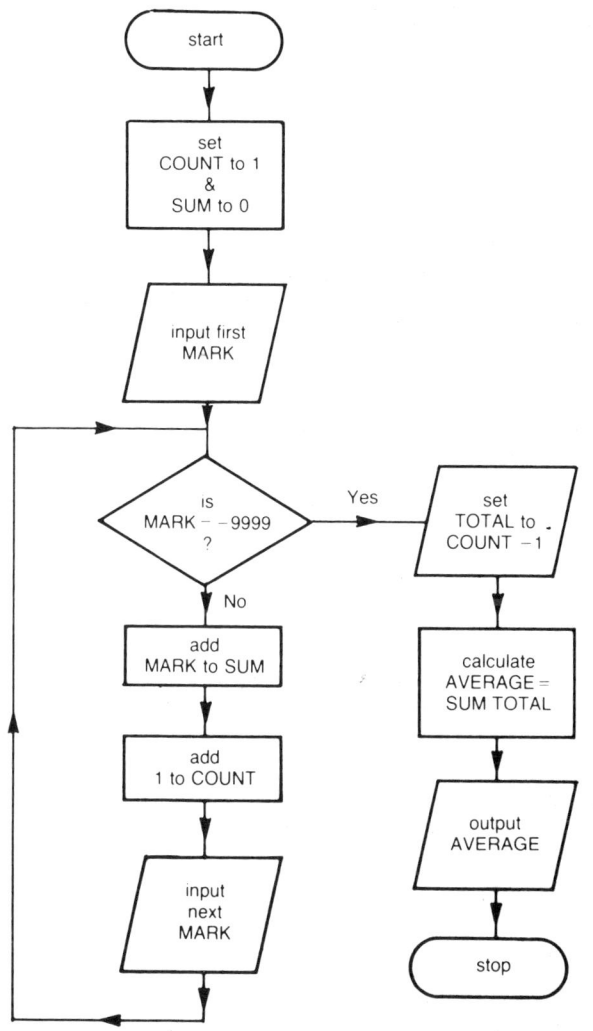

(Figure 2   Flowchart for arithmetic mean)

```
 10 REM**ARITHMETIC MEAN**
 20 LET COUNT=0
 30 LET SUM=0
 40 READ NUMBER
 50 WHILE NUMBER<>-9999
 60 LET SUM=SUM+NUMBER
 70 LET COUNT=COUNT+1
 80 READ NUMBER
 90 WEND
100 REM*****************
110 PRINT "AVERAGE=";SUM/COUNT
120 REM*****************
130 DATA 56,47,52,65,24,34,59,37,49,66
140 DATA 38,24,62,76,31,47,66,61,74,45
150 DATA 66,44,55,67,36,56,54,54,50,43
160 DATA 18,83,23,79,29,-9999
OK
```
Program 1 Arithmetic mean

```
RUN
AVERAGE=50.57143
```

K Program 1.

Exercise 1
Write a program to find the average length of the words in the 'Jude' DATA statements of Example 2 of Unit 5. You can do this by grafting a routine onto Program 1 of Unit 5 which already finds the lengths of words.

Exercise 2
Write a program to find the average score in a simulated experiment of tossing a die 100 times. Run it 10 times to see what range of results you get.

Simulation
The expected average score when throwing a die a large number of times is:

$$\frac{1+2+3+4+5+6}{6} = \frac{21}{6} = 3.5$$

However, running Exercise 2 will not necessarily produce exactly that result. By way of experiment we tried running the program 30 times (i.e. a total of 3,000 throws) and got an exact result of 3.5 only once, with values ranging from 3.24 to 3.76. So you might well ask, 'Is the random number generator biased?' (We did call it 'pseudo' anyway!). How many experiments do we need to convince us that it is, or is not, biased?

To explore that question fully we need to go into statistical theory which is beyond the scope of this course, but we can at least find the mean of these means. All we have to do is to take data from the 30 runs of the program:

3.56,3.47,3.52,3.65,...

and enter them into the DATA statements of Program 1 above. This gives us the mean of the means.

You will notice below that we have entered only the decimal parts of the numbers in order to make our data entry a little easier, e.g. 56 instead of 3.56. (We can do this because all the numbers are 3.something.)

```
130 DATA 56,47,52,65,24,34,59,37,49,66
140 DATA 38,24,62,76,31,47,66,61,74,45
150 DATA 66,44,55,67,36,56,54,54,50,43
160 DATA -9999
RUN
AVERAGE=51.26667
OK
```

(Figure 3)

Thus the overall mean of 3,000 throws is 3.51 to 2 decimal places – a bit more convincing!

Simulation summarised
Simulation is rather a grand word for what we have just done. However, we wanted to emphasise that we can simulate a real-life activity without getting deeply involved in statistics. We couldn't toss a die 3,000 times in a classroom but with a computer we can collect and process data fairly rapidly.

If your curiosity has been aroused, then try the following exercise.

Exercise 3
Write a program to find the average score in a simulated experiment of tossing two dice 100 times.

What would you expect the average score to be in this case and in experiments with three, four ... dice? Are your expectations justified by your experiments?

7.3 Range

While discussing the results of Exercise 2, we quite naturally used the idea of range. We said that the values ranged from 3.24 to 3.76. The process involves finding the lowest and highest values of the set.

Example 3
Devise an algorithm and write a routine to find the maximum and minimum values of the numbers stored in the DATA statements in Example 2. Add this routine to the program to find the arithmetic mean as written as a solution to Example 2.

(If you feel confident enough, treat this Example as an exercise before working through our solution.)

Solution
You may feel we've been here before, in Unit 4, when we found the lowest member of a list. We could use that approach again, but to do so we would first have to put the data in a list form and then sort it twice with the interchange routine. That's a lot of work, so we will look at a shorter approach: trying to find the lowest and highest marks as the data is read in.

We know how to read in the data (lines 10 to 90 in Program 1) but what do we do with it as each item is read?

(a) First we create two stores:
MAX for top mark so far
MIN for bottom mark so far
(b) Then we read the first mark and put it into both MIN and MAX. After all, it is the lowest and highest so far!

(c) Then we read each mark and if it is higher than MAX, put it into MAX or, if lower than MIN, put it into MIN. If neither, just read the next mark.

So a descriptive solution is:

Description
1. Start
2. Set counter to 1
3. Read number
4. Start WHILE ... WEND ... loop; if number=−9999 then exit loop
5. If number>max then make number become new max
6. If number<min then make number become new min
7. Increment counter
8. Read next number
9. Loop back to 4
10. Output min, max and average

(Figure 4)

And a flowchart:

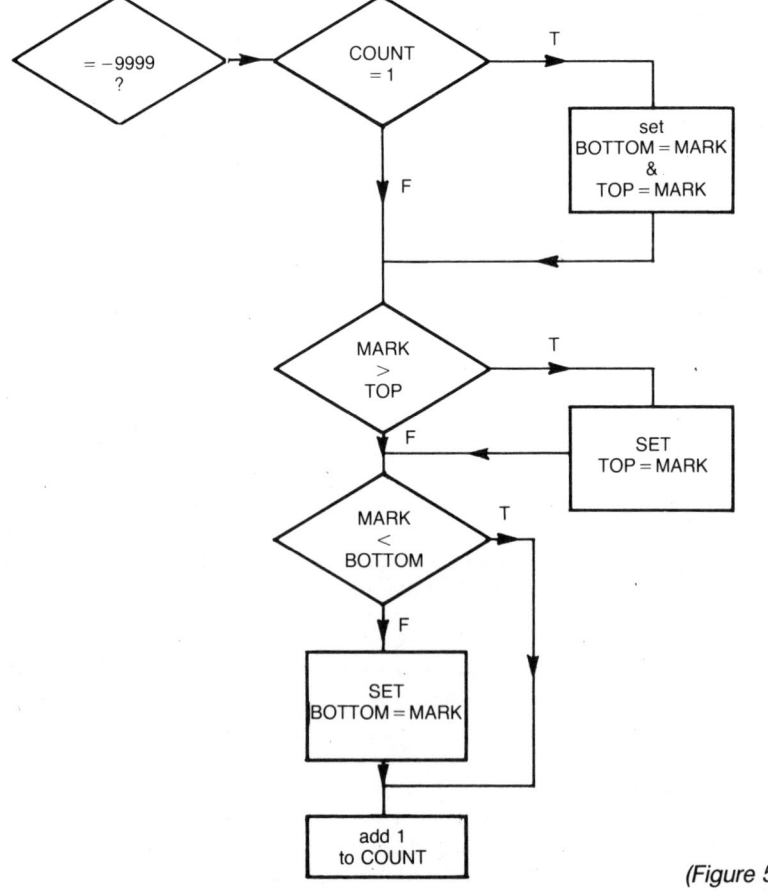

(Figure 5)

```
 10 REM**MAX AND MIN**
 20 LET COUNT=0
 30 LET MAX=0
 40 LET MIN=0
 50 READ NUMBER
 60 LET MAX=NUMBER
 70 LET MIN=NUMBER
 80 LET SUM=0
 90 WHILE NUMBER<>-9999
100 LET SUM=SUM+NUMBER
110 IF NUMBER>MAX THEN LET MAX=NUMBER
120 IF NUMBER<MIN THEN LET MIN=NUMBER
130 COUNT=COUNT+1
140 READ NUMBER
150 WEND
160 REM*********************
170 PRINT
180 PRINT "MAX=";MAX;" MIN=";MIN
190 PRINT "AVERAGE=";SUM/COUNT
200 REM*********************
210 DATA 56,47,52,65,24,34,59,37,49,66
220 DATA 38,24,62,76,31,47,66,61,74,45
230 DATA 66,44,55,67,36,56,54,54,50,43
240 DATA 18,83,23,79,29,-9999
RUN
MAX=83     MIN=18
AVERAGE=50.57143
```

Program 2.

K Program 2.

Exercise 4
Write a program to draw up a frequency table for the data in Program 2, using categories:

0–9, 10–19, 20–29, . . . 90–99

Suggestion
You could use a score-list

S(0), S(10), S(20), . . . S(90)

And for each mark read in, test whether it is less than the top of the second band (10), less than the top of the third band (20), etc. until you find

MARK<K true

then increment S(K−10). This is the approach we have used (see answer).

7.4 Number crunching

We have avoided anything other than fairly simple arithmetic so far in the course, and will continue to do so. But it would be wrong not to give a brief insight into the computer's arithmetic capacity. If your heart sinks at the sight of the following few pages, you will miss no vital programming information if you pass on to the next section on dry-running and tracing, but we hope you will give it a try. Our machine certainly does take the drudgery out of arithmetic.

Here is a simple program which calculates for the numbers 1 to 10 their *squares*, *cubes* and *reciprocals* and then tabulates the result.

```
10 REM**TABULATES THE SQUARES, CUBES AND
20 REM**RECIPROCALS FOR THE FIRST TEN
30 REM**NATURAL NUMBERS
40 PRINT "N","N*N","N*N*N","1/N"
50 PRINT
60 FOR N=1 TO 10
70 PRINT N,N*N,N*N*N,1/N
80 NEXT N
90 END
```
Program 3

```
RUN
N          N*N            N*N*N          1/N

1          1              1              1
2          4              8              .5
3          9              27             .333333
4          16             64             .25
5          25             125            .2
6          36             216            .166667
7          49             343            .142857
8          64             512            .125
9          81             729            .111111
10         100            1000           .1
OK
```

K Program 3.

Raising to a power

We expect that you are familiar with the notation:

$4 \times 4 = 4^2$ (4-squared or 4 raised to the power 2)
$7 \times 7 \times 7 = 7^3$ (7-cubed or 7 raised to the power 3)
$10 \times 10 \times 10 \times 10 \times 10 = 10^5$ (10 raised to the power 5)

In BASIC raised to the power is shown as ↑ or simply ∧. Any number N raised to the power P is shown as N ↑ P. P is called the exponent and, would you believe it, raising to a power is called exponentiation.

Similarly for negative powers:

		N	P	N↑P
$\frac{1}{4} \times \frac{1}{4} = \frac{1}{4 \times 4} = 4^{-2}$		4	−2	4↑(−2)
$\frac{1}{7} \times \frac{1}{7} \times \frac{1}{7} = \frac{1}{7 \times 7 \times 7} = 7^{-3}$		7	−3	7↑(−3)
$\frac{1}{10} \times \frac{1}{10} \times \frac{1}{10} \times \frac{1}{10} \times \frac{1}{10} = \frac{1}{10 \times 10 \times 10 \times 10 \times 10} = 10^{-5}$		10	−5	10↑(−5)

Fractional powers (positive and negative) are also possible but we will not be concerned with them.

We can use the ↑ notation instead of * in Program 3. Thus Program 3 re-written with ↑ becomes:

```
10 PRINT "N","N∧2","N∧3","N∧-1"
20 FOR N=1 TO 10
30 PRINT N,N∧2,N∧3,N∧-1
40 NEXT N
50 END
```

Program 4

Sequences and their sums

Calculating the individual terms in a sequence, or the sum of the first N terms, is a very great labour without a computer. Think how long it would take you to evaluate the terms of

$$\frac{1}{1^2}, \frac{1}{2^2}, \frac{1}{3^2}, \cdots \frac{1}{N^2}?$$

Well, it's very easy with Program 5.

```
10 PRINT "N","N∧-2"
20 FOR N=1 TO 10
30 PRINT N,N∧-2
40 NEXT N
50 END
```

Program 5

```
RUN
N         N∧-2
 1        1
 2        .25
 3        .1111111
 4        .0625
 5        .04
 6        2.777778E-02
 7        2.040816E-02
 8        .015625
 9        1.234568E-02
10        .01
OK
```

(Your computer will show numbers with E in them in column 2. This will be explained in Section 7.6)

[K] Program 5.

Exercise 5

Write a program to find how many terms of the series

$$1, \frac{1}{2}, \frac{1}{3}, \frac{1}{4}, \cdots$$

are needed to make their sum exceed 2.4

Exercise 6

Modify the program from Exercise 5 to find out how many terms are needed for

$$\text{sum} = 1 + \frac{1}{2^2} + \frac{1}{3^2} + \frac{1}{4^2} + \ldots$$

to exceed 1.5

Exercise 7
Factorials are interesting numbers. Factorial $4 = 4 \times 3 \times 2 \times 1$ and is usually written 4! So

Factorial $7 = 7 \times 6 \times 5 \times 4 \times 3 \times 2 \times 1 = 7!$

Factorial $N = N \times (N-1) \times (N-2) \times \ldots \times 1 = N!$

Write a program to evaluate the factorial of any positive integer.

Exercise 8
We wrote a rather clumsy program to evaluate the yield (Y) on a deposit (D) at compound interest percentage (P) way back in Unit 1. A neater formula is $Y = D \times (1 + P/100)^T$

where T is the number of years of the investment

Write a program to evaluate the yield, using this formula, for various deposits, percentages and time periods.

7.5 Dry running

Often we find that a program either does not work at all, or not to our complete satisfaction. If we have reasonable access to a computer we may sit at the machine until we trace the fault, but when all else fails we may be forced to sit down with pencil and paper and think hard. Stepping through an algorithm line by line with pencil and paper is called *dry running*.

We shall illustrate dry running by looking at Program 17, which is the solution to Exercise 5 (page 177).

```
10 REM**SUM OF RECIPROCALS**
20 LET SUM=0
30 LET NUMBER=1
40 WHILE SUM<=2.4
50 LET SUM=SUM+1/NUMBER
60 LET NUMBER=NUMBER+1
70 WEND
80 PRINT "SUM=";SUM;" THE NO. OF TERMS IS";NUMBER-1
90 END
```
Program 17 (from Exercise 5)

```
RUN
SUM=2.45 THE NO.OF TERMS IS 6
OK
```

Tracing means finding and recording each step, the line number executed at that step and the values of the variables *after* that line has been executed. So, for Program 17 we need the headings:

step no.	line no.	N	S
1			
2			
etc			

We omit from the trace, lines which don't affect the variables, i.e.:

```
REM      10
WHILE    40
```
etc.

Apart from these, the program steps are as follows:

step no.	line no.	N	S
1	20	–	0
2	30	1	0
3	50	1	1
4	60	2	1
5	50	2	1.5
6	60	3	1.5
7	50	3	1.83
8	60	4	1.83
9	50	4	2.08
10	60	5	2.08
11	50	5	2.28
12	60	6	2.28
13	50	6	2.45
14	60	7	2.45
15	80	6	2.45

Note the effect of WHILE ... WEND ... repeating lines 50 and 60.

(Figure 6)

Tracing
Most BASIC interpreters provide a TRACE command, but these often provide so much information that it is difficult to see the wood for the trees. A carefully designed trace routine of your own often works best. We shall not, therefore, show the TRACE command at work but will show you later in this Unit how to write your own trace into a program.

SAQ 2
Complete a dry-run on the following program, starting when line 20 has just been executed and continuing until the condition in line 40 is broken. Draw up the table with the same headings as in the above example.

```
10 REM**SUM OF SQUARES**
20 SUM=0
30 NUMBER=0
40 WHILE SUM<50
50 SUM=SUM+NUMBER^2
60 NUMBER=NUMBER+1
70 WEND
80 PRINT "SUM=";SUM;" NO OF TERMS=";NUMBER
90 END
```

Program 6

7.6 The representation of numbers

So far in the course we have left in abeyance a number of questions about the representation of numbers in our programs. We do not intend to consider the mathematics of number representation in computers in general but we need to tidy up our ideas about numbers.

In general terms computers must be able to process and store the following types of number:

(a) positive and negative whole numbers (integers or counting numbers);
(b) fractions and numbers which are partly whole and partly fractional (measuring numbers);
(c) very large numbers and very small numbers;
(d) the number zero.

The single most important piece of advice that we can give you at this stage is that if a number has been involved in any sort of calculation within a program then consider it with a certain amount of suspicion. The reason for this statement is that numbers within a computer are stored and manipulated in binary form, that is to the base 2, rather than to the base 10 with which we are familiar. In our familiar decimal notation you will recall that a number like $1/3$ or $1/7$ is incapable of exact expression, e.g. $1/3 = 0.3333\ldots$ We assume that by adding on as many 3s to this number as we wish, we can achieve an acceptable level of accuracy in any particular problem. In the binary system, in just the same way, some numbers cannot be expressed exactly, e.g. in decimal form we can say that $1/10 = 0.1$ exactly but when this number is changed into binary form it cannot be represented exactly.

The BASICA interpreter allows for numbers to be expressed to an accuracy of seven decimal digits. In decimal form, then, the number $3^1/_{10}$ could be represented as 3.100000 to seven decimal digit accuracy. However, if this number had been the result of some calculation within a computer, we might find that the number output was 3.099999 or 3.100001. So, in general, you must always be suspicious of the least significant digit in any answer (i.e. the digit on the far right of the number).

Program 7 shows how this type of inaccuracy may occur. The FOR . . . NEXT . . . loop adds 4.0, 4.1 and 4.25 into locations S, T and U one thousand times. Now 4.0 and 4.25 are exactly represented in binary form, but 4.1 is not. We can see that the result of this repetitious summation is exact in respect of 4.0 and 4.25, but not for 4.1 where the error is 0.04 in 4100.00. Obviously, we would avoid writing programs involving such repetitions wherever possible, but we hope that the program will act as a warning about possible inaccuracies.

```
 10 REM**ACCURACY DEMONSTRATION**
 20 LET S=0
 30 LET T=0
 40 LET U=0
 50 FOR I=1 TO 1000
 60 LET S=S+4.0
 70 LET T=T+4.1
 80 LET U=U+4.25
 90 NEXT I
100 PRINT S,T,U
110 END
```

Program 7

```
RUN
4000      4100.04     4250

OK
```

K Program 7.

Small and large numbers

Seven decimal digits do not allow us to cope with very small or very large numbers. So these numbers are represented in BASIC in exponential form.

Small numbers

0.000586321 means $\dfrac{586321}{1{,}000{,}000{,}000} = \dfrac{586321}{10^9}$

which could be expressed 586321×10^{-9}. We could also express 0.000586321 as

$\dfrac{0.586321}{1000} = 0.586321 \times 10^{-3}$

in BASIC this last number would be written as 0.586321E−3 or 0.586321E−03.

Similarly,

$0.0234539 = 2.34539 \times 10^{-2} = 2.34539E-2$

and

$0.00000000959734 = 0.959734 \times 10^{-8} = 0.959734E-8$

E stands for exponent, and the base for exponentiation is 10. So E−4 means move the decimal point 4 places to the left, and E+9 means move the decimal point 9 places to the right.

Large numbers

$12368500 = 1.23685 \times 10^7 = 1.23685E+7$
$935.432 = 0.935432 \times 10^3 = 0.935432E+3$
$959734000000000000000 = 0.959734E+21$

The BASICA interpreter has a range of E−39 to E+38.

[K] Find out how your computer represents small and large numbers with this program.

```
10 REM**NUMBER DEMONSTRATION**
20 PRINT "NUMBER","REPRESENTATION"
30 FOR I=-10 TO 10
40 PRINT "10^";I,10^I
50 NEXT I
```

Program 8

7.7 The ABS-function

An arithmetic function related to the above ideas, is to find the *modulus*, or *absolute value* of a number. It sounds rather grand, but is very simple.

ABS(X) simply gives us the positive value of X.
e.g. ABS(23)=23, ABS(−23)=23.

The following program illustrates the function.

```
 10 REM**THE ABS FUNCTION**
 20 PRINT "X","Y","X+Y","ABS(X+Y)"
 30 FOR I=1 TO 4
 40 READ X,Y
 50 PRINT X,Y,X+Y,ABS(X+Y)
 60 NEXT I
100 DATA 5,7,5,-7,-5,7,-5,-7
```

Program 9

```
RUN
X        Y        X+Y      ABS(X+Y)
5        7        12       12
5        -7       -2       2
-5       7        2        2
-5       -7       -12      12
OK
```

[K] Program 9.

SAQ 3
What will the print-out table be if we change line 100 to

`100 DATA 9,14,11,-2,-4,13,-7,-8`

7.8 Iteration

The process of making a guess at a value, testing it, making a better guess and testing again, etc., until we home in on an item or value is known as *iteration*. The essence of iteration involves:

- making an arbitrary guess
- testing how accurate this point is
- refining this in a sequence of repeated operations.

Square root by iteration

BASIC can do square roots directly, as this program demonstrates:

```
10 FOR X=33 TO 63 STEP(10)
20 PRINT X,X^(.5),SQR(X)
30 NEXT X
```

Program 10

SQR(X) gives the square root of X provided that X>=0

```
RUN
33      5.744562      5.744563
43      6.55739       6.55739
53      7.280111      7.28011
63      7.937253      7.937254
```

However, we shall also show you how to find a square root by an iterative method, not because that's how you would normally do it but because it's an easy example through which to demonstrate iteration.

The method

If you want to square root a number N, then:

- take a guess at the square root, say G;
- work out N/G;
- then the average of G and N/G will be an even better guess than your first one, i.e. it will be closer to the unknown square root than your first guess:
- go back to the beginning using this new 'better' guess;

We shan't prove this here (it's in plenty of maths textbooks) but we shall show its working in a simple case.

To square root $N = 12$
Guess $G = 2$
Work out $N/G = 6$
Take average $\dfrac{G + N/G}{2} = \dfrac{2 + 6}{2} = 4$

So 4 is the new guess:

Guess $G = 4$
$N/G = 3$
$\dfrac{G + N/G}{2} = 3.5$

So 3.5 is the new guess.

In table form this looks like

G	N/G	$\frac{G+N/G}{2}$
2	12/2=6	(2+6)/2=4
4	12/4=3	(4+3)/2=3.5
3.5	12/3.5=...	....

(Figure 5)

SAQ 4
To make sure that you have grasped the process draw up a table similar to that above, but make your first guess 1.

Iteration ... stop
The question now is: 'How do we stop the process?' Well, we want to stop the process when the square of our guess becomes as close as possible to N. What do we mean by 'as close as possible'? The answer is that it's up to you. You're in charge! How accurate do you want the square root to be? If, for example, we wish to find the square root of 12 to 2 decimal places, then the difference between G*G and N would have to be

`<0.005`

We don't need to know whether G*G is bigger or smaller than N — only the difference matters. So we are back to ABS. If

`ABS(N-G*G)<0.005`

then stop, is what we are after.

Descriptive algorithm for square root iteration
1. Start
2. Input the number whose square root is sought
3. Input the accuracy required
4. Make first iteration
5. Start WHILE ... WEND ... loop. If result is to required accuracy then exit loop
6. Make another iteration
7. Loop back to 5
8. Output result
9. Stop

(Figure 6)

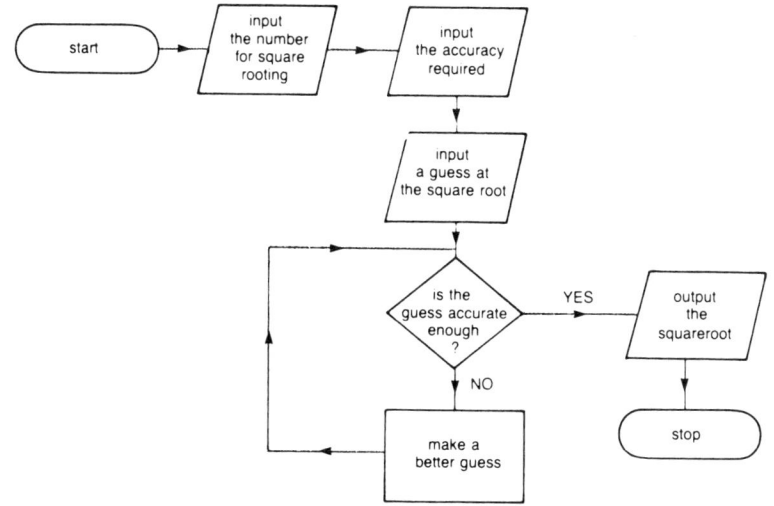

(Figure 7   Flowchart for square root iteration)

```
10  REM**SQRT BY ITERATION**
20  INPUT "NO.FOR SQUARE-ROOTING";NUMBER
30  INPUT "ACCURACY REQUIRED";ACCURACY
40  INPUT "YOUR GUESS";GUESS
60  WHILE ABS(NUMBER-GUESS*GUESS)>ACCURACY
70  LET GUESS=.5*(GUESS+(NUMBER/GUESS))
80  WEND
90  PRINT
100 PRINT "THE SQRT OF ";NUMBER;" IS ";GUESS
110 END
```

Program 11   Square root iteration

```
RUN
NO. FOR SQUARE-ROOTING? 12
ACCURACY REQUIRED? .005
YOUR GUESS? 2

THE SQRT OF 12 IS 3.464286
OK

RUN
NO. FOR SQUARE-ROOTING? 12
ACCURACY REQUIRED? .00005
YOUR GUESS? 2

THE SQRT OF 12 IS 3.464102
OK
```

K Program 11.

Tracing the iterative process

Now the result of Program 11 is not very startling. As we pointed out earlier on, we can find square roots directly with a computer. But we wanted a simple example to demonstrate iteration at work so we will now take a closer look at what is happening. We will put a trace into Program 11 as follows:

```
45 PRINT "OLD","NEW","ABS(NUMBER-GUESS*GUESS)"
65 PRINT GUESS,
75 PRINT GUESS,ABS(NUMBER-GUESS*GUESS)
```

In each pass round the loop (i.e. each iteration), lines 65 and 75 print out a report on how the calculation is going.

```
 10 REM**SQRT BY ITERATION**
 20 INPUT "NO.FOR SQUARE-ROOTING";NUMBER
 30 INPUT "ACCURACY REQUIRED";ACCURACY
 40 INPUT "YOUR GUESS";GUESS
 45 PRINT "OLD","NEW","ABS(NUMBER-GUESS*GUESS)"
 60 WHILE ABS(NUMBER-GUESS*GUESS)>ACCURACY
 65 PRINT GUESS,
 70 LET GUESS=.5*(GUESS+(NUMBER/GUESS))
 75 PRINT GUESS,ABS(NUMBER-GUESS*GUESS)
 80 WEND
 90 PRINT
100 PRINT "THE SQRT OF ";NUMBER;" IS ";GUESS
110 END
```

Program 12   Iterative square root with trace

```
RUN
NO. FOR SQUARE-ROOTING? 12
ACCURACY REQUIRED? .005
YOUR GUESS? 2

OLD        NEW           ABS(NUMBER-GUESS*GUESS)
2          4             4
4          3.5           .25
3.5        3.464286      1.276016E-03  ──── 3 loops only

THE SQRT OF 12 IS 3.464286
OK
```

```
RUN
NO. FOR SQUARE-ROOTING? 12
ACCURACY REQUIRED? .0005  ─────────── increasing the accuracy tenfold
YOUR GUESS? 2                         still only takes 4 loops

OLD        NEW           ABS(NUMBER-GUESS*GUESS)
2          4             4
4          3.5           .25
3.5        3.464286      1.276016E-03
3.464286   3.464102      0

THE SQRT OF 12 IS 3.464102
OK
```

K Program 12.

```
RUN
NO. FOR SQUARE-ROOTING? -67 ──── if we give it a negative number
ACCURACY REQUIRED? .005
YOUR GUESS? 8
```

```
OLD            NEW            ABS(NUMBER-GUESS*GUESS)
8              -.1875         67.03516
-.1875         178.5729       31955.29
178.5729       89.09886       8005.607
89.09886       44.17345       2018.293
44.17345       21.32835       521.8983
21.32835       9.093494       149.6916
9.093494       .8627939       67.74441
.8627939       -38.39595      1541.249
-38.39595      -18.32549      402.8235
-18.32549      -7.334688      120.7977
-7.334688      .8999939       67.80999
.8999939       -36.77248      1419.215
-36.77248      -17.47523      372.3837
-17.47523      -6.820617      113.5208
^C
BREAK IN 75                                  it doesn't like it, and we have
OK                                           to pull the plug!
```

Exercise 9
Change the square root program above to produce cube roots. If G is a guess at the cube root of N then $\frac{1}{2}(G+N/G^2)$ will be a better guess.

Assignment 7

1. If G is a guess at the solution of the quadratic equation $X^2+BX+C=0$, then a better guess is $-C/(B+G)$. Devise an algorithm and write a BASIC program to find the solution of any quadratic equation.

   Notes:

   (a) By solution we mean a value of X which makes the left-hand side of the equation equal to zero.
   (b) When testing your algorithm choose values of B and C such that $B^2>4C$.

Objectives of Unit 7

Calculate (manually) an arithmetic mean	☐
Write a program to calculate arithmetic means	☐
Write a program to find the largest and smallest item in a data list	☐
Use *, / and ↑ in programs	☐
Dry run a program	☐
Interpret numbers in E notation	☐
Use ABS(X)	☐

Write programs for iterative routines to include terminating procedures ☐
Insert trace print lines in a program ☐

Answers to SAQs and Exercises
SAQ 1
Sum=8+4+2+6+1+7+6+1+4=39
There are 9 numbers
So the arithmetic mean is 39/9=4.333 . . .

Exercise 1

```
 10 REM**AVERAGE LENGTH**
 20 LET SUM=0
 30 LET COUNT=1
 40 READ WORD$
 50 WHILE WORD$<>"ZZZZ"
 60 LET LENGTH=LEN(WORD$)
 70 LET SUM=SUM+LENGTH
 80 LET COUNT=COUNT+1
 90 READ WORD$
100 WEND
110 LET NUMBER=COUNT-1
120 LET AVERAGE=SUM/NUMBER
130 PRINT "AVERAGE LENGTH OF THE WORD IS ";AVERAGE
140 END
150 DATA THE,HORSE,STOOD,STILL,TILL,HE,HAD,FINISHED,
    THE,HYMN
160 DATA WHICH,JUDE,REPEATED,UNDER,THE,SWAY,OF,
    A,POLYTHEISTIC
170 DATA FANCY,THAT,HE,WOULD,NEVER,HAVE,THOUGHT,
    OF,HUMOURING
180 DATA IN,BROAD,DAYLIGHT,ZZZZ
```
Program 13

[K] Program 13.

Exercise 2

```
 10 REM**MEAN OF 100 THROWS**
 20 REM**OF 1 DIE**
 30 RANDOMISE VAL(RIGHT$(TIME$,2))
 40 LET SUM=0
 50 FOR I=1 TO 100
 60 LET TOSS1=INT(6*RND(1)+1)
 70 LET SUM=SUM+TOSS1
 80 NEXT I
 90 PRINT "AVERAGE SCORE=";SUM/100
100 END
```
Program 14

[K] Program 14.

Exercise 3

```
 60 REM**MEAN OF 100 THROWS**
 20 REM**OF 2 DICE**
 30 RANDOMISE VAL(RIGHT$(TIME$,2))
 40 LET SUM=0
 50 FOR I=1 TO 100
 60 LET TOSS1=INT(6*RND(1)+1)
 70 LET TOSS2=INT(6*RND(1)+1)
 80 LET SUM=SUM+TOSS1+TOSS2
 90 NEXT I
100 PRINT "AVERAGE SCORE=";SUM/100
110 END
```

Program 15

K Program 15.

Exercise 4

```
  5 OPTION BASE 1
 10 REM**HISTOGRAM**
 20 DIM SCORES(100)
 30 READ MARK
 40 WHILE MARK<>-9999
 50 CAT=10
 60 WHILE MARK>=CAT ───────────────── CAT for score category
 70 CAT=CAT+10                        or class interval
 80 WEND
 90 SCORES(CAT-10)=SCORES(CAT-10)+1── correct category found.
100 READ MARK                         Increment counter for
110 WEND                              that category.
120 FOR I=0 TO 90 STEP 10
130 PRINT I,SCORES(I)
140 NEXT I
150 END
160 DATA 56,47,52,65,24,34,59,37,49,66
170 DATA 38,24,62,76,31,47,66,61,74,45
180 DATA 66,44,55,67,36,56,54,54,50,43
190 DATA 18,83,23,79,29,-9999
```

Program 16

```
RUN
  0       0
 10       1
 20       4
 30       5
 40       6
 50       8
 60       7
 70       3
 80       1
 90       0
```

K Program 16.

Exercise 5

```
10 REM**SUM OF RECIPROCALS**
20 LET SUM=0
30 LET NUMBER=1
40 WHILE SUM<=2.4
50 LET SUM=SUM+1/NUMBER
60 LET NUMBER=NUMBER+1
70 WEND
80 PRINT "SUM=";SUM;" THE NO. OF TERMS IS";NUMBER-1
90 END
```
Program 17

```
RUN
SUM=2.45 THE NO. OF TERMS IS 6
```

K Program 17.

Exercise 6

```
10 REM**SUM OF N^-2**
20 SUM=0
30 NUMBER=1
40 WHILE SUM<=1.5
50 SUM=SUM+NUMBER^-2
60 NUMBER=NUMBER+1
70 WEND
80 NUMBER=NUMBER-1
90 PRINT "SUM=";SUM;" NO. OF TERMS=";NUMBER
100 END
```
Program 18

```
RUN
SUM=1.511797 NO. OF TERMS=7
```

You can, of course, change line 40 to explore the number of terms needed for the sum to exceed other values, e.g.

```
40 WHILE SUM<1.6
```

to find the number of terms needed to make 1.6.

What a good starting point these and similar programs would make to lessons about limits and convergence of numbers series!

K Program 18.

Exercise 7

```
10 REM...FACTORIALS
20 PRINT "TO END THE RUN, ENTER -9999"
30 PRINT
40 INPUT "FIRST FACTORIAL";NUMBER
50 WHILE NUMBER<>-9999
60 LET FACTORIAL=1
```

```
 70 FOR I=1 TO NUMBER
 80 FACTORIAL=FACTORIAL*I
 90 NEXT I
100 PRINT NUMBER,FACTORIAL
110 INPUT "NEXT FACTORIAL";NUMBER
120 WEND
130 END
```

Program 19

```
RUN
TO END THE RUN, ENTER -9999

FIRST FACTORIAL? 1
 1            1

NEXT FACTORIAL? 3
 3            6

NEXT FACTORIAL? 5
 5           120

NEXT FACTORIAL? 7
 7          5040

NEXT FACTORIAL? 9
 9        362880

NEXT FACTORIAL? 11
 11      3.99168E+07  ──────  what's happened here?
                               See the section on number representation
NEXT FACTORIAL? -9999
OK
```

K Program 19.

Exercise 8

```
10 REM**COMPOUND INTEREST**
20 PRINT "ENTER DEPOSIT, PERCENTAGE, TIME"
30 INPUT DEPOSIT,PERCENTAGE,YEARS
40 PRINT "TIME","YIELD"
50 FOR I=1 TO YEARS
60 PRINT I,DEPOSIT*(1+PERCENTAGE/100)^I
70 NEXT I
80 END
```

Program 20

```
ENTER DEPOSIT, PERCENTAGE, TIME
500, 11.5, 5
TIME     YIELD
1        557.5
2        621.612
3        693.098
4        772.8041
5        861.6766
```

K Program 20.

SAQ 2

Step No	Line No	N	S
1	20		0
2	30	0	0
3	50	1	1
4	60	2	1
5	50	2	5
6	60	3	5
7	50	3	14
8	60	4	14
9	50	4	30
10	60	5	30
11	50	5	55

SAQ 3

```
RUN
X         Y         X+Y        ABS(X+Y)
 9        14         23         23
11        -2          9          9
-4        13          9          9
-7        -8        -15         15
```

SAQ 4

G	N/G	$\frac{G+N/G}{2}$
1	12	6.5
6.5	1.8	4.15
4.15	2.89	3.52
3.52	3.41	3.46 etc

Exercise 9

```
 10 REM**CUBEROOT ITERATION**
 20 INPUT "NUMBER FOR CUBEROOTING";NUMBER
 30 INPUT "ACCURACY REQUIRED";ACCURACY
 40 LET GUESS=NUMBER/2  ── the machine makes the first guess at NUMBER/2
 50 COUNTER=1
 60 WHILE ABS(NUMBER-GUESS*GUESS*GUESS)>ACCURACY
 70 LET GUESS=.5*(GUESS+NUMBER/(GUESS*GUESS))
 80 LET COUNTER=COUNTER+1
 90 WEND
100 PRINT "THE NO. OF LOOPS=";COUNTER
110 PRINT "THE CUBEROOT OF";NUMBER;"=";GUESS
120 END
```

Program 21

```
RUN
NUMBER FOR CUBEROOTING? 28
ACCURACY REQUIRED? .005
THE NO. OF LOOPS=14
THE CUBEROOT OF 28=3.03641
OK

RUN
NUMBER FOR CUBEROOTING? 10101
ACCURACY REQUIRED? .005
THE NO. OF LOOPS=28
THE CUBEROOT OF 10101=21.61664
OK

RUN
NUMBER FOR CUBEROOTING? -937
ACCURACY REQUIRED? .005
THE NO. OF LOOPS=21
THE CUBEROOT OF-937=-9.785419
OK
```

K Program 21.

UNIT 8
An introduction to data processing

8.1	Introduction	196
8.2	Sorting	196
8.3	Subroutines	199
8.4	Searching	203
8.5	Tables	208
	Assignment 8	214
	Objectives of Unit 8	214
	Answers to SAQs and Exercises	215

8.1 Introduction

In this Unit we shall emphasise again how important it is to impose some sort of order on data. In particular, we shall analyse in detail one method of ordering data: the interchange procedure for sorting. Having sorted the data we shall then show how to search through it quickly using the bisection search procedure. Finally we shall look at how to handle data in tabular form.

These activities will also give us a chance to see how subroutines can help us perform many of those little repetitive tasks which can occur in programs of any size.

8.2 Sorting

In Unit 4 we spent some time discussing the procedure for finding the lowest value item in a list. We did this by an interchange procedure that put the lowest item into position 1 on the list. We said that we could repeat the procedure for the rest of the list, placing the second lowest value into position 2, etc., and we left you with the problem of sorting the whole list as an assignment. Because of the interchange sort's importance, we are now going to look at it in greater detail.

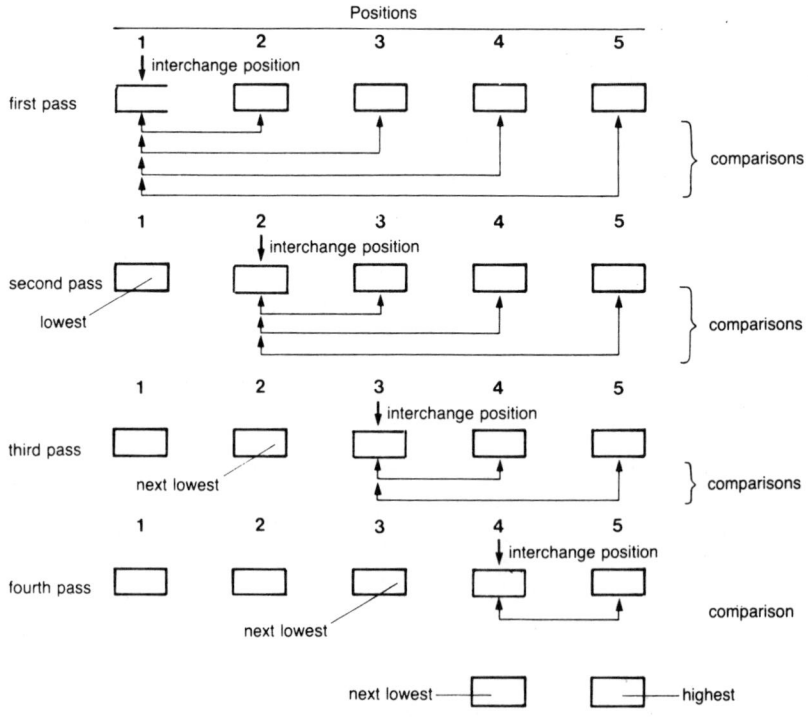

(Figure 1   The sort procedure for a list of 5 items)

Figure 1 illustrates the procedure for placing the items into locations 1 to 5 with the lowest item in 1, the next lowest in 2 and so on.

First pass
On the first pass all items are compared with the item in position 1 and the lowest is then placed in position 1.

Second pass
Position 1 can now be ignored and the procedure repeated on positions 2 to 5. This will find the next lowest which is placed in position 2.

Third pass
Now positions 1 and 2 can be ignored since they contain 'lowest' and 'next to lowest'. The procedure is repeated on positions 3 to 5. This finds the third lowest which goes in position 3.

Fourth pass
This is performed on items 4 and 5 only and results in the fourth lowest going into the fourth position. The remaining item must be the highest and will already be in the fifth position so no further passes are needed.

We can summarise the sort procedure as:

loop number	interchange point	remaining sub-sequence	
		start	end
1	1	2	5
2	2	3	5
3	3	4	5
4	4	5	5

(Figure 2   Four sorts in a list of 5 items)

Or, more generally, if we want to sort a list of N items:

loop number	interchange point	remaining sub-sequence	
		start	end
1	1	2	N
2	2	3	.
3	3	4	.
.	.	.	N
K	K	K+1	.
.	.	.	N
.	.	.	N
N−1	N−1	N	N

(Figure 2a   (N−1 sorts in a list of N items)

Since each pass involves a repetitive series of comparisons, it is an obvious candidate for a FOR ... NEXT ... loop. Then we need a further loop to decide which loop we are going round:

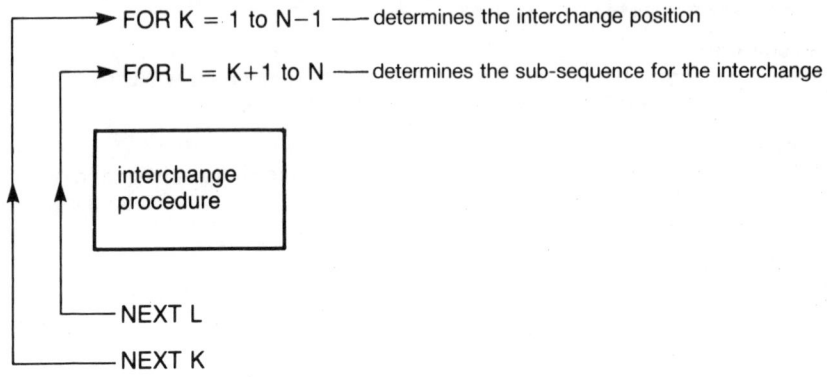

(Figure 3 The nested loops of interchange sorting)

SAQ 1
Use the interchange sort to place the following in order. Show the numbers stored at each location after each run

6, 1, 4, 0, 2, 3, 7, 8

The program is:

outer loop decides
interchange point

```
120 REM**SORT ROUTINE**
130 FOR K=1 TO NUMBER-1
140 FOR L=K+1 to NUMBER
150 WHILE ANAME$(L)<ANAME$(K)
160 TEMP$=ANAME$(L)
170 ANAME$(L)=ANAME$(K)
180 ANAME$(K)=TEMP$
190 WEND
200 NEXT L
210 NEXT K
220 REM**END OF SORT ROUTINE**
```

if the item in the sub-sequence is < the item in the interchange position then interchange

the 'power-house': should be condensed onto one line to speed up the process

Program 1 Interchange sort

inner loop decides the sub-sequence

Using the sort program
The sort program can be used whenever it is needed. Here is one particular use: to sort a list of names into alphabetical order.

lines 40 to 80   read in the data
lines 120 to 220   carry out the sort
lines 230 to 280   print out the sorted list
the data has been stored in line 300

```
  5 OPTION BASE 1
 10 REM**SORT ROUTINE**
 20 DIM ANAME$(100)
 30 I=1
 40 READ BNAME$
 50 WHILE BNAME$<>"ZZZZ"
 60 ANAME$(I)=BNAME$ : I=I+1
 70 READ BNAME$
 80 WEND
 90 REM******
100 NUMBER=I-1
110 REM**GET ZZZZ OUT OF LIST
120 REM**SORT ROUTINE**
130 FOR K=1 TO NUMBER-1
140 FOR L=K+1 TO NUMBER
150 WHILE ANAME$(L)<ANAME$(K)
160 TEMP$=ANAME$(L)
170 ANAME$(L)=ANAME$(K)
180 ANAME$S(K)=TEMP$
190 WEND
200 NEXT L
210 NEXT K
220 REM**END OF SORT ROUTINE**
230 PRINT "FINAL SORTED LIST"
240 FOR P=1 TO NUMBER
250 PRINT ANAME$(P);" ";
260 NEXT P
270 PRINT
280 END
290 REM***********
300 DATA TONY,SAM,PETE,JOE,BILL,ZZZZ
```

- reads in the data
- sort routine
- printing out the result

Program 2   Using the sort routine

```
RUN
FINAL SORTED LIST
BILL JOE PETE SAM TONY
OK
```

8.3 Subroutines

By the time you have reached this stage you will begin to distinguish the wood from the trees. You will be aware that programs have an overall structure and are assemblies of smaller parts, like the paragraphs of an essay. It is usual to break a program down into its constituent parts, and to write and test each part separately. Certain operations are often repeated several times throughout a program. The structure of a program may be simplified and tidied up by including these repetitive operations as subroutines.

We shall illustrate subroutines by taking a final look at the sort procedure. We are going to insert two extra trace print lines into the program so that we can see what is happening at each of the three stages of the sort routine:

Sort routine		Trace print line to show
1.	Input	The list as taken in
2.	Sort	The list after each sub-sequence
3.	Output	The final, sorted, list

Figure 4 shows the overall structure and how we can use one PRINT subroutine for all three PRINT operations.

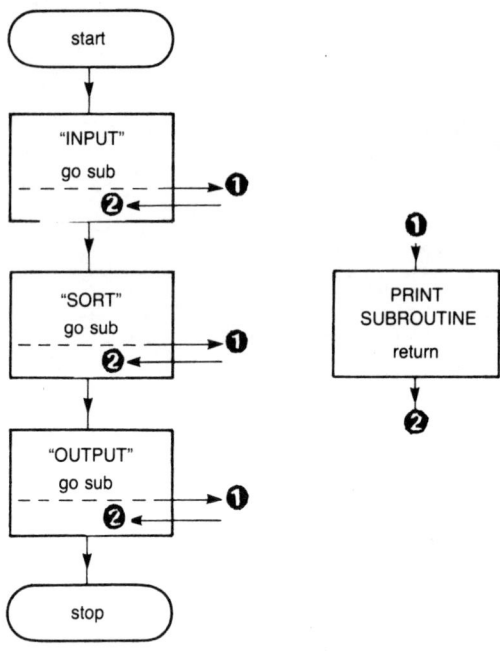

(Figure 4   Print subroutine in the sort program)

GOSUB
In BASIC to go to a subroutine we say:

GOSUB

followed by the line number of the start of the subroutine. Each subroutine must end with the statement

RETURN

which will return control to the next line in the main body of the program after the appropriate GOSUB statement. Thus in the following program segment line 30 transfers control to line 200 and lines 200 and 210 are executed. The line 220 returns control to line 40 for the program to continue in the normal way.

```
    10 INPUT A
    20 INPUT B
    30 GOSUB 200
    40 S=A+B
    50 ...

    200 PRINT "A","B"          GOSUB 200
    210 PRINT A,B
    220 RETURN
```

200

SAQ 2
What is the value of B after this program has been run: (a) if 5 is inputted; (b) if 3 is inputted?

```
10 INPUT A
20 IF A>4 THEN GOSUB 60
30 B=A*A
40 PRINT B
50 END
60 REM**SUBROUTINE**
70 B=1/A
80 PRINT B
90 RETURN
```

Program 3

Here is the sort program with a print subroutine (lines 330–390) which is used each time the program executes line 120, line 240 and line 310.

```
  5 OPTION BASE 1
 10 REM**SORT ROUTINE**
 20 DIM ANAME$(100)
 30 I=1
 40 READ BNAME$
 50 WHILE BNAME$<>"ZZZZ"
 60 ANAME$(I)=BNAME$
 70 I=I+1
 80 READ BNAME$
 90 WEND
100 NUMBER=I-1 : REM**LENGTH OF LIST**
110 PRINT "LIST AT START"
120 GOSUB 330
130 PRINT
140 REM*******************
150 REM**SORT ROUTINE***
160 FOR K=1 TO NUMBER-1
170 PRINT "PASS NO.";K
180 FOR L=K+1 TO NUMBER
190 WHILE ANAME$(L)<ANAME$(K)
200 TEMP$=ANAME$(L)
210 ANAME$(L)=ANAME$(K)
220 ANAME$(K)=TEMP$
230 WEND
240 GOSUB 330
250 NEXT L
260 PRINT
270 NEXT K
280 REM**END OF SORT ROUTINE**
290 REM***********************
300 PRINT "FINAL SORTED LIST"
310 GOSUB 330
320 END
330 REM**PRINT SUBROUTINE**        ⎤
340 FOR P=1 TO NUMBER              |
350 PRINT ANAME$(P);TAB(P*6);      |── subroutine
360 NEXT P                         |
370 PRINT                          |
380 RETURN                         ⎦
390 REM**END OF PRINT SUBROUTINE**
400 REM
410 DATA TONY,SAM,PETE,JOE,BILL,ZZZZ
```

Program 4   Print subroutine in sort program

```
RUN
LIST AT START                                              printed by GOSUB
TONY              SAM     PETE    JOE     BILL ]   ——  at line 120.

PASS NO. 1
SAM               TONY    PETE    JOE     BILL
PETE              TONY    SAM     JOE     BILL ┐
JOE               TONY    SAM     PETE    BILL │
BILL              TONY    SAM     PETE    JOE  │
                                                │        each bock printed
PASS NO. 2                                      │        by GOSUB at line
BILL              SAM     TONY    PETE    JOE   │        240 on the four
BILL              PETE    TONY    SAM     JOE   │        occasions the
BILL              JOE     TONY    SAM     PETE  ├——      program executes
                                                │        the loop controlled
PASS NO. 3                                      │        by K.
BILL              JOE     SAM     TONY    PETE  │
BILL              JOE     PETE    TONY    SAM   │

PASS NO. 4
BILL              JOE     PETE    SAM     TONY ┘

FINAL SORTED LIST                                         printed by GOSUB
BILL              JOE     PETE    SAM     TONY ]——     at line 310
```

Examples of subroutines
The purpose of a subroutine is to simplify and shorten long programs. By its very nature, then, it is difficult to get short, meaningful programs which illustrate subroutines without their often being a little contrived. We need a program where the same or similar function is repeated at different points in the program.

Example 1
The game of dice ('craps' in the USA) provides a simple example. A pair of dice is thrown twice and the total score on each throw is noted. If the two scores are the same, the game ends. If they are different, the dice are thrown again. Write a program to simulate the game which prints out the number of throws required to obtain equal scores and what that score was.

Solution

```
10  REM**2 EQUAL THROWS**
20  RANDOMISE VAL(RIGHT$(TIME$,2))
30  COUNT=1
40  GO1=2
50  GO2=1
60  WHILE GO1<>GO2
70  GOSUB 150
80  GO1=SCORE
90  GOSUB 150
100 GO2=SCORE
110 COUNT=COUNT+1
120 WEND
130 PRINT "EQUAL SCORE";GO1;"IN";COUNT;"THROWS"
140 END
150 REM**DICE ROLLING ROUTINE**
160 TOSS1=INT(6*RND(1)+1)
170 TOSS2=INT(6*RND(1)+1)
180 SCORE=TOSS1+TOSS2
190 RETURN
```

Program 5 Simulation of 'craps'

```
RUN
EQUAL SCORE 7 IN 9 THROWS
RUN
EQUAL SCORE 8 IN 21 THROWS
RUN
EQUAL SCORE 8 IN 7 THROWS
RUN
EQUAL SCORE 5 IN 4 THROWS
RUN
EQUAL SCORE 10 IN 22 THROWS
RUN
EQUAL SCORE 10 IN 7 THROWS
```

Exercise 1
(a) Write a segment of program to print a line of dashes '-------' across the screen or printer, probably 40 for the screen and 60 for the printer,

(b) Write one line of program to print a 'submarine' (see Exercise 2 below) or <=>, at any point across the screen or printer where the variable XPOS determines the position.

(c) Write a program to print on successive lines:
   (i)   a line of dashes;
   (ii) a submarine at any point;
   (iii) another line of dashes;
   with the printing in (i) and (iii) in a subroutine.

Exercise 2
Now you must admit that the solution to Exercise 1(c) looks like an aerial view of a vessel in a canal. So why not a submarine, as we are concerned with subroutines? Instead of battleships in a 2–dimensional sea, we have a submarine in a 1–dimensional canal. Anyway, we have the picture for a simple game.

Write a program to generate a random number between 1 and 38 for a screen, or 1 and 58 for a printer. (Or, of course, any width convenient for your machine.) The submarine is going to take up the last three positions of the width (38, 39, 40 or 58, 59, 60). Use the random number to print the submarine in random positions along the canal.

Exercise 3
The essence of the game we are going to play with the machine will be clear from Exercise 2. The computer generates a random number and invites you to find the submarine by guessing a number between 1 and 40, or 1 and 60. If you guess the correct position, i.e. between XPOS and XPOS+2 if XPOS is the random number (remember the submarine takes up 3 places in the line), then the machine records a 'hit' and the game ends. If you don't find the submarine, the machine will record a 'miss' and invite you to try again. Write a program to do this.

(We advise you to write the program to give yourself the option to stop playing before you find the submarine, because it is infuriating to have to try every position across the screen just to stop the program running. You could just pull the plug out, and then it would sink!)

8.4 Searching

The submarine problem gives us a good lead into discussions about searching data. The only methodical way to find the submarine was to search the canal successively position by position, starting from one end. How much easier it would have been had the program responded with 'too high' or 'too low', as appropriate, after each guess. No doubt you can immediately think of a procedure for 'homing-in' on the submarine as quickly as possible!

Similarly, if dictionaries, telephone directories, encyclopedias and library catalogues were not arranged in alphabetical order, think how difficult it would be to find the desired information.

But if we've gone to a lot of trouble to sort our data into numerical or alphabetical order, then we need an efficient search technique to find any given item. If we consult a dictionary or telephone directory for an item, we don't start looking at the first page and work methodically through the volume page by page until the item is found. We take a rough guess, e.g. if the name begins with 'P' then we try to open the directory at just over half-way through it, and start looking at that point.

Bisection search

A 'rough' guess is too imprecise a term for a computer. However, we can specify guessing points as follows:

(a) Divide the range of items into half and ask 'Is the item above or below the half-way mark?'
(b) if it is below then we define a new range with the middle item now acting as the upper limit;
(c) If above then the middle item becomes our lower limit.
(d) Either way we discard half the old range and repeat our halving or bisection procedure with the new range.

So the bisection search is, in outline:

Is 7 in the list 1, 2, 3, 4, 5, 6, 7, 8, 9, 10?

List in order: | 1 | 2 | 3 | 4 | 5 | 6 | 7 | 8 | 9 | 10 |

Halve list: | 1 | 2 | 3 | 4 | 5 | 6 | 7 | 8 | 9 | 10 |

Is 7=middle item?   No.
Is 7<middle item?   No.
So 7 is in top half.

Halve list: | 6 | 7 | 8 | 9 | 10 |

Is 7=middle item?   No.
Is 7<middle item?   Yes.

Halve list: | 6 | 7 | 8 |

Is 7=middle item? Yes.
So 7 is in list.

This outline illustrates the principle of the bisection search but in practice we need to distinguish between the values of the items in a list and the indexes of those items.

Example 2
An ordered list contains the items A, F, I, M, P, T, U, Z. Use the bisection search procedure to find whether or not P is in the list.

We call P, Query – the value we wish to enquire about:

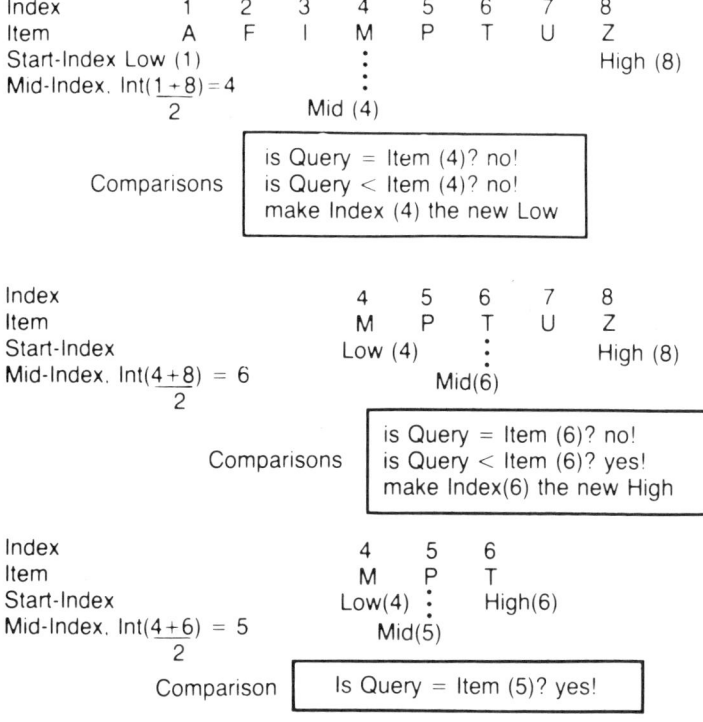

(Figure 5   Bisection search)

Exercise 4
Carry out the bisection search procedure on the list in Example 2 but looking for the letter I.

We had to make only 3 comparisons to home-in on the item 'P' in Example 2, but they were a bit long-winded, and the whole procedure may seem to have little advantage over simply searching straight through the list. The effectiveness of the method is not really apparent in short lists. We will demonstrate its power in searching longer lists later, but first we still have some loose ends to tie up.

Some problems with bisection search
(a) How to stop

Example 3
Carry out the same procedure as before, but search for the letter 'Q'.

The method would proceed exactly the same as before as far as the 3rd comparison, so we'll pick up the story there.

Query = Q

		4	5	6
Index		4	5	6
Item		M	P	T
Start-Index		Low(4)	:	High(6)
Mid-Index, Int(4 + 6) = 5			Mid(5)	
2				

Comparisons:
is Query = Item(5)? no!
is Query < Item(5)? no!
make Index(5) the new Low

		4	5	6
Index		4	5	6
Item			P	T
Start-Index			Low(5)	High(6)
Mid-Index, Int(5 + 6) = 5			Mid(5)	
2				

Comparisons:
is Query = Item(5)? no!
is Query < .... we have done this before?!

So we don't seem able to stop. Q is not there but we are stuck looking for it between P and T. We have already met the problem of stopping the process in the last example. If the indexes Low and High have moved so close that they are at adjacent positions, and Query is not yet found, then Query is not a member of the list. That is the end and outcome of the search. So the end is either when the Query has been found, or when Low and High occupy adjacent indexes (High–Low=1).

(b) How to start
To start the process seemed straightforward enough. We make Index (1)=Low and Index(N)=High. Trouble would occur, however, if Item (1) and Item (N) were not the lowest and highest possible values.

E.g. consider the following list which does not include letters before C or after S;

1	2	3	4	5
C	F	G	P	S
Low				High

If Query was A or B or higher than S, then the process would not work. The easiest solution is to ensure that the items at the ends of the list will always have the extreme values, e.g. in a list of names make Item (1)=AAAA and Item (N)=ZZZZ.

We will now outline the algorithm in flowchart form.

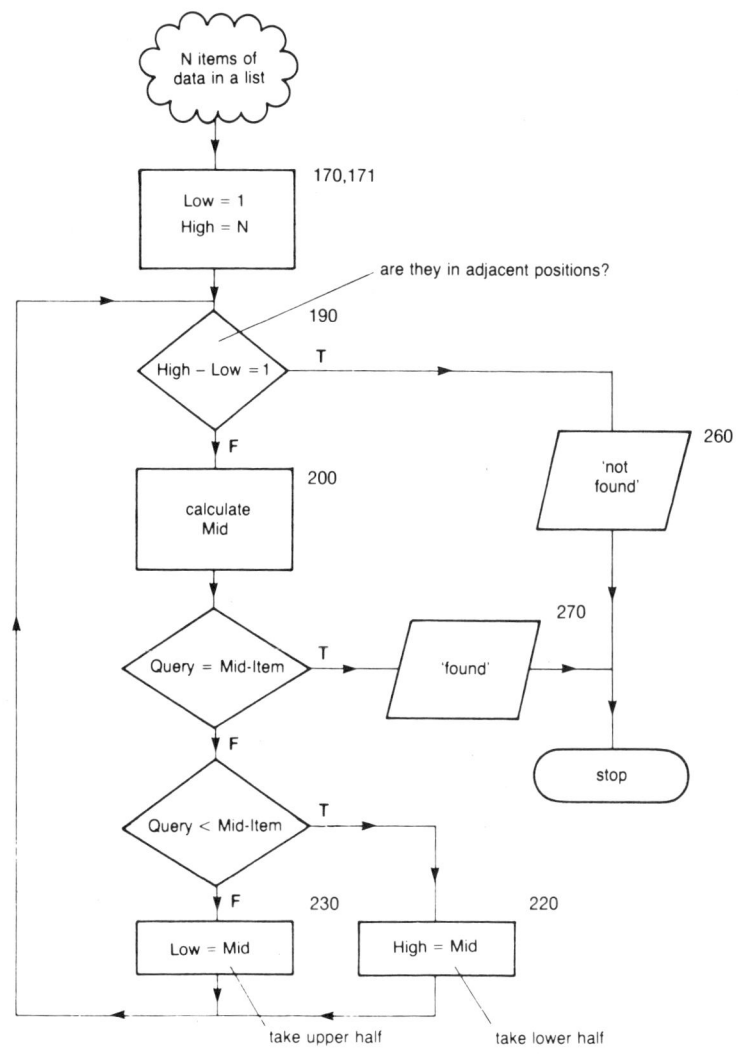

(Figure 6   Flowchart for bisection search)

All we have to do now is to write the program:

```
 5 OPTION BASE 1
10 REM**BISECTION SEARCH**
20 DIM ANAME$(20),PHONE$(20)
30 I=1
40 READ BNAME$,APHONE$
50 WHILE BNAME$<>"ZZZZ"
60 ANAME$(I)=BNAME$
70 PHONE$(I)=APHONE$
```

```
 80 I=I+1
 90 READ BNAME$,APHONE$
100 WEND
110 REM***************
120 NUMBER=I : REM**WE ARE USING ZZZZ THIS TIME**
130 REM***************
140 INPUT "QUERY NAME";QUERY$
150 REM**START OF SEARCH**
160 PRINT "LOW";TAB(5);"HIGH";TAB(15);"MID";TAB(20);
    "ANAME$(MID)"
170 LOW=1
180 HIGH=NUMBER : MID=INT((LOW+HIGH)/2)
190 WHILE HIGH-LOW<>1 AND QUERY$<>ANAME$(MID)
200 MID=INT/((LOW+HIGH)/2)
210 PRINT LOW;TAB(5);HIGH;TAB(10);MID;TAB(15);ANAME$(MID)
220 IF QUERY$<ANAME$(MID) THEN HIGH=MID
230 IF QUERY$>ANAME$(MID) THEN LOW=MID
240 WEND
250 REM**END OF SEARCH**
260 IF HIGH-LOW=1 THEN PRINT QUERY$;" IS NOT IN LIST"
270 IF QUERY$=ANAME$(MID) THEN PRINT QUERY$;
    "'S NUMBER IS ";PHONE$(MID)
280 END
290 REM**DATA FOR LIST**
300 DATA AAAA,0000
310 DATA BENNY,1234
320 DATA COPPER,9832
330 DATA DRAPER,1980
340 DATA EDDIE,7294
350 DATA GWYNNE,5821
360 DATA HETTY,8632
370 DATA MORLEY,7832
380 DATA PROSSER,1383
390 DATA SMYTHE,1147
400 DATA WEEKS,5529
410 DATA WILSON,9936
420 DATA ZZZZ,9999
```

Program 6 Bisection search program

```
RUN
QUERY NAME? MORLEY
L    H    M
1    13   7    HETTY
7    13   10   SMYTHE
7    10   8    MORLEY
MORLEY'S TELE NO. IS 7382

RUN
QUERY NAME? WEEK
L    H    ANAME$(MID)
1    13   7    HETTY
7    13   10   SMYTHE
10   13   81   WEEKS
WEEK IS NOT IN THE LIST
```

8.5 Tables

When we want to store a lot of information there are various methods open to us. One is lists (see Unit 4), which are sometimes called one-dimensional arrays. A second method is tables or two-dimensional arrays.

Suppose you want to store the following data:

	1st qtr	2nd qtr	3rd qtr	4th qtr
Car sales	20	70	80	40
Servicing	10	14	18	11
Petrol	30	45	50	30

(Figure 7   Income for Main Road Service Station (£000s))

Now you could put this in one list but it would be hard to use. The first four items would be income for car sales, the next four for servicing, etc. Alternatively you could have three lists: one for car sales, one for servicing and one for petrol. But BASIC allows you to have a two-dimensional table named by any variable name, e.g.:

TELNO (,)

Comparison of lists and tables

Lists need one index to describe a position in the list. Tables need two, which are usually called subscripts not indices (or indexes, as we have called them).

List

L(1), L(2), L(3) . . . L(l) . . .
      |
      └── index of this item = 3

Array

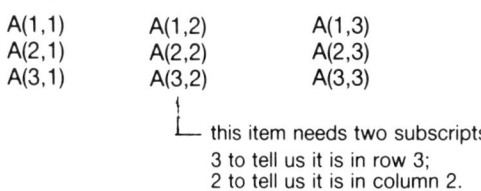

└── this item needs two subscripts:
   3 to tell us it is in row 3;
   2 to tell us it is in column 2.

Tables
- A table must contain either all string variables, or all numerical variables. (Numbers can of course be stored as strings, and their values found by the VAL-function.)
- We use one of the variable names allowed in our BASIC to describe the table as a whole. e.g. A table, B$ table, M3$ table.

Generally a table comprises:

	col.1	col.2	col.3	col.4
row 1	r1c1	r1c2	r1c3	....
row 2	r2c1	r2c2	r2c3	....
row 3	r3c1	r3c2	r3c3	....
etc	....	....	....	....

(Figure 8   The rows and columns of a table)

For the service station data, T needs three rows and four columns and so contains 12 items:

$T(1,1) \quad T(1,2) \quad T(1,3) \quad T(1,4)$
$T(2,1) \quad T(2,2) \quad T(2,3) \quad T(2,4)$
$T(3,1) \quad T(3,2) \quad T(3,3) \quad T(3,4)$

So

$T(2,1) = 10$
$T(3,3) = 50$ etc.

This is very similar to the idea of tables which you have previously met. There we said that a file consists of a series of records each of which consists of fields. In table form this would look like:

	Field 1	Field 2
	Name	Telephone number
Record 1	BENNY	1234
Record 2	COPPER	9823
Record 3	DRAPER	1950
Record 4	EDDIE	7294

Or, more generally:

	Field 1	Field 2	Field 3	etc
Record 1	R1F1	R1F2	R1F3	....
Record 2	R2F1	R2F2	R2F3	....
Record 3	R3F1	R3F2	R3F3	....
etc	....	....	....	....

If the telephone numbers table is called T$ then the individual items will be labelled:

	Field 1	Field 2
	Name	Telephone number
Record 1	T$(1,1)=BENNY	T$(1,2)=1234
Record 2	T$(2,1)=COPPER	T$(2,2)=9823
Record 3	T$(3,1)=DRAPER	T$(3,2)=1950
Record 4	T$(4,1)=EDDIE	T$(4,2)=7294

- The whole table is called T$ table.
- Each item in the table is described by two subscripts. Thus 1950 (3rd row, 2nd column) is

  T$(3,2)

- The 3 and 2 describe the position of item T$(3,2), not its value. Its value is 1950. So we say

  T$(3,2)=1950

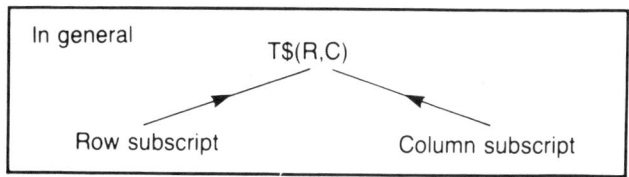

In general T$(R,C)

Row subscript   Column subscript

Example 4
The N$-table below has 9 values as shown. What are their variable names?

N$(,)

C\R	1	2	3
1	BENNY	COPPER	DRAPER
2	EDDIE	GWYNNE	HETTY
3	MORLEY	PROSSER	SMYTHE

Solution

BENNY = N$(1,1)   COPPER = N$(1,2)   DRAPER = N$(1,3)

EDDIE = N$(2,1)   GWYNNE = N$(2,2)   HETTY = N$(2,3)

MORLEY = N$(3,1)   PROSSER = N$(3,2)   SMYTHE = N$(3,3)

SAQ 3
In the following A$ table identify the variables and their values as in Example 4.

ARCHER	BENNY	COPPER
DRAPER	EDDIE	FRAME
GWYNNE	HETTY	KEMP
LAMB	MORLEY	NOAKES
PROSSER	SMYTHE	TAIT

Tables and nested loops
If FOR . . . NEXT . . . loops and lists seemed to be made for each other, then even more so do nested FOR . . . NEXT . . . loops and tables seem complementary.

For example, suppose you want to read:

ARCHER,BENNY,COPPER,DRAPER,EDDIE,FRAME,GWYNNE,HETTY, KEMP,LAMB,MORLEY,NOAKES,PROSSER,SMYTHE,TAIT,WEEKS

in a table ANAME$ with 4 rows and 4 columns. (We need a string array because we are storing string data.) This can be done with a READ statement in two nested loops:

```
 60 FOR I=1 TO 4
 70 FOR J=1 TO 4
 80 READ ANAME$(I,J)
 90 NEXT J
100 NEXT I
```

This process is carried out in full by lines 5 to 100 of Program 7.

It's all very well to store the value in a table, but of course we cannot see the result of this until we print it out. The second half of the program prints the table values out in a column with I and J accompanying them so that you can identify clearly how I and J are used.

```
  5 OPTION BASE 1
 10 REM**TABLE READ AND PRINT**
 20 REM**SET UP 2D ARRAY**
 30 DIM ANAME$(20,5)  ──────────── DIM statement for 2-D array.
 40 REM**READ ROUTINE**            We are asking for space for
 50 REM**WITH 2 LOOPS**             20 rows and 5 columns
 60 FOR I=1 TO 4
 70 FOR J=1 TO 4
 80 READ ANAME$(I,J)
 90 NEXT J
100 NEXT I
110 REM**PRINT ROUTINE**
120 PRINT " I"," J","ANAME$(I,J)"
130 FOR I=1 TO 4 ──────────────── rows
140 FOR J=1 TO 4 ──────────────── columns
150 PRINT I,J,ANAME$(I,J)
160 NEXT J
170 NEXT I
180 REM****************
190 DATA ARCHER,BENNY,COPPER,DRAPER,EDDIE,FRAME,GWYNNE,
    HETTY
200 DATA KEMP,LAMB,MORLEY,NOAKES,PROSSER,SMYTHE,TAIT,
    WEEKS
```

Program 7 Reading data into a 4×4 array

```
RUN
I          J          ANAME$(I,J)
1          1          ARCHER
1          2          BENNY
1          3          COPPER
1          4          DRAPER
2          1          EDDIE
2          2          FRAME
2          3          GWYNNE
2          4          HETTY
3          1          KEMP
3          2          LAMB
3          3          MORLEY
3          4          NOAKES
4          1          PROSSER
4          2          SMYTHE
4          3          TAIT
4          4          WEEKS
```

SAQ 4
The following amendments are made to Program 7. Write out what the output table will look like.

```
 60 FOR I=1 TO 3
 70 FOR J=1 TO 5
130 FOR I=1 TO 3
140 FOR J=1 TO 5
```

Table output
The output of Program 7 is not very satisfactory since we want to see the table in table form. To do this we insert a new print routine and delete line 120.

```
110 REM**PRINT ROUTINE**              the first column starts at position 1−1=0
130 FOR I=1 TO 5
140 FOR J=1 TO 3
150 PRINT TAB(10*(J-1));ANAME$(I,J);
160 NEXT J
170 PRINT                  columns 10 characters wide
180 NEXT I
```

Program 8

The output then is:

```
ARCHER      BENNY       COPPER
DRAPER      EDDIE       FRAME
GWYNNE      HETTY       KEMP
LAMB        MORLEY      NOAKES
PROSSER     SMYTHE      TAIT
```

Assignment 8

1. A salesman has 4 product lines. The value (in £) of his firm orders for one week are shown in the table.

day \ product	1	2	3	4	totals
1	500	300	20	25	e
2	600	700	40	0	f
3	200	550	60	20	g
4	250	450	100	5	h
5	400	200	100	11	i
totals	a	b	c	d	t

Write a program which will help him analyse his week's work by giving:

(i) his day totals (e, f, g, h, i)
(ii) his product totals (a, b, c, d)
(iii) his overall weekly total (t)

2. Write a program to extend the submarine game to a 10×10 grid. If the guess is close to the submarine then the program should give a 'near miss' clue. You decide what is meant by 'close'.

Objectives of Unit 8

Now that you have completed this Unit, check that you are able to:

Use the interchange sort (manually) on a set of data ☐

Write two nested program loops to perform the interchange sort ☐

Follow GOSUB in programs ☐

Write GOSUBs into programs ☐

Use the bisection search (manually) on a set of data ☐

Write a program for the bisection search ☐

Put data into two-dimensional arrays ☐

Write a program to read data into a two-dimensional array ☐

Write a program to print data out of a two-dimensional array ☐

Write a program to find the row sums and the column sums in a two-dimensional array ☐

Answers to SAQs and Exercises

SAQ 1

```
0  6  4  1  2  3  7  8
0  1  6  4  2  3  7  8
0  1  2  6  4  3  7  8
0  1  2  3  6  4  7  8
0  1  2  3  4  6  7  8
0  1  2  3  4  6  7  8
0  1  2  3  4  6  7  8
```

FINAL SORT LIST
```
0   1   2   3   4   6   7   8
```

SAQ 2
(a) B=0,2,25
(b) B=9

Exercise 1
(a)
```
10 FOR I=1 TO 60
20 PRINT "-";
30 NEXT I
40 PRINT
```

Program 9

or in one line:

```
FOR I=1 TO 60:PRINT"-";:NEXT I:PRINT
```

(b) `PRINT TAB(XPOS);"<=>"`

(c)
```
10 INPUT XPOS
20 GOSUB 100
30 PRINT TAB(XPOS);"<=>"
40 GOSUB 100
50 END
100 FOR I=1 TO 60
110 PRINT "-";
120 NEXT I
130 PRINT
140 RETURN
```

Program 10

The value that we give XPOS will determine the position of the submarine along the canal, and we get a picture like this:

```
------------------------------------------------------------
                         <=>
------------------------------------------------------------
```

Exercise 2

```
 10 REM**SUBMARINE**
 20 RANDOMISE VAL(RIGHT$(TIME$,2))
 30 XPOS=INT(58*RND(1)+1)
 40 GOSUB 500
 50 PRINT TAB(XPOS);"<=>"
 60 GOSUB 500
 70 END
500 REM**PRINT SUBROUTINE**
510 FOR I=1 TO 60
520 PRINT "-";
530 NEXT I
540 RETURN
```

Program 11

```
RUN
------------------------------------------------------------
                            <=>
------------------------------------------------------------
RUN
------------------------------------------------------------
  <=>
------------------------------------------------------------
RUN
------------------------------------------------------------
                                       <=>
------------------------------------------------------------
```

Exercise 3

```
 10 REM**SUBMARINE**
 20 RANDOMISE VAL(RIGHT$(TIME$,2))
 30 REM**PRINT CHALLENGE**
 40 GOSUB 190
 50 PRINT "A NUMBER FROM 1 TO 60 MIGHT FIND ME"
 60 GOSUB 190
 70 XPOS=INT(58*RND(1)+1)
 80 TRY$=""
 90 PRINT
100 INPUT "FIRST GUESS";GUESS
110 WHILE GUESS<>XPOS AND TRY$<>"NO"
120 GOSUB 190
130 INPUT "ANOTHER TRY";TRY$
140 IF TRY$="NO" THEN GOSUB 300
150 IF TRY$<>"NO" THEN GOSUB 370
160 WEND
170 IF GUESS=XPOS THEN GOSUB 250
180 END
190 REM**PRINT SUBROUTINE**
200 FOR I=1 TO 60
210 PRINT"-";
220 NEXT I
230 PRINT
240 RETURN
250 REM**HIT SUBROUTINE**
260 GOSUB 190
```

```
270 PRINT "A HIT"
280 GOSUB 190
290 RETURN
300 REM**GIVE UP SUBROUTINE**
310 GOSUB 190
320 PRINT "I WAS HERE"
330 GOSUB 190
340 PRINT TAB(XPOS);"<=>"
350 GOSUB 190
360 RETURN
370 GOSUB 190
380 INPUT "ANOTHER GUESS";GUESS
390 RETURN
```

Program 12

Exercise 4

```
    1   2   3   4   5   6   7   8
    A   F   I   M   P   T   U   Z
                    ⋮
                  Mid (4)
```

> Query = Item (4)? No.
> Query < Item (4)? Yes.
> make Index (4) the new high

```
    1   2   3   4
    A   F   I   M
            ⋮
```

$\text{Mid-Index} = \text{Int}(\frac{1+4}{2}) = 2$

> Query = Item (2)? No.
> Query < Item (2)? No.
> make Index (2) the new low

```
    2   3   4
    F   I   M
        ⋮
```

> Query = Item (3)? Yes.
> Therefore I is in list

SAQ 3

A$(1,1) = ARCHER   A$(1,2) = BENNY   A$(1,3) = COPPER
A$(2,1) = DRAPER   A$(2,2) = EDDIE   A$(2,3) = FRAME
A$(3,1) = GWYNNE   A$(3,2) = HETTY   A$(3,3) = KEMP
A$(4,1) = LAMB   A$(4,2) = MORLEY   A$(4,3) = NOAKES
A$(5,1) = PROSSER   A$(5,2) = SMYTHE   A$(5,3) = TAIT

SAQ 4

RUN

I	J	ANAME$
1	1	ARCHER
1	2	BENNY
1	3	COPPER
1	4	DRAPER
1	5	EDDIE
2	1	FRAME
2	2	GWYNNE
2	3	HETTY
2	4	KEMP
2	5	LAMB
3	1	MORLEY
3	2	NOAKES
3	3	PROSSER
3	4	SMYTHE
3	5	TAIT

(Note that WEEKS was not read into the table. A 5×3 table will read only the first 15 items.)

UNIT 9
File handling

9.1	Saving programs	220
9.2	LPRINT	221
9.3	Sequential files	221
9.4	Create and access	222
9.5	Files in flowcharts	225
9.6	Sorting filed data	227
9.7	Merge	229
9.8	Deletion	233
	Postscript	236
	Assignment 9	236
	Objectives of Unit 9	236
	Answers to Exercises	237

9.1 Saving programs

The course so far has largely been concerned with a system of only three devices, viz. keyboard, processor and monitor. That system is volatile, i.e. when you switch off the power your programming efforts are lost. If you wish to run a program again you will have to type it in again. But most microcomputers provide facilities for saving a program on disks (floppy disks). Once the program is on disk, you can switch off your computer and still be able to re-run the program whenever you want in the future.

There are two occasions on which you will wish to store programs:

(a) when you have a complete program that you want to keep; and
(b) to save part of a program which you are developing.

If you save every time you have a screen-full, you will never lose too much when you have an accident with the part currently in your computer. When the complete program has been entered and saved, you can always erase your intermediate part-programs.

The process of saving

Before you can save your program you have to select the appropriate disk drive for the program to be saved to. You must consult your DOS manual to find which drive has which letter. Generally hard disks are called either C or E and disk drives are called A or B. To select the chosen drive, type the following in BASIC:

SHELL "A:"   for drive A

or

SHELL "B:"   for drive B

etc.

Having selected the appropriate drive you may wish to see what is already on the disk. To do this type

FILES

followed by RETURN

and you will see a response like this:

A:\
MATHS.BAS   GAMES.BAS   PROG7-5.BAS   CIRCLE.BAS
PROG1.BAS

Or just A:\ if you have a blank disk. Once you have chosen a suitable name for your program you can save it. To do this type:

SAVE "PROGNAME" — insert your program's name between the quotes

The name can be up to 8 letters long; if it is longer the extra letters are discarded.

The process of loading
Having saved a program you may wish to use it at a later date. It can be loaded back in your machine with the LOAD command.

Having selected the appropriate drive, and used FILES to see if the program is on your disk, type the following

```
LOAD "PROGNAME"
```

The computer will now load your program into memory.

9.2 LPRINT

Sooner or later you will want a copy on paper of a program or data. Copy printed on paper is usually referred to as 'hard copy'.

So far in the course we have written all our programs so that all the responses you see on your screen would be printed onto paper if your computer were attached to a printer. You have seen these responses being printed out in the runs which we have shown from our computer. This was done to help you to trace the runs of all parts of the programs. But we would not normally wish to have all of the screen responses printed out on paper. For example, in the run of Program 11 or 12 of Unit 7, we would want printed out on paper the final result perhaps, but not all of the input prompts:

```
ACCURACY REQUIRED?    etc.
```

These would be needed by the user to set up the run on the screen, but not to be printed out as a permanent record.

LPRINT allows us to direct output to the line-printer.

Similarly LLIST will print the program currently in memory at the line-printer.

9.3 Sequential files

We have used the term 'file' several times through the course, to mean 'a collection of data items'. However, when a program is saved we refer to its having a file-name, and we think of both saved programs and data as files.

Data
So far we have either inputted data from the keyboard during the course of a program's execution, or have read from DATA statements which formed part of the program. On several occasions we have made a program handle different sets of data by over-writing or substituting new DATA statements for old ones. This latter method can be quite effective for a small computer system without file-handling facilities. But if we wish to handle collections of data of meaningful size,

we need the facility to be able to store this data on disk. We need to be able to store new data on a file on disk and to read data from these files to use in program runs.

Sequential files
As a simplification we shall consider only sequential file-handling. Sequential files are where we read in every item of data from the file in the sequence in which it was originally created.

9.4 Create and access

Create refers to a program's activity of writing data from the program in the computer's memory to a peripheral device: in our case, disk. Access is when data is read from the peripheral device to the program in memory.

Because you cannot 'see' what's stored on disk, the activities of create and access must be complementary. You do not know whether your program to create has been successful until you've written an access program to read the data back in. Only then can you see it on the screen or printer.

In order to keep this Unit as simple as possible, we shall keep create and access as separate as possible.

Create
To create a new file, or to write into an existing one, we have to tell the computer:

(a) the name of the file;
(b) that we wish to OPEN the file for output to it;
(c) then we write out to it;
(d) then we CLOSE it.

Notice that:

(a) during the create run, the computer needs a temporary number for that file to identify it during execution;
(b) that between OPEN and CLOSE, the computer is under control of the disk drive.

So creating a file in BASICA is like this:

```
1000 REM**CREATING A DATA FILE**
1010 OPEN "NAME"FOR OUTPUT AS #1
```

```
1060 CLOSE #1
```

Notes

OPEN "NAME"   tells the computer to create a file called 'name'

FOR OUTPUT   tells the computer we will be writing to the file, in our case creating a new one.

AS #1	is our internal reference number for the file.
CLOSE #1	this closes the file and puts the "end of file marker" (EOF) on the disk.

So let's see this in use.

Example 1a
Write a program to create a data file of 10 names.

Solution

```
1000 REM**CREATE A DATA FILE**
1010 OPEN "FRED" FOR OUTPUT AS #1
1020 FOR I=1 TO 10
1030 READ ANAME$
1040 PRINT #1,ANAME$
1050 NEXT I
1060 CLOSE #1
1070 PRINT "FILE HAS BEEN CREATED"
1080 DATA ARCHER,BENNY,COPPER,DRAPER,EDDIE,FRAME,GWYNNE,
     HETTY
1090 DATA KEMP,LAMB,MORLEY,NOAKES,PROSSER,SMYTHE,TAIT,
     WEEKS
```

Program 1   Create a data file

```
RUN
FILE HAS BEEN CREATED
OK
```

Once we have opened the file for output (line 1010) we can write to it. Here we used it as follows.

```
1020 FOR I=1 TO 10
1030 READ ANAME$
1040 PRINT #1,ANAME$
1050 NEXT I
```

The only new bit here is PRINT #1,ANAME$. This writes the value ANAME$ into the file #1. (You can see why we wanted a number for the file to use during the program.)

At the end of all that, the 10 names (ARCHER, BENNY, etc.) are all on the disk drive under the file-name "FRED". If you switch off your computer, it should still be there.

Access
Now you want the data back to use. For this you need an access program. This has the following structure:

```
10 REM**ACCESS A DATA FILE**
20 OPEN "FRED" FOR INPUT AS #1
30 WHILE EOF(1)=0
40 INPUT #1,ANAME$
```

```
100 WEND
110 CLOSE #1
```

Notes

OPEN "FRED"	tells the computer to open the file named "FRED"
FOR INPUT	tells the computer we want to read data from the file.
AS #1	is the number for the file.
EOF(1)	tells the computer to look for the end of file. If EOF(1)=0 then the end of file has not yet been reached.
CLOSE #1	tells the computer to close file no. 1.

In use, our program works as follows:

Example 1b
Write a program to access the data file "FRED" which was created in Example 1a, and to print out the 10 names in the file.

```
10 REM**ACCESS A DATA FILE**
20 OPEN "FRED" FOR INPUT AS #1
30 WHILE EOF(1)=0
40 INPUT #1,ANAME$
50 PRINT ANAME$
60 WEND
70 CLOSE #1
```

Program 2   Access a data file

```
RUN
ARCHER
BENNY
COPPER
DRAPER
EDDIE
FRAME
GWYNNE
HETTY
KEMP
LAMB
```

Once we have opened the file, we input the data with:

```
40 INPUT #1,ANAME$
```

Then we can use the data in any other program. In this case, we simply want to print it, so we write

```
50 PRINT ANAME$
```

Exercises preamble
A fairly serious defect of Programs 1 and 2 is that they both work only for a specifically named file, viz, "FRED". Now if a file-handling program is going to be of general use, we don't want to have to edit the program just to create or access data from a file of different names. We can overcome this by entering the file name into a variable store location, FILE$, in the following example.

```
INPUT "NAME OF THE DATE FILE";FILE$
OPEN FILE$ FOR OUTPUT AS A1
```

Also it was rather artificial to read into a file from a DATA statement. Let's write some programs which remedy these two points.

Exercise 1
Modify Program 1 to write a sequence of names to a file directly from the keyboard, and allow the file thus created to have a variable name.

Exercise 2
Modify Program 2 to access the file created in Exercise 1 and to print out the list.

Exercise 3
Write a program to access the file created in Exercise 1 and to search through it to find and print out all those names whose initial letter is 'N'.

Exercise 4
Write a program to access the file created in Exercise 1 and to enter the names into a list, and to print out the list with indexes.

9.5 Files in flowcharts

The solution to Exercise 4 holds the key to the development of future programs. It's our old friend the list again, which makes all the difference! Having got the data into list form we can do much more with it. Before we do, however, let's try to summarise the position we've reached.

The program solution to Exercise 1 may be summarised as in Figure 1.

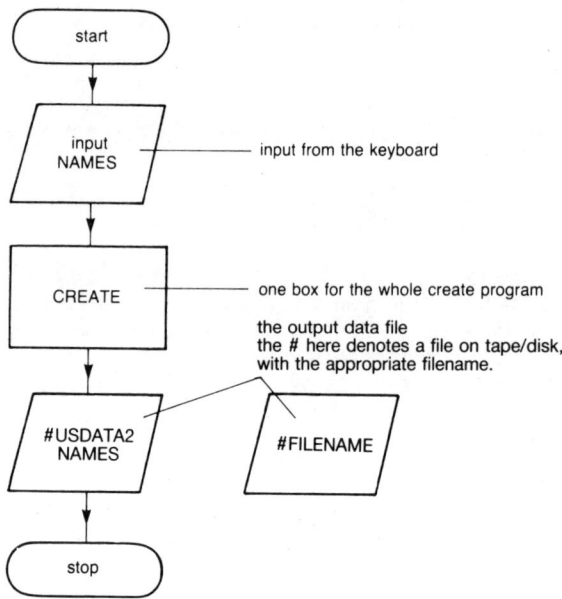

(Figure 1   Flowchart for 'create a file')

The flowchart solution for Exercise 4 is given in Figure 2.

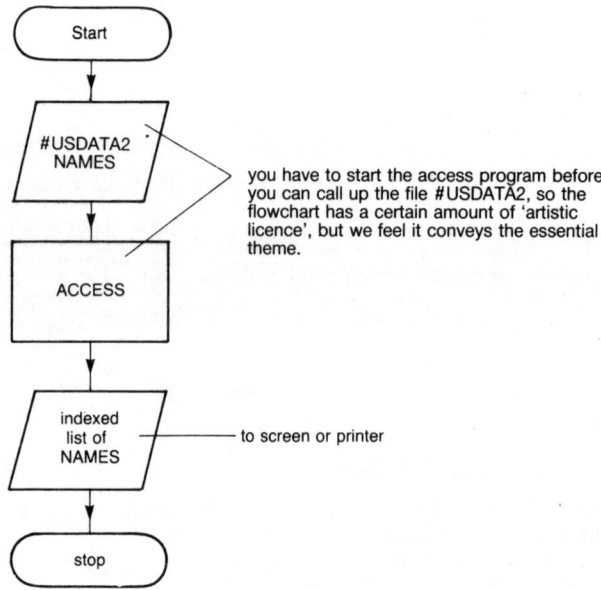

(Figure 2   Access a file and index as a list)

9.6 Sorting filed data

The list of names in the answer to Exercise 2 is just asking to be sorted! We have an access routine and we developed a sort routine in Unit 8. All we have to do now is to link the two together. Before we do, let's sketch the algorithm.

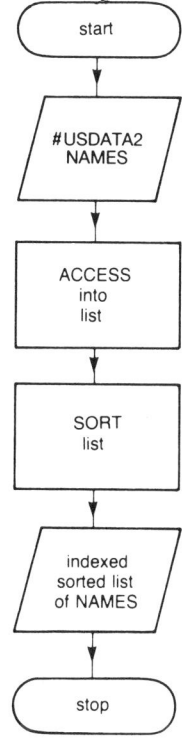

(Figure 3   Access and sort)

The program is simply three routines (access, sort and print) that you have already met, joined together.

```
  5 OPTION BASE 1
 10 REM**ACCESS AND SORT**
 20 DIM ANAME$(50)
 30 COUNT=1
 40 INPUT "NAME OF DATA FILE";FILENAME$
 50 OPEN FILENAME$ FOR INPUT AS #1
 60 WHILE EOF(1)=0
 70 INPUT #1,ANAME$(COUNT)
 80 COUNT=COUNT+1
 90 WEND
100 CLOSE #1
110 REM**END OF ACCESS**
120 NUMBER=COUNT-1
```

```
130 REM**SORT ROUTINE**
140 FOR K=1 TO NUMBER-1
150 FOR L=K+1 TO NUMBER
160 IF ANAME$(L)<ANAME$(K) THEN TEMP$=ANAME$(L) :
    ANAME$(L)=ANAME$(K) : ANAME$(K)=TEMP$
170 NEXT L
180 NEXT K
190 REM**END OF SORT ROUTINE**
200 PRINT "FINAL SORTED LIST"
210 FOR P=1 TO NUMBER
220 PRINT P,ANAME$(P)
230 NEXT P
240 PRINT
250 END
260 REM***********
```

Program 3   Access and sort

```
RUN
NAME OF THE DATA FILE? USDATA2
FINAL SORTED LIST
 1        ASHTON
 2        BANKS
 3        BARR
 4        BURNS
 5        CAREY
 6        COMPTON
 7        DOYLE
 8        EDGE
 9        GRANT
10        HOWSON
11        ICKERY
12        NASH
13        NEILS
14        NUNN
15        PRIEST
16        PURVISS
17        SCALES
18        SHIPTON
19        TEELE
20        TURNER
21        WATERS
22        WATTS
23        WELLS
24        WEST
```

Exercise 5
We don't necessarily wish to print out the list as we did for demonstration purposes in Program 3, but we definitely would want the sorted data to be saved in a data file for future use.

Modify Program 3 to write the sorted data list to a file, SDATA, say.

How will you test that it is successful?

Exercise 6
Having created a file of sorted data you will sooner or later wish to search through it quickly.

Combine the list-access routine of Program 3 with the bisection search routine of Unit 8 to make this file-search utility program.

Exercise 7
Write a program to access a file and input the data into a table.

You are in charge of the dimensions of the table and the data you use.

9.7 Merge

We've created, accessed, sorted and searched files. What else is there to do? Well, very seldom does a data file which is doing useful work, stay static for long. We usually want to add or delete items, or make amendments to it. The rest of this Unit will be spent considering how to add and delete items to and from a file.

No doubt you have already visualised how you would go about these tasks, and we hope that you follow up your ideas. We will develop a fairly standard approach. To add items to a file we will merge two files together. You've done this if you have ever played cards. You have a hand which you have sorted and have spread out fan-like before you. You pick up another card and slot it into its appropriate place in your hand.

The process of merging involves a master file (sorted into order) and a list of new items to go in (also sorted into order).

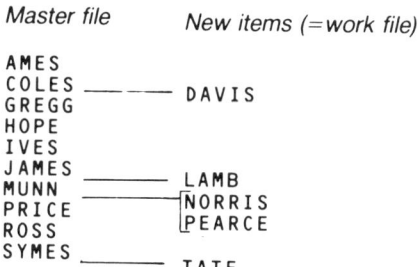

Master file   *New items (=work file)*

```
AMES
COLES ————— DAVIS
GREGG
HOPE
IVES
JAMES
MUNN  ————— LAMB
PRICE       ┌NORRIS
ROSS        └PEARCE
SYMES
            ————— TATE
```

But before we develop a program for the merge, we must anticipate and remove one problem: the extremes of the master file. Both in the bisection search (Unit 8) and in Exercise 6 we found it necessary to ensure that the master file included the extremes. So we now develop a program routine to ensure that this will be so.

The extremes of the master file
The following routine takes any sorted file (FILE$) and places "AAAA" as the first item and "ZZZZ" as the last.

```
  5 OPTION BASE 1
 10 REM**ACCESS A DATA FILE**
 20 DIM WORDS$(50)
 30 COUNT=1
 40 WORDS$(1)="AAAA"                       lowest item made AAAA
 50 INPUT "NAME OF DATA FILE",FILE$        before accessing the file
 60 OPEN FILE$ FOR INPUT AS #1
 70 WHILE EOF(1)=0
 80 COUNT=COUNT+1
 90 INPUT #1,WORDS$(COUNT)
100 WEND
110 CLOSE #1
120 REM***************
130 NUMBER=COUNT+1
```

```
140 WORDS$(NUMBER)="ZZZZ"                    highest made ZZZZ after
150 REM***************                       closing the file
160 FOR I=1 TO NUMBER
170 PRINT I,WORDS$(I)
180 NEXT I
```

Program 4   Adding AAAA and ZZZZ to a file

```
RUN
NAME OF THE DATA FILE? SDATA3
   1        AAAA ———————  lowest item
   2        AMES  ⎤
   3        COLES │
   4        GREGG │
   5        HOPE  │
   6        IVES  ├── original file SDATA3
   7        JAMES │
   8        MUNN  │
   9        PRICE │
  10        ROSS  │
  11        SYMES ⎦
  12        ZZZZ ———————  highest item
```

The merge program

A picture of the overall process is shown in Figure 4. Once again there is a certain amount of artistic license. The program does not really have two starting points, but as you will see when the program is run, there are two quite distinct entry points for the two input files.

The essential point to remember is that SDATA3 and SDATA4 have been sorted into alphabetical order before entry into the program. This was done using programs developed earlier in this Unit

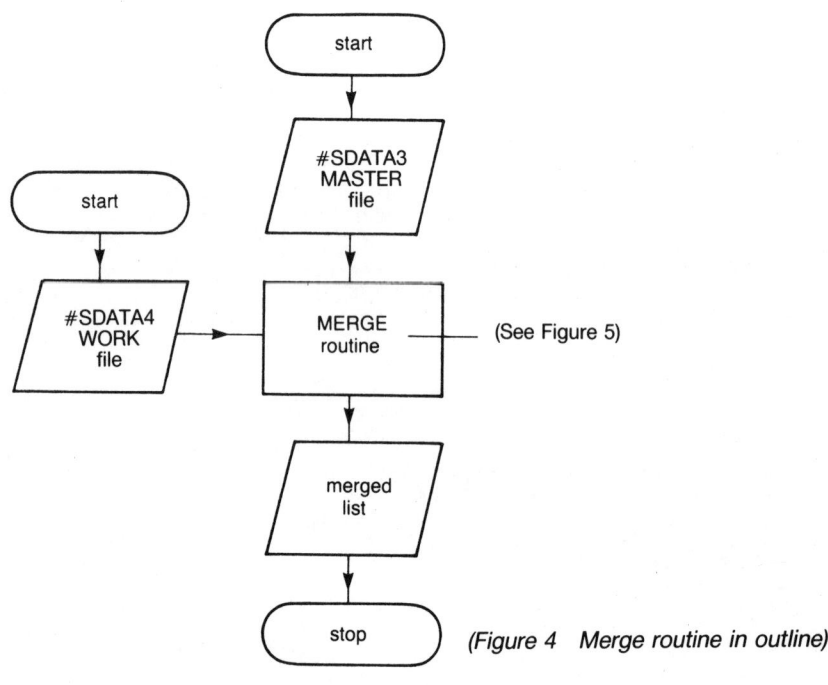

(Figure 4   Merge routine in outline)

The merge routine

The central idea is:

(a) if the item in the Master file is lower in order than the item from the Work file,
(b) then write the item from the Master file into the New file;
(c) otherwise write the item from the Work file into the New file.

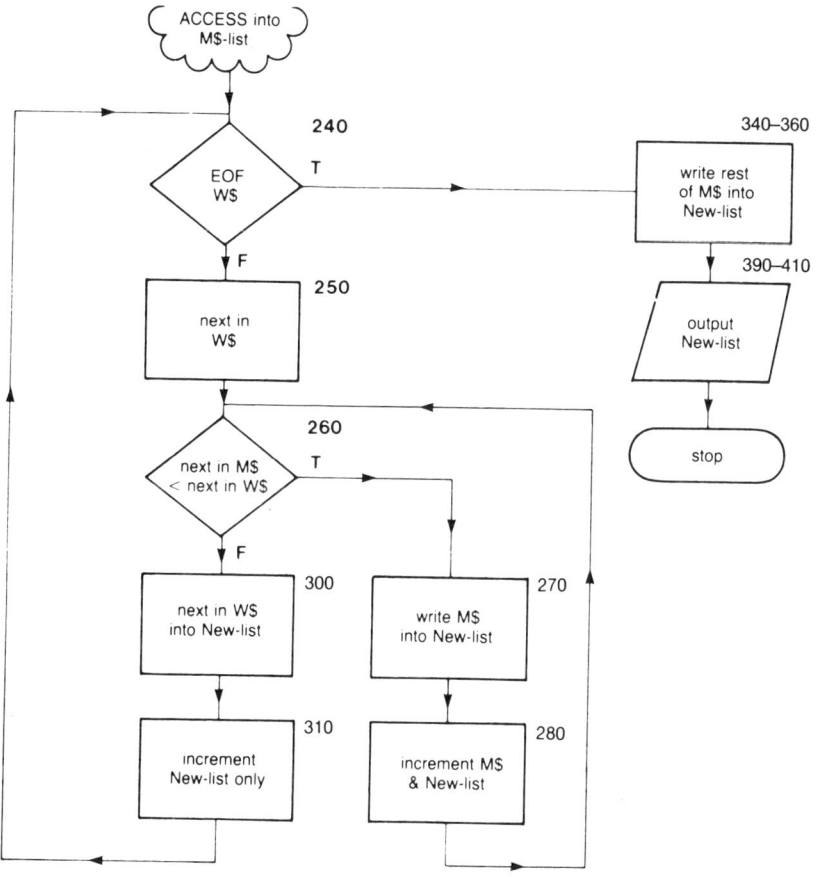

(Figure 5   The merge routine in detail)

```
  5 OPTION BASE 1
 10 REM**ACCESS A DATA FILE**
 20 DIM WORDS$(50),ANEWLIST$(50)          ──── ANEWLIST$ will be the new-list
 30 COUNT=1
 40 WORDS$(1)="AAAA"
 50 INPUT "NAME OF DATA FILE";FILE$
 60 OPEN FILE$ FOR INPUT AS #1
 70 WHILE EOF(1)=0
 80 COUNT=COUNT+1                              accessing Master file WORDS$,
 90 INPUT #1,WORDS$(COUNT)                     and inserting AAAA and ZZZZ
100 WEND                                       at ends
110 CLOSE #1
120 REM***************
130 NUMBER=COUNT+1
140 WORDS$(NUMBER)="ZZZZ"
150 REM***************
160 FOR I=1 TO NUMBER                          print-out of Master file
170 PRINT I,WORDS$(I)                          before merge
180 NEXT I
190 REM**MERGE*********
200 I=1
210 K=1
220 INPUT "NAME OF WORK FILE";WORK$
230 OPEN WORK$ FOR INPUT AS #2
240 WHILE EOF(2)=0
250 INPUT #2,WORD$
260 WHILE WORDS$(K)<WORD$
270 ANEWLIST$(I)=WORDS$(K)
280 K=K+1 : I=I+1                              merge
290 WEND
300 ANEWLIST$(I)=WORD$
310 I=I+1
320 WEND
330 CLOSE #2
340 WHILE K<NUMBER
350 ANEWLIST$(I)=WORDS$(K)
360 K=K+1 : I=I+1
370 WEND
380 REM*************
390 FOR L=2 TO I-2                        ──── I is one too high at 360 (last time)
400 PRINT L,ANEWLIST$(L)                       and we don't want "ZZZZ" either:
410 NEXT L                                     hence I−2
```

Program 5   The complete merge program

Runs of merge program
First using SDATA3 as the Master file:

```
RUN
NAME OF DATA FILE? SDATA3
   1       AAAA
   2       AMES
   3       COLES
   4       GREGG
   5       HOPE
   6       IVES
   7       JAMES
   8       MUNN
   9       PRICE
  10       ROSS
  11       SYMES
  12       ZZZZ
```

```
NAME OF WORK FILE? SDATA4
   2      AMES
   3      COLES
   4      DAVIS
   5      GREGG
   6      HOPE
   7      IVES
   8      JAMES
   9      LAMB
  10      MUNN
  11      NORRIS
  12      PEARCE
  13      PRICE
  14      ROSS
  15      SYMES
  16      TATE
```

Second using SDATA4 as the Master file:

```
RUN
NAME OF DATA FILE? SDATA4
   1      AAAA
   2      DAVIS
   3      LAMB
   4      NORRIS
   5      PEARCE
   6      TATE
   7      ZZZZ

NAME OF WORK FILE? SDATA3
   2      AMES
   3      COLES
   4      DAVIS
   5      GREGG
   6      HOPE
   7      IVES
   8      JAMES
   9      LAMB
  10      MUNN
  11      NORRIS
  12      PEARCE
  13      PRICE
  14      ROSS
  15      SYMES
  16      TATE
```

We have run the program using data files SDATA3 and 4 as Master file. You can see that it doesn't really matter which one we call the Master and which the Work file. (It is interesting to note that entering the smaller of the two first (SDATA4) takes up slightly less room in the memory.)

If we wanted the New-list in a data file, we would have to add a create routine to the end of the program.

9.8 Deletion

Deletion may seem a very different process from addition and merging but it can be achieved by modifying the merge program only very slightly.

First, the items for deletion are collected into a Work file.

Then:

(a) if the item in the Master list = that in the Work list then do not write the Master list item into the New-list;
(b) otherwise do write the Master list item into the New-list.

We will not give a flowchart in this case, but hope that you can follow the changes to the merge program as shown in the delete program below. In this case a moment's thought will convince you that the Work and Master lists are no longer interchangeable.

Master file (SDATA)
ASHTON
BANKS
BARR
BURNS
CAREY
COMPTON
DOYLE
EDGE
GRANT
HOWSON
ICKERY
NASH
NEILS
NUNN
PRIEST
PURVISS
SCALES
SHIPTON
TEELE
TURNER
WATERS
WATTS
WELLS
WEST

Work file (SDATA5)
= deletions to be made

BURNS
DOYLE
NASH
TEELE
WATTS

```
  5 OPTION BASE 1
 10 REM**ACCESS A DATA FILE**
 20 DIM WORDS$(50),ANEWLIST$(50)
 30 COUNT=1
 40 WORDS$(1)="AAAA"
 50 INPUT "NAME OF DATA FILE";FILE$
 60 OPEN FILE$ FOR INPUT AS #1
 70 WHILE EOF(1)=0
 80 COUNT=COUNT+1
 90 INPUT #1,WORDS$(COUNT)
100 WEND
110 CLOSE #1
120 REM***************
130 NUMBER=COUNT+1
140 WORDS$(NUMBER)="ZZZZ"
150 REM***************
160 FOR I=1 TO NUMBER
170 PRINT I,WORDS$(I)
180 NEXT I
190 REM**MERGE*********
200 I=1
210 K=1
220 INPUT "NAME OF WORK FILE";WORK$
```

```
230 OPEN WORK$ FOR INPUT AS #2
240 WHILE EOF(2)=0
250 INPUT #2,WORD$
260 WHILE WORDS$(K)<>WORD$ ─────────── Master item not in
270 ANEWLIST$(I)=WORDS$(K)              Work list, therefore write
280 K=K+1 : I=I+1                        Master item into New list
290 WEND
300 REM DON'T TRANSFER ITEM TO BE DELETED
310 REM JUST SKIP OVER IT IN WORDS$(K)
320 K=K+1 ─────────────────────── If Master item = Work item,
330 WEND                                 do nothing, just go for next
340 CLOSE #2                             Master item.
350 WHILE K<NUMBER
360 ANEWLIST$(I)=WORDS$(K)
370 K=K+1 : I=I+1
380 WEND
390 REM**************
400 FOR L=2 TO I-2
410 PRINT L,ANEWLIST$(L)
420 NEXT L
```

Program 6 Deletion program

```
RUN
NAME OF THE DATA FILE? SDATA

 1            AAAA
 2            ASHTON
 3            BANKS
 4            BARR
 5            BURNS
 6            CAREY
 7            COMPTON
 8            DOYLE
 9            EDGE
10            GRANT
11            HOWSON
12            ICKERY          ──── Master list
13            NASH
14            NEILS
15            NUNN
16            PRIEST
17            PURVISS
18            SCALES
19            SHIPTON
20            TEELE
21            TURNER
22            WATERS
23            WATTS
24            WELLS
25            WEST
26            ZZZZ

NAME OF THE WORK FILE? SDATA5

 2            ASHTON
 3            BANKS
 4            BARR
 5            CAREY
 6            COMPTON
 7            EDGE
 8            GRANT
 9            HOWSON
10            ICKERY          ──── New list ... the old Master
11            NEILS                 with five items deleted
12            NUNN
```

```
13        PRIEST
14        PURVISS
15        SCALES
16        SHIPTON
17        TURNER
18        WATERS
19        WELLS
20        WEST
```

Postscript

Our file-handling techniques have been fairly rough and ready. We've aimed at simplicity rather than sophistication.

You will have noticed that we have 'written out to' and 'read in from' files one field at a time. The INPUT# and PRINT# statements can handle more than one variable, *but great care must be taken over details to ensure success.*

We have also had only one file open at any one time. This means that the data must be read into the computer's memory for processing before being outputted again. If the file is large the machine must have a large memory to hold the file. To overcome this we would have to have input and output files open simultaneously; and to read in from one, process and output to the other within one routine.

Despite all these simplifications we have managed to leave you with programs to carry out the basic file-handling operations.

Assignment 9

1. Write a program to create a library Master loan file in alphabetical order by borrower's name, with records of the form:

    BORROWER   DATE DUE   BOOK TITLE
    (a) Write a routine to merge new records with this Master file.
    (b) Write a routine to access and search through the file to find those books which are overdue.

2. Write a program to access a table of numerical values, to complete row and column sums, and to create a new file to include this extra information.

Objectives of Unit 9

Check that you are able to write programs to:

Create a data file (open for output) ☐

Access a data file (open for input) ☐

Sort a data file ☐

Add new items to a data file (merge) ☐

Delete items from a data file ☐

Answers to Exercises

Exercise 1

```
10  REM**CREATE A DATA FILE**
20  INPUT "NAME OF THE DATA FILE";FILE$
30  OPEN FILE$ FOR OUTPUT AS #1
40  INPUT "NEXT NAME";ANAME$
50  WHILE ANAME$<>"ZZZZ"
60  PRINT #1,ANAME$
70  INPUT "NEXT NAME";ANAME$
80  WEND
90  CLOSE #1
100 PRINT FILE$;" HAS BEEN SAVED"
```

Program 7

```
NAME OF THE DATA FILE? USDATA2
NEXT NAME? BARR
NEXT NAME? SHIPTON
NEXT NAME? HOWSON
NEXT NAME? WELLS
NEXT NAME? CAREY
NEXT NAME? WEST
NEXT NAME? NEILS
NEXT NAME? ASHTON
NEXT NAME? NASH
NEXT NAME? TURNER
NEXT NAME? COMPTON
NEXT NAME? BURNS
NEXT NAME? EDGE
NEXT NAME? NUNN
NEXT NAME? PRIEST
NEXT NAME? DOYLE
NEXT NAME? SCALES
NEXT NAME? WATERS
NEXT NAME? GRANT
NEXT NAME? BANKS
NEXT NAME? PURVISS
NEXT NAME? TEELE
NEXT NAME? WATTS
NEXT NAME? ICKERY
NEXT NAME? ZZZZ
USDATA2 HAS BEEN SAVED
```

Exercise 2

```
10  REM**ACCESS A DATA FILE**
20  INPUT "NAME OF THE DATA FILE";FILE$
30  OPEN FILE$ FOR INPUT AS #1
40  WHILE EOF(1)=0
50  INPUT #1,WORD$
60  PRINT WORD$
70  WEND
80  CLOSE #1
```

Program 8

```
RUN
NAME OF THE DATA FILE? USDATA2
BARR
SHIPTON
HOWSON
WELLS
CAREY
WEST
NEILS
ASHTON
NASH
TURNER
COMPTON
BURNS
EDGE
NUNN
PRIEST
DOYLE
SCALES
WATERS
GRANT
BANKS
PURVISS
TEELE
WATTS
ICKERY
```

Exercise 3

```
10 REM**ACCESS A DATA FILE**
20 INPUT "NAME OF THE DATA FILE";FILE$
30 OPEN FILE$ FOR INPUT AS #1
40 WHILE EOF(1)=0
50 INPUT #1,WORD$
60 IF LEFT$(WORD$,1)="N" THEN PRINT WORD$
70 WEND
80 CLOSE #1
```

Program 9

```
RUN
NAME OF THE DATA FILE? USDATA2
NEILS
NASH
NUNN
```

Exercise 4

```
  5 OPTION BASE 1
 10 REM**ACCESS A DATA FILE**
 20 DIM WORDS$(50)
 30 COUNT=0
 40 INPUT "NAME OF DATA FILES";FILE$
 50 OPEN FILE$ FOR INPUT AS #1
 60 WHILE EOF(1)=0
 70 COUNT=COUNT+1
 80 INPUT #1,WORDS$(COUNT)
 90 WEND
100 REM**********
110 FOR I=1 TO COUNT
120 PRINT I,WORDS$(I)
130 NEXT I
140 CLOSE #1
```

Program 10

```
RUN
NAME OF THE DATA FILE? USDATA2
   1       BARR
   2       SHIPTON
   3       HOWSON
   4       WELLS
   5       CAREY
   6       WEST
   7       NEILS
   8       ASHTON
   9       NASH
  10       TURNER
  11       COMPTON
  12       BURNS
  13       EDGE
  14       NUNN
  15       PRIEST
  16       DOYLE
  17       SCALES
  18       WATERS
  19       GRANT
  20       BANKS
  21       PURVISS
  22       TEELE
  23       WATTS
  24       ICKERY
```

Exercise 5

Instead of the print routine of lines 200 to 260 of Program 3, we have to write a create routine as follows:

```
  5 OPTION BASE 1
 10 REM**ACCESS AND SORT**
 20 DIM ANAME$(50)
 30 COUNT=1
 40 INPUT "NAME OF DATA FILE";FILENAME$
 50 OPEN FILENAME$ FOR INPUT AS #1
 60 WHILE EOF(1)=0
 70 INPUT #1,ANAME$(COUNT)
 80 COUNT=COUNT+1
 90 WEND
100 CLOSE #1
110 REM**END OF ACCESS**
120 NUMBER=COUNT-1
130 REM**SORT ROUTINE**
140 FOR K=1 TO NUMBER-1
150 FOR L=K+1 TO NUMBER
160 IF ANAME$(L)<ANAME$(K) THEN TEMP$=ANAME$(L) :
    ANAME$(L)=ANAME$(K) : ANAME$(K)=TEMP$
170 NEXT L
180 NEXT K
190 REM**END OF SORT ROUTINE**
200 REM***********
210 REM**CREATE A DATA FILE**
220 INPUT "NAME FOR THE DATA FILE";FILE$
230 OPEN FILE$ FOR OUTPUT AS #2
240 FOR P=1 TO NUMBER
250 PRINT #2,ANAME$(P)
260 NEXT P
270 CLOSE #2
280 PRINT FILE$;" HAS BEEN SAVED"
290 REM***********
```

Program 11

```
RUN
NAME OF DATA FILE? USDATA2
NAME FOR THE DATA FILE? SDATA
SDATA HAS BEEN SAVED
```

To test whether it has been successful we can load and run the access program for the file SDATA.

```
NAME OF DATA FILE? SDATA
ASHTON
BANKS
BARR
BURNS
CAREY
COMPTON
DOYLE
EDGE
GRANT
HOWSON
ICKERY
NASH
NEILS
NUNN
PRIEST
PURVISS
SCALES
SHIPTON
TEELE
TURNER
WATERS
WATTS
WELLS
WEST
```

Exercise 6

```
  5 OPTION BASE 1
 10 REM**ACCESS AND SEARCH**
 20 DIM ANAME$(50)
 30 COUNT=0
 40 INPUT "NAME OF THE DATA FILE";FILE$
 50 OPEN FILE$ FOR INPUT AS #1
 60 WHILE EOF(1)=0
 70 COUNT=COUNT+1                            ├── Access
 80 INPUT #1,ANAME$(COUNT)
 90 WEND
100 CLOSE #1
110 REM**NUMBER IS THE LENGTH OF THE LIST**
120 NUMBER=COUNT
130 INPUT "QUERY NAME";QUERY$
140 REM**START OF SEARCH**
150 LOW=1 : HIGH=NUMBER
160 MID=INT((LOW+HIGH)/2)
170 WHILE HIGH-LOW<>1 AND QUERY$<>ANAME$(MID)   Bisection search
180 MID=INT((LOW+HIGH)/2)
190 IF QUERY$<ANAME$(MID) THEN HIGH=MID
200 IF QUERY$>ANAME$(MID) THEN LOW=MID
210 WEND
220 REM**END OF SEARCH**
230 IF HIGH-LOW=1 THEN PRINT QUERY$;" IS NOT IN THE
    LIST"
240 IF QUERY$=ANAME$(MID) THEN PRINT "YES ";QUERY$;" IS
    IN THE LIST"
250 END
```
Program 12

```
RUN
NAME OF THE DATA FILE? SDATA ────── The sorted data file. (We couldn't use
QUERY NAME? HOWSON                   the bisection search on the
YES HOWSON IS IN THE LIST            unsorted file.)
OK

RUN
NAME OF THE DATA FILE? SDATA
QUERY NAME? SMITH
SMITH IS NOT IN THE LIST
OK
```

Note: We have combined an access program with the bisection search program of Unit 8, and it works. To make the program foolproof, however, we must be careful about its limits: remember ANAME$(1)="AAAA" and ANAME$(N)="ZZZZ" in Unit 8! We will deal with this problem in Unit 9 Program 5.

Exercise 7

```
  5 OPTION BASE 1
 10 REM**ACCESS A DATA FILE**
 20 DIM WORDS$(30,30)
 30 INPUT "NO. OF ROWS AND COLUMNS";ROWS,COLUMNS
 40 INPUT "NAME OF THE DATA FILE";FILE$  ⎤
 50 OPEN FILE$ FOR INPUT AS #1           │
 60 WHILE EOF(1)=0                       │
 70 FOR I=1 TO ROWS                      │
 80 FOR J=1 TO COLUMNS                   │
 90 INPUT #1,WORDS$(I,J)                 │  Access and input into
100 NEXT J                               │  table combined
110 NEXT I                               │
120 WEND                                 │
130 CLOSE #1                             ⎦
140 REM**********
150 REM**PRINT OUT THE TABLE**           ⎤
160 FOR I=1 TO ROWS                      │
170 FOR J=1 TO COLUMNS                   │
180 PRINT TAB(10*(J-1));WORDS$(I,J);     │  table printout
190 NEXT J                               │
200 PRINT                                │
210 NEXT I                               │
220 END                                  ⎦
```

Program 13

Run on SDATA

```
RUN
NO. OF ROWS AND COLUMNS? 6 , 4
NAME OF THE DATA FILE? SDATA

ASHTON      BANKS       BARR        BURNS
CAREY       COMPTON     DOYLE       EDGE
GRANT       HOWSON      ICKERY      NASH
NEILS       NUNN        PRIEST      PURVISS
SCALES      SHIPTON     TEELE       TURNER
WATERS      WATTS       WELLS       WEST
```

Appendix A

American Standard Code for Information Interchange or ASCII Code

That part of the code which concerns us here is shown below.

0	NUL	38	&	57	9	76	L
7	BEL	39	'	58	:	77	M
9	HT	40	(	59	;	78	N
10	LF	41	)	60	<	79	O
11	VT	42	*	61	=	80	P
12	FF	43	+	62	>	81	Q
13	CR	44	,	63	?	82	R
14	SO	45	-	64	@	83	S
15	SI	46	.	65	A	84	T
18	DC2	47	/	66	B	85	U
20	DC4	48	0	67	C	86	V
24	CAN	49	1	68	D	87	W
27	ESC	50	2	69	E	88	X
32	SP	51	3	70	F	89	Y
33	!	52	4	71	G	90	Z
34	"	53	5	72	H	91	[
35	#	54	6	73	I	92	\
36	$	55	7	74	J	93	]
37	%	56	8	75	K	94	∧

95	—	104	h	113	q	122	z
96	'	105	i	114	r	123	{
97	a	106	j	115	s	124	|
98	b	107	k	116	t	125	}
99	c	108	l	117	u	126	~
100	d	109	m	118	v	128	NUL
101	e	110	n	119	w		
102	f	111	o	120	x		
103	g	112	p	121	y		

Special Characters

The list of BASIC special characters is summarised below.

CHARACTER	ACTION
	Blank
=	Equals sign or assignment symbol
+	Plus sign
-	Minus sign
*	Asterisk or multiplication symbol
/	Slash or division symbol
^	Up arrow or exponentiation symbol
(	Left parenthesis
)	Right parenthesis
%	Per cent sign or integer type declaration character
#	Number (or pound) sign or double precision type declaration character
$	Dollar sign or string type declaration character
!	Exclamation point or single precision type declaration character
[	Left bracket
]	Right bracket
,	Comma
.	Period or decimal point
'	Single quotation mark (apostrophe)
"	Double quotation mark (string delimiter)
;	Semicolon
:	Colon
&	Ampersand
?	Question mark (print abbreviation)
<	Less than
>	Greater than
\	Backslash or integer division symbol
@	At sign
—	Underscore

Appendix B

Reserved words

BASIC comprises a set of statements, commands, function names, and operator names which are treated as reserved words, and which cannot be used as variable names. The total list of BASIC reserved words is as follows:

ABS	EOF	LPRINT	RND
AND	EQV	LSET	RSET
ASC	ERASE	MERGE	RUN
ATN	ERDEV	MID$	SAVE
AUTO	ERDEV$	MKDIR	SCREEN
BEEP	ERL	MKD$	SGN
BLOAD	ERR	MKI$	SHELL
BSAVE	ERROR	MKS$	SIN
CALL	EXP	MOD	SOUND
CALLS	FIELD	MOTOR	SPACE$
CDBL	FILES	NAME	SPC
CHAIN	FIX	NEW	SQR
CHDIR	FNXXXXXXXX	NEXT	STEP
CHR$	FOR	NOT	STOP
CINT	FRE	OCT$	STR$
CIRCLE	GET	ON	STRING$
CLEAR	GOSUB	OPEN	SWAP
CLOSE	GOTO	OPTION	SYSTEM
CLS	HEX$	OR	TAB
COLOR	IF	OUT	TAN
COM	INKEY$	PAINT	THEN
COMMON	INP	PALETTE	TIMER
CONT	INPUT	PEEK	TIME$
COS	INPUT$	PEN	TO
CSNG	INPUT#	PLAY	TROFF
CSRLIN	INSTR	PMAP	TRON
CVD	INT	POINT	UNLOCK
CVI	IOCTL	POKE	USING
CVS	IOCTL$	POS	USR
DATA	KEY	PRESET	VAL
DATE$	KILL	PRINT	VARPTR
DEF	LEFT$	PRINT#	VARPTR$
DEFDBL	LEN	PSET	VIEW
DEFINT	LET	PUT	WAIT
DEFSGN	LINE	RANDOMISE	WEND
DEFSTR	LIST	READ	WHILE
DELETE	LLIST	REM	WIDTH
DIM	LOAD	RENUM	WINDOW
DRAW	LOC	RESET	WRITE
EDIT	LOCATE	RESTORE	WRITE#
ELSE	LOCK	RESUME	XOR
END	LOF	RETURN	
ENVIRON	LOG	RIGHT$	
ENVIRON$	LPOS	RMDIR